Dialogues with Patriarch Athenagoras

Dialogues with Patriarch Athenagoras

with Foreword by
His Eminence Archbishop Elpidophoros of America

Olivier Clément
Translated by Jeremy N. Ingpen
Introduction by John Chryssavgis

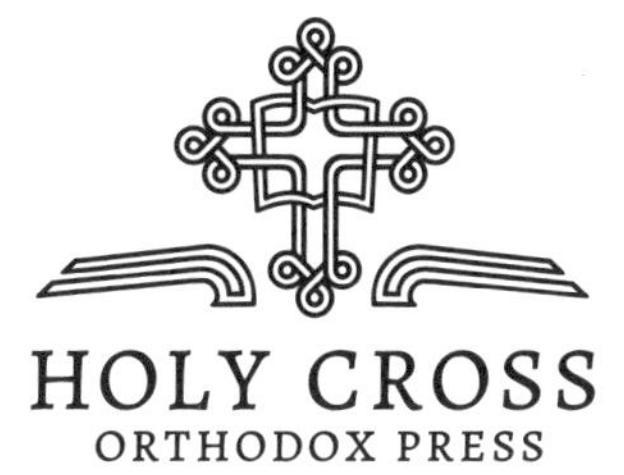

Brookline, Massachusetts

Published by Holy Cross Orthodox Press
Hellenic College, Inc.
50 Goddard Avenue
Brookline, MA 02445

ISBN 13: 978-1-935317-73-9
ISBN 1-935317-73-3

Dialogues avec le Patriarche Athénagoras
Paris, Librairie Arthème Fayard, 2nd Edition, 1976

This translation and publication was made possible with a generous grant from The Archbishop Iakovos Leadership 100 Endowment Fund.

Library of Congress Cataloging-in-Publication Data

Names: Clément, Olivier, author. | Ingpen, Jeremy N., translator.
Title: Dialogues with Patriarch Athenagoras / Olivier Clement ; translated by Jeremy N. Ingpen ; introduction by John Chryssavgis.
Other titles: Dialogues avec le Patriarche Athénagoras. English
Description: Brookline , Massachusetts : Holy Cross Orthodox Press, 2022. | Summary: "The text is a series of conversations between the author, Olivier Clement, and then Ecumenical Patriarch Athenagoras, which took place in the late 1960s in Istanbul, Turkey. In the conversations, the two discuss the Patriarch's life and his work as Ecumenical Patriarch of the Orthodox Church. In the discussions the two reflect on various aspects of Orthodox Christian theology and experience. They spend a great deal of time discussing the historic meetings of Patriarch Athenagoras and Pope Paul VI, which lifted the Great Schism of 1054 between Eastern and Western Christianity. Patriarch Athenagoras also shares his vision for Christianity globally"—Provided by publisher.
Identifiers: LCCN 2022011127 | ISBN 9781935317739 (paperback)
Subjects: LCSH: Orthodox Eastern Church—Doctrines. | Athēnagoras I, Ecumenical Patriarch of Constantinople, 1886-1972—Interviews.
Classification: LCC BX320.3 .C57713 2022 | DDC 281.9—dc23/eng/20220503
LC record available at https://lccn.loc.gov/2022011127

Contents

FOREWORD

Ecumenical Patriarch Athenagoras is one of those rare hierarchs who has shaped profoundly and permanently the destiny of world Orthodoxy. Throughout the twentieth century, from his ministry on Kerkyra (Corfu), in America, and ultimately as Ecumenical Patriarch, his initiatives and determination to serve the most vulnerable as a fundamental expression of our Christian faith, have proved an inspiration for many Christians, regardless of denomination or confession, over many generations. Fifty years after his blessed repose, Orthodox Christianity still lives into his vision.

The translation of these unique *Dialogues with Ecumenical Patriarch Athenagoras* was long overdue. I am particularly happy that this publication is taking place during the centennial celebration of the Greek Orthodox Archdiocese of America. Indeed, before his election to the See of the Mother Church of Constantinople, Ecumenical Patriarch Athenagoras presided over vital developments of Orthodoxy in America for over a decade, profoundly shaping the identity and nature of our presence in this country.

Throughout these pages, readers will discover the importance of encounter through dialogue. The fruit of these intimate conversations with French Orthodox theologian Olivier Clément is more than a spiritual legacy; it is the key that unlocks the treasure-chest of Orthodox Christianity, an experiential faith that unfolds through engagement with other people by embracing through love and understanding the diversity of the world. It is crucial for us today to hear this prophetic voice calling us to embody our Orthodox ethos as a dialogical commitment to serve our neighbor and the world. Dialogue is illumination. Dialogue is knowledge. Dialogue transcends discrimination. Dialogue is a promise of communion and is transformed into prayer as it functions for the glory of God.

Ecumenical Patriarch Athenagoras especially articulated and exemplified two forms of dialogue: the dialogue of love and the dialogue of truth. These two principles continue to constitute the basis whereby we are committed to building a society that is just and equitable, marked by God's presence in peace and reconciliation. As the righteous Gideon proclaimed, "the Lord is peace" (Judges 6:24). This is the legacy and lesson bequeathed to us all by Ecumenical Patriarch Athenagoras.

I pray that countless people, clergy and laity, will benefit from these inspiring conversations, which can assist and guide us in promoting the mission and vision of the Greek Orthodox Archdiocese of America over the next one hundred years.

† ELPIDOPHOROS
Archbishop of America

Introduction

Preliminary Remarks

It was during the winter of 1976—fresh out of high school and preparing to commence undergraduate studies in theology at the University of Athens—that I first came across this extraordinary book by Olivier Clément at a popular bookstore in the center of Athens. I was seventeen at the time—an impressionable age—and the imposing photograph of Ecumenical Patriarch Athenagoras on the cover immediately captured my attention. The volume that I held in my hands combined my delight in the French language, my devotion to the Ecumenical Patriarchate, and my imagination of how theology should speak to the modern world.

Published in Paris by Fayard in 1969,[1] the nearly 600-page original was irresistibly inviting for a budding novice in theology and spirituality. The publication in your hands comprises the first English translation, produced more than fifty years after it first appeared, but today it is a slightly condensed volume; we do, after all, live in the age of the internet.

The current Ecumenical Patriarch Bartholomew was himself a young impressionable student at the Theological School of Halki when he first became acquainted with Athenagoras. It is hardly surprising then that, as patriarch, Bartholomew went on to sustain and strengthen the legacy of unity pioneered by his visionary predecessor, who provided the promising student with a scholarship for his canonical and ecumenical studies abroad. Bartholomew proceeded to pursue a doctoral program at

1 The book was reprinted in 1976.

the Pontifical Oriental Institute in Rome during a period when the Second Vatican Council was in full swing. It was at this time that the young Bartholomew encountered Pope Paul VI and interacted with influential Roman Catholic scholars, including German Jesuit Karl Rahner and German professor Joseph Ratzinger (later Pope Benedict XVI), as well as French Dominican Yves Congar and French Jesuit Henri de Lubac.

Over the last five decades since the publication of Clément's book, the ecclesiastical and ecumenical trajectory of the Ecumenical Patriarchate has revealed an uncommon and uncanny sense of continuity grounded on the conviction of these two prominent and pioneering prelates—Athenagoras and Bartholomew—who have permanently shaped and determined the role of the Orthodox Church in a rapidly changing world. It came as no surprise, then, that in 1997 Olivier Clément published a sequel dedicated to Ecumenical Patriarch Bartholomew, addressing—in addition to many of the same subjects broached with Athenagoras—the impact of the technological revolution on the ecological crisis, as well as the rise of secularism and of radical fundamentalism.[2]

An Engaging Professor

This book contains the intimate discussions and reflections between a professor and a patriarch.[3] Olivier-Maurice Clément was one of the most significant religious thinkers and prolific theological writers of twentieth-century Europe. Born on November 17, 1921, in the small town of Aniane, near Montpellier in the Cévennes region of southwestern France, he became known for pioneering a renewal of Orthodox theology and spirituality, while spearheading a renaissance of religious intellectualism and mysticism. He was a faithful supporter of Christian unity, a fervent advocate for interfaith dialogue, and a firm apologist for the engagement of church and society.

Clément's religious disbelief and leftist culture, along with the prevailing Christian divisions between Catholicism and Protestantism of his time, marked his early formation and horizon. His spiritual

2 Olivier Clément, *Conversations with Ecumenical Patriarch Bartholomew I* (Crestwood, NY: St. Vladimir's Seminary Press, 1997).

3 *The Professor and the Patriarch* is the title of a book published in Italian by Andrea Riccardi, (Milan: Jaca Books, 2018), also translated into French (Cerf: Paris, 2020) and Greek (Athens: Apostoliki Diakonia, 2020).

autobiography[4] recounts his upbringing in an atheist family, his influence by eastern and existential thought around the time of the Second World War, and even his flirtation with nihilism and despair. It also describes his love for truth and beauty—or truth as beauty—and his encounter with Orthodox iconography and theology, specifically an icon of the *deisis* (a supplication of the Theotokos and John the Baptist facing Christ) and Vladimir Lossky's *The Mystical Theology of the Eastern Church*.[5]

Such was the inward journey of a passionate seeker of the genuine "sun of righteousness" (Mal. 4:2), of a profound thinker that discerned the way through the impasse of the frenetic slogans of the student movement against authority and establishment in the late 1960s. Clément pursued a new paradigm that generated reconciliation—East and West, primacy and collegiality, past and present, old and new, clergy and laity—through dialogue and communion. In the church, he believed, there was always room for others; and there was certainly more room for lay members.

All of this led to a discovery by Clément of a passion for ecumenical exchange in the search for unity and a rediscovery of the early Christian sources of the Orthodox Church. The first eventually resulted in a personal friendship with Pope John Paul II (1920–2005) and Brother Roger of Taizé (1915–2005), while the second defined his personal relationship with theologians of the Russian diaspora, including Vladimir Lossky (1903–1958) and Paul Evdokimov (1901–1970), as well as Ecumenical Patriarch Athenagoras in Constantinople (1886–1972) and Fr. Sophrony of Essex (1896–1993). In 1952, at the age of thirty, he was baptized into the Orthodox Church at the Russian Orthodox parish of Saint-Denys in Paris within the Moscow Patriarchate.

An educator by profession, teaching for many years at the Louis-le-Grand lyceum in Paris, Clément also taught at St. Sergius Orthodox Theological Institute established in 1925. He read and wrote on a wide range of subjects, from poetry to literary criticism, as well as from philosophy to theology. And of course his work extended to book-length interviews with

4 See Olivier Clément, *L'autre soleil* (Paris: Stock, 1975). For an English translation, with an introduction and notes, see Michael Donley, *The Other Sun* (Herefordshire, UK: Gracewing, 2021).

5 V. Lossky, *The Mystical Theology of the Eastern Church* (Crestwood: St. Vladimir's Seminary Press, 1976), which originally appeared in French (Paris: Aubier, 1944).

contemporary Ecumenical Patriarchs Athenagoras and Bartholomew. All of his writing is revealing and refreshing, as well as insightful and inspiring, while avoiding the temptation of moralizing and self-indulgence.

The author of over thirty books and countless articles,[6] Olivier Clément died at the age of eighty-seven on January 15, 2009. He was admired for his kind demeanor, his ecumenical commitment, and his love for the Orthodox tradition.

An Enlightening Patriarch

Clément's theological trajectory proved particularly energetic and effective as he engaged in dialogue with Ecumenical Patriarch Athenagoras, whose groundbreaking initiative to meet with Pope Paul VI in January 1964 during a historic pilgrimage to Jerusalem that launched the modern-day Orthodox-Catholic rapprochement. It was, moreover, Athenagoras and Paul VI who in 1965 instigated the "lifting of the anathemas" that had divided the two "sister churches" for over one thousand years.

A graduate of the famous Theological School of Halki off the coast of Istanbul and equipped with the experience of contemplation on Mt. Athos, Athenagoras originally served the Church of Greece in various capacities. When Athenagoras was elected Greek Orthodox Archbishop of North and South America on August 13, 1930, his appointment marked the end of a long era of instability and the beginning of a new era of growth in the United States, Canada, and Latin America.

In many ways, the history of what is today the Greek Orthodox Church in America is intimately connected to the personality and ministry of Archbishop Athenagoras. When he arrived, the church had already been declared an eparchy of the Ecumenical Patriarchate eight years earlier—a result of political divisions in the Church of Greece and the implementation of canonical jurisdiction by the Church of Constantinople. The legacy of Athenagoras was formative and remains palpable throughout the archdiocese.

---

6 His most popular book, entitled *L'Eglise Orthodoxe*, PUF, 1965 Que sais-je? [What do I know?], No. 949, 8th Edition, 2002 with questions and answers about the Orthodox Church, was originally published in 1961 and reprinted many times in French. Many of his articles appeared in the French Orthodox journal *Contacts* (Paris), founded in 1949.

Thus, in order to bring order to the fractured church in the Americas, Athenagoras increased the number of diocesan districts, each with an assistant bishop; he recognized the importance of a new charter for the church, for which the highest legislative body is the biennial Clergy-Laity Congress;[7] having arrived during the Great Depression, he strengthened the finances of the church; and he moved the archdiocesan headquarters from an inadequate structure in Astoria to its present offices in Manhattan. Furthermore, beyond instituting an archdiocesan registry and prompting parishes to do likewise for births, marriages, and deaths, Athenagoras encouraged the formation of the National Clergy Association, whose priorities included the creation of a pension fund and medical insurance for clergy; he founded the National Ladies Philoptochos Society and St. Basil's Academy; and he established Holy Cross Greek Orthodox School of Theology.

Elected to the Throne of Constantinople on November 1, 1948, Athenagoras "displayed the visionary qualities of a statesman" (p. 39) that he had acquired and revealed in America. His tenure as patriarch, however, was marred by a crisis over Cyprus and the resulting pogrom in Istanbul in the late 1950s, which led the patriarch to admit that "when you are completely at a loss, you place yourself completely in the hands of God, in his mercy. Then there is no more fear. Only trust" (p. 66).

There is no doubt that Ecumenical Patriarch Athenagoras attained inconceivable goals by any standard or measure of productivity and success. Ultimately, however, he imparted much more than a mere legacy. Athenagoras was a spiritual and cultural leader, who left behind a treasure of principles and deposit of values that breathed a spirit of openness and dialogue. As such, there is no doubt that he continues and will long continue to shape the Orthodox Church for many years to come. One might say that Athenagoras did not simply leave something behind; rather, he moved the entire church *forward* with his vision and aspiration to establish an open and constructive conversation between church and society, but also between the Orthodox Churches themselves and every community of believers throughout the world.

---

7 The first Clergy-Laity Congress took place in September 1921 at the initiative of Archbishop Meletios Metaxakis, who—like Athenagoras—also later became Ecumenical Patriarch. See George Papaioannou, *The Odyssey of Hellenism in America* (Thessaloniki: Patriarchal Institute of Patristic Studies, 1985).

An Extraordinary Publication

Clément's book presents the mind and heart of Patriarch Athenagoras through the lenses of the Incarnation and the Resurrection. These dimensions provide the fundamental sources and justifications for the patriarch's spiritual and ecumenical vision. They also promote a unified perspective that transcends customary dissensions and conventional dichotomies through the "record of an encounter," as the author describes it, with a burning timelessness. Here is how the author describes his conversations with Athenagoras:

> In 1968, I spent several weeks with the Patriarch, first in Istanbul and then in the offshore Princes Islands, at the Halki Theological Academy, where the Patriarch had come to relax during the quiet time of the summer holidays. At first, the Patriarch thought I might be one of those intellectuals who bury life under a pile of books (some even believe that they have managed to bury God)—one of those theologians that he disliked, because they turn the living God into a concept, a matter for polemical debate. I kept my silence, I waited, and I entered into the rhythms of silence, respect and invitation that are so important in the East. And so began an encounter. (p. xxiv)

The book remains faithfully rooted within the framework of the early church and patristic tradition, while also firmly resting within the continuity of the historical church and contemporary tradition alike. Clément weaves the life of the Ecumenical Patriarch into the fabric of the social and political context of the Orthodox Church. The charismatic and compelling ministry of Athenagoras emerges through a sincere search for the light of Christ's Resurrection—"the hidden means of transforming death into transfiguration" (p. xxiii). Thus the patriarch discerns and discovers the transparent "body of the Resurrected Christ" (p. 59) in the poor and hungry, rather than in what he calls the "pseudo-science of theology and vague moral creed of Christianity" (see p. 78).

In fact, everything starts and ends with the Resurrection. For the patriarch, the Resurrection is the center and the circumference, the alpha and the omega:

> Everything is straining toward the universal Resurrection, in ways in which we cannot know. Everything is oriented

> toward the Resurrection. The Resurrection is the only total event in history, one that contains all human reality and all cosmic reality. The Resurrection gives history its meaning and direction, like a universal force of gravity. (pp. 74–75)

It is this vision that gives him the confidence to speak openly about "the pathological fear of women" (p. 81) and "obligatory celibacy" (ibid.) in the church, as well as about "political systems . . . [and] political power" (p. 122) and "the ultimate meaning of science and technology" (p. 127) in the world. And it is the same vision that affords him the insight to anticipate the need for "a joint Catholic-Orthodox commission . . . to go into the depths of the living tradition of the Church . . . and look dispassionately into our differences" (431).[8] "Only the union of the Western 'mind' and the Eastern 'heart,' in the fire of the Holy Spirit, can reveal the true dimensions of the 'citizen of the world'" (p. 125).

As for bilateral contacts with Protestant confessions and inter-church organizations, Athenagoras realistically believed that these should lead our ecumenical partners to "little by little . . . discover their own ecclesial roots" (p. 237). "Spiritually, the various Protestant communities have no independent existence. They only exist in relation to the Western Church that they wished to reform. Orthodoxy can only act as a mediator if it encounters the whole of Western Christianity, even if this wholeness is broken apart" (p. 178). Nonetheless, as he claimed elsewhere, we Orthodox are "neither archeologists of Christianity nor sociologists of a revolutionary Church. All of that is radically old. We shall be the prophets of renewal, beholders of the risen Christ" (495–497).[9]

PLUS ÇA CHANGE . . .

The final section of the book is devoted to relations and impediments of the Ecumenical Patriarchate with other Orthodox Churches—estrangement and isolation, nationalistic tensions, and conflicts—especially as these are unraveled and addressed in the pre-conciliar meetings held at Rhodes and Geneva from 1960 to 1968 on the way toward the Holy and Great Council of the Orthodox Church. Clément hoped that such a council would ensure not only the adaptation of our tradition to today's world

8 Page number refers to French edition, but does not appear in the English translation.

9 As above, the page number refers to French, but does not appear in the English translation.

but would ultimately restore its force of inspiration and regeneration. As Clément forecasts, "[t]he Orthodox Churches are fiercely independent, in reaction to anything that might resemble an 'Eastern Papacy', but also out of national pride. In particular, some Russians think their Church should assume a de facto leadership role, on account of its size, while the primacy of the ecumenical patriarch should become a purely honorary role, of no practical importance" (p. 245).

Of course, any renewal in the Orthodox Church is inseparable from heritage and unity: "Today, the Orthodox Church needs to resolve a situation that is the reverse of the burning concern in Catholicism. The Catholics want to re-introduce synodality. For the Orthodox, the question is how the unity and the universality of the Church should be expressed" (p. 245). The patriarch argues: "The Russian Church has never claimed to deny the 'rights of seniority' to the patriarchates of Antioch, Alexandria or Constantinople. And Constantinople is their mother church, that brought them the light of Christ." The professor retorts: "Not that they did not want to!" (ibid.)

As I noted above, in terms of the vision and ministry of those seated on the Throne of Constantinople, there has clearly always been a sense of succession, even progression—especially in the transition from the vision of Athenagoras to the service of Bartholomew. Nevertheless, what is disappointing and disheartening for the reader of Clément's exchanges with Athenagoras and Bartholomew is the realization that by contrast, during the same period and for the better part of an entire century, the Church of Moscow has not changed in the least—whether under Stalin or under Putin. Indeed, if anything, Moscow's antagonism and intrigue have only heightened, even hardened. In an obituary notice published exactly fifty years ago on Patriarch Athenagoras, then Archimandrite (and now Metropolitan of Diokleia) Kallistos Ware wrote:

> When Athenagoras became Patriarch, there was an urgent need to reaffirm the traditional primacy of the Ecumenical Throne. A vigorous challenge had come from the north. Following the restoration of the Moscow Patriarchate in 1943, Slav propagandists reanimated the idea of Rome as the Third Rome in a new form. With the disappearance of the Ottoman Empire, so they suggested, the Ecumenical Patriarchate had become an anachronism, and it was now the Patriarchate of Moscow which should assume the leadership of world

Orthodoxy. A determined attempt had been made to carry these ideas into practice immediately before the accession of Athenagoras.

In spring 1947, Patriarch Aleksii announced his intention to summon a Pan-Orthodox Council the following November. The Ecumenical Patriarchate at once protested that the initiative in summoning such a gathering could come only from itself, as primus inter pares. Moscow accordingly postponed the proposed Council but revived the same plan in the following year under a slightly different form. In spring 1948, all the Orthodox Churches were invited to Moscow to celebrate the fifth centenary of the autocephaly of the Russian Church, and also to remain for a Pan-Orthodox Conference immediately after the celebrations. This was once more a clear challenge to Constantinopolitan primacy. In the event Constantinople and Greece attended the celebrations but took no part in the subsequent Conference.[10]

ΩΩΩ

The image of the church that emerges in these *Dialogues with Patriarch Athenagoras* by Olivier Clément, while timeless and priceless, is neither romantic nor idealistic. In the epilogue to his autobiography, Clément writes about the church, that "she does not disappoint once one has understood what she is":

> [N]utrient soil, a great life force offered to us. It is up to us whether or not we avail ourselves of it. As a child, I wanted to live close to the sea. To console me, my grandfather would hold a shell to my ear and get me to hear the sound of the waves. The church is the sea that sings forever in the shell of the world.
>
> I have lost the naive and somewhat blinkered attitude of the recent convert. I have taken stock of the historical weakness of Orthodoxy, also of its tenacious patience and, in many places, its fruitful passion. I have observed the modesty, the temptation to withdraw into itself, and yet the reality, of the Orthodox presence [in the world]. I too have become more than modest. But I walk close to the sea.[11]

---

10 K. Ware, "The Ecumenical Patriarch Athenagoras I," *Eastern Churches Review* IV, 2 (Autumn, 1972), 159–60.
11 See Michael Donley, *The Other Sun*, 191.

This book is a timeless gem and deserves to be read by all those genuinely interested in the history of the Ecumenical Patriarchate and the Greek Orthodox Church in America, as well as by anyone earnestly devoted to inter-Orthodox unity, inter-Christian dialogue, and inter-religious cooperation.

We should be grateful for the initiative of His Eminence Archbishop Elpidophoros of America—through the Archdiocesan Department of Inter-Orthodox, Ecumenical and Interfaith Relations—to commission and publish this English translation on the occasions of the 50th anniversary since the repose of Ecumenical Patriarch Athenagoras and the 100th anniversary since the establishment of the Greek Orthodox Archdiocese in America, the foremost and largest eparchy of the Ecumenical Patriarchate.

John Chryssavgis

Translator's Introduction

In 1968, the French Orthodox theologian, Olivier Clément, spent several weeks at the side of Patriarch Athenagoras, accompanying him everywhere and in constant conversation. The resulting Dialogues with Patriarch Athenagoras has been called Clément's masterpiece. It has remained untranslated for over fifty years.

We owe this translation to the initiative of Archbishop Elpidophoros and Father Nicolas Kazarian of the Greek Orthodox Archdiocese of America, who wanted to celebrate the 100th Anniversary of the founding of the Greek Orthodox Archdiocese and the 50th Anniversary of the death of Patriarch Athenagoras. I had also been looking for someone to sponsor this project, so it was a happy day when Father Nicolas contacted me in early 2021. He worked with me closely throughout the translation, together with our editorial assistant, Anthony Ladas. We are happy to be able, at last, to bring the *Dialogues with Patriarch Athenagoras* to an English-speaking audience.

The book is in three parts. Part One introduces us to the Patriarch and vividly describes his life as a child in Tsaraplana, on the borders of Greece and Albania; in Monastir, now part of North Macedonia; as a student at Halki; and as Archbishop in America. Part Two contains the dialogues with Olivier Clément, between the Patriarch and the Professor. These take you into the heart of the Church's relationship with the world, the heart of what it means to be a Christian in today's world. At times, they read like a play script, at other times like a poem. They have an immediacy that cuts through theological abstractions and academic jargon.

Part Three is more historical and analytical, presenting the record of the encounters between Patriarch Athenagoras and Pope John XXIII, Pope Paul VI, and with the other Orthodox Churches, in search of the unity of the one Church, in the one communion cup. Here one begins to see how long and hard Patriarch Athenagoras labored in search of Church unity.

Because of its genesis, the book is conversational and, at times, colloquial in tone. Athenagoras' language is terse and telegraphic. He is given to short, punchy statements, with discontinuities and exclamations. Clément's language is more complex, given to long, sustained thoughts in complex paragraphs. But his is the tone of an inspired speaker, not that of a dry academic. Clément piles up his metaphors until, on occasion, his thought seems to end in silence. One is the old, wise patriarch. The other is the young, enthusiastic professor. One has to remind oneself that at the time of their meeting, Olivier Clément was already forty-seven years old, not some eager graduate student.

The interplay between the Patriarch and the Professor is masterful, as is the interweaving of themes throughout the book. In addition to the two protagonists, there are four other 'actors' whose presence is felt throughout the book. In the background, the Greek people of Asia Minor, whose tragic history acts almost as a chorus. In the foreground, the city of Byzantium, in its historical manifestations as Constantinople and Istanbul. Towering over all like a sleeping giant, the temple of Hagia Sophia, the Temple of Wisdom. And finally, the life of the Patriarch and the life of the whole city is guarded by the constant presence of the Mother of God, the Theotokos.

What emerges is a deep meditation on the church in the modern world, on the nakedness of modern man, on hell, on paradise, on world religions, on communion. Interwoven with the dialogues is the history of the Greeks of the Ottoman Empire, the history of modern Turkey, the forced exchange of populations of 1922, the religious riots of 1955, and the long and slow path of ecumenical and inter-Orthodox outreach by the Phanar. Clément goes on to examine the Patriarch's historic meeting in Jerusalem with Pope Paul VI in 1964, the lifting of the anathemas between the two Churches, and the exploration of the possibility of shared communion.

In his definitive *Il professore e il patriarca*, Andrea Riccardi has demonstrated, through his detailed review of Clément's letters and notebooks, just how closely the dialogues, especially of Part Two, record the actual conversations. In the evening, Clément made a record of the day's meetings and conversations in his notebooks and in letters to his wife, Monique Clément. In places, the Dialogues with Patriarch Athenagoras quote verbatim from this contemporaneous record.[12]

This translation assumes no knowledge of theological terminology. Because the setting is the Orthodox Church of Constantinople, we have used the terminology and service books of the Greek Orthodox Church, The Patriarch wears an *exorason*, not a Russian *ryassa* or a western cassock. On his head he wears a Greek monk's *kalimavkion*. The Biblical quotations are taken from the New Oxford Annotated Bible – Revised Standard Version, adapted where necessary to reflect Clément's French version. Editorial comments, where necessary, are indicated by [square brackets].

We did not include chapters that mainly provided background information: Chapter 2 – What is the Orthodox Church; Chapter 17 – The Prayer of Jesus; Chapter 23 – An Ecclesiology of Communion; and Chapters 32–35 that cover developments in ecumenical and inter-Orthodox discussions up to 1968 and have been largely superseded by subsequent events.[13]

A good introduction to the Orthodox Church can be found in Metropolitan Kallistos Ware, *The Orthodox Church*. Clément's introduction to the prayer of the heart can be found in *The Roots of Christian Mysticism*, Part 3, On Prayer. The history of ecumenical discussions up to the year 2000 is covered in Clément's *Conversations with Patriarch Bartholomew* (Part 1) and *You Are Pete*r (ch. 10). *You Are Peter* also provides an introduction to the ecclesiology of the Church in the first millennium. *The Dialogues with Patriarch Athenagoras* were translated into German in 1982, in a greatly abbreviated form, and into Italian, partially in 1972 and then in full in 2013.[14] The German translation, *A Portrait of a Prophet*, has a valuable introduction by two Catholic scholars, Johannes Bold and Albert Rauch.

I would like to thank Archbishop Elpidophoros and Father Nicolas Kazarian, and also Professor Michel Stavrou, Dean of the St. Serge

12 Andrea Riccardi, *Il professore e il patriarca, Milan*, Jaca Book, 2018, translated as Le Professor et le Patriarche, Paris, Cerf, 2020

13 The chapter numbers refer to the French editions of 1969 and 1976.

14 *Porträt eines Propheten*, Munich, Verlag Neue Stadt, 1982 and *Umanesimo Spirituale, Dialoghi tra oriente e occidente*, Milan, Cinisello Balsamo, 2013

Theological Institute in Paris, for entrusting me with the translation of Olivier Clément's complex and poetic French. This has been a very personal journey. Olivier Clément was born one week after my mother in November 1921. Athenagoras became Patriarch in the year of my birth, 1949. My brother-in-law Peter Bouteneff gave me a photo of the Patriarch warmly holding the hand of my father-in-law, Michael Bouteneff, at the Phanar. In America, Athenagoras is remembered as Archbishop and as the founder of St. Basil's Academy, Garrison, NY, where I worked for two years after my retirement. "Yes," a parishioner of Prophet Elias Greek Orthodox Church in Yonkers, NY, told me, "Athenagoras visited here in the late 1940s." Finally, I would like to thank my wife, Dr. Manya Bouteneff, for her constant support during the six-month marathon of this book's translation.

Completed on the 100th Anniversary of the birth of Mercy Ray in Shillong, India, and of Olivier Clément in Aniane, France.

Jeremy N. Ingpen
Hartsdale, New York
November, 2021

For Further Reading:

Metropolitan Kallistos Ware, *The Orthodox Church*, London and New York, Penguin, 1993
Olivier Clément, *The Roots of Christian Mysticism*, Hyde Park, NY, New City Press, 2013
Olivier Clément, *On Human Being, Hyde Park*, NY, New City Press, 2000
Olivier Clément, *Conversations with Patriarch Bartholomew*, Hyde Park, NY, New City Press, 1997
Olivier Clément, *You Are Peter*, Hyde Park, NY, New City Press, 2003
Olivier Clément, *Transfiguring Time*, Hyde Park, NY, New City Press, 2019
Olivier Clément, *The Other Sun*, Leominster, UK, Gracewing, 2021
Andrea Riccardi, *Le Professeur et le Patriarche*, Paris, Cerf, 2020
Judith Herrin, *Byzantium*, London, Penguin, 2008
Philip Mansel, *Constantinople*, New York, St. Martins's Press, 1996
Orhan Pamuk, *Istanbul*, London, Faber and Faber, 2006

Preface

This book is the story of an encounter, an encounter that introduces a man and his spirituality (the word is loaded but it is the only word). When Patriarch Athenagoras' tall silhouette appeared on television screens and in news magazines in the 1960s, Western Christians, and, thanks to the mass media, the Western public, became aware of their deep unity with the Christian 'East' that the Patriarch revealed through his acts and symbolic gestures. In a society that advances blindly towards death while exalting youthfulness, Athenagoras' icon-like face spoke of the wisdom of old age, the wisdom of one who perhaps knows the hidden means of transforming death into transfiguration. Carl Jung would have called him an archetype of the old sage, who could discern how life is fulfilled in the moment of its transcendence, and how at the root of all things is found, not a nihilistic void, but love.

As one who was born into atheism, just as others are born into a church, I had already for many years been engaged in a pilgrimage towards an internal 'East.' My lucidly chosen baptism into the Orthodox Church was a decisive initiation. I had followed the actions of the Patriarch and had seen how richly they bore fruit. In the dark night of the soul that today overshadows the Western world, that in the words of St. John of the Cross perhaps is a "mystical night," I watched as one whole part of Western Christianity—the least vocal but the most prayerful—rediscovered its 'Eastern' roots. And I watched as some of those in revolt against the Western world came to understand that the only real alienation is that which cuts a person off from the infinite. That is why, when asked, I agreed to write this book, to serve our common unity.

In 1968, I spent several weeks with the Patriarch, first in Istanbul and then in the offshore Princes Islands, at the Halki Theological Academy, where the Patriarch had come to relax during the quiet time of the summer holidays. At first, the Patriarch thought I might be one of those intellectuals who bury life under a pile of books (some even believe that they have managed to bury God)—one of those theologians that he disliked, because they turn the living God into a concept, a matter for polemical debate. I kept my silence, I waited, and I entered into the rhythms of silence, respect and invitation that are so important in the East. And so began an encounter. The Patriarch began to see that I was more alert to him as a person, than to the roles that he had from time to time to assume. He could feel my love for his people and for Byzantium. A more profound convergence emerged: each in our own way we began to be aware of a new face of the Unknown, of the Living God, that, in the full light of the Gospel, transcended the limitations of the Churches. The face of the Unknown, of the Living God, revealed in a history that has become that of the whole planet, of a cosmos that has become immeasurably vast. The Patriarch loved to play with words and one day he said I was a theologian, clement, and that clemency was one of those most beautiful names of God. On that day, he adopted me. "Here, you are my monk and you must obey me." And I obeyed. It was as if I had rediscovered a father. And when he so wished, I sat close to him, like a disciple at the feet of his master. "And so," he said to me one day, "the old man confesses to the young man."

These dialogues are in no way imaginary. It is true that they were not interviews, and that I never took notes while the Patriarch was talking, but I "kept all these things in my heart." In composing the dialogues that are in this book, I proceeded rather in the manner of the historians of antiquity, whose starting point was the underlying thread of the conversation. I sought to shed light on the topic under discussion, sometimes making use of the Patriarch's recent announcements to expand his allusions. But at the same time, I have sought to capture the turn of phrase and the rich vocabulary. As a portrait, this is not a photographic reproduction, rather, it is that of a painter who seeks to reveal the depths of the person.

As I was writing, the one thing that bothered me was the form of the dialogue itself. The word dialogue—which exemplifies the best of

Western tradition—implies the equality of the participants. While personal communications in the East have a warm simplicity that we have lost, they are governed by a sense of respect. To properly understand a grand old man, a patriarch, a man of wisdom, demanded a framework of respect, more vertical than horizontal. I listened more than I spoke. I asked questions more than I voiced my opinion. My side of the dialogue should be seen more as an echo of the Patriarch's words, an echo which at times I have put into words and at times left silent.

To make the man and his words understood, I needed to place them in their spiritual context. Now, I was already very familiar with the role of translator and intermediary of spiritual worlds. And so the book took shape. First you will see his life unfold. I listened as he talked to his sister about their childhood, sitting in the evening in the garden at Halki. He spoke to me of the many difficult episodes of his life. This life was deeply rooted in a world that the West hardly knows. This landscape and history forms the background, sometimes hinted at impressionistically, sometimes given with the meticulous clarity of a folk artist. Then come the dialogues themselves. In them you can, I hope, feel how the living tradition of the Church is perpetually renewed and made young in the Spirit, *juvenescens*, as Irenaeus, first Bishop of Lyons, wrote in the second century. The third part of the book explores the Patriarch's work in the renewal of ecumenical relations, freeing them from the grip of the Protestant-Catholic dialogue in which they had been trapped. And, in this final section, the book explores the gathering of the Orthodox Churches in a movement of renewed Orthodox awareness, that can only be of great service to the search for Christian unity.

This book is written in gratitude. For Patriarch Athenagoras, who helped me to 'disarm'—to use one of his favorite expressions—to shed my secret fears and prejudices, who showed me how to find the pathways of a prophetic creation in the history of today. For the Orthodox Church, my spiritual home, which is summoned to bear humble witness to the undivided Church, as it breaks through its historical confines: a Church in which there is not opposition but synergy between freedom and mystery. For those who helped bring this book into being. And finally, for Byzantium, the Byzantium that today exists only as light, of which Patriarch Athenagoras I is perhaps the ultimate incarnation.

Olivier Clément, 1969

Part One: A Man Called Athenagoras

1. The Phanar

When you leave the new districts of Istanbul to cross the innermost bridge of the Golden Horn—just where on the further bank you can see a massive highway cutting through the Byzantine and Turkish body of the old city—you have to take a right turn and follow the road that climbs the Golden Horn. The Roman Aqueduct of Valens still strides triumphantly across the highway. In the 1960s, this was an industrial area with sawmills for the logs brought by sea from the coastal forests of Asia Minor. Sawmills everywhere, the shrill whine of the saws cutting into the trunks, the movement of trucks stirring up dust and mud, the stacked lumber-drying sheds.

Where there is an occasional small, dusty park laid out next to the wharfs, you get a fleeting glimpse of the bay: small, overloaded freighters working the shoreline from the old Theodosian walls to the sacred ground of the Eyüp Sultan Mosque, where the last of the Prophet's comrades-in-arms died in a vain attack on Byzantium. There are boats in dry dock for repainting, surrounded by rusty barrels; in the summer, there are children swimming between the billowing sails of the feluccas. The leaves of the plane trees are turning yellow.

On the farther bank, across the calm waters of the Golden Horn, there is a green hillside and the white tombstones of a Muslim cemetery. At the base of the hill, naval shipyards and the din of the hammers riveting metal. Where we are standing, the road rises steeply and once past the reddish remains of the sea wall—today these have almost completely vanished—you discover elegant Turkish houses, with wooden balconies, and the whole drama of a Mediterranean city. Already, however, the women's presence is hidden. Men wet down the road in front of their house, vines and wisteria climb up the facades, there are piles of musk melons and watermelons. Further up the hill, the cobbled street turns into a dirt road. There are fig trees, a small mosque in ruins, surrounded by gravestones—a stone flower for the women, a column capped by a turban for the men. Here, animal power still rules over the machine: there are few trucks or American cars. There are fine-looking horses with blue-pearled collars, to ward off the evil-eye. Seagulls and vultures swirl above the garbage.

All of a sudden, halfway up the hill, incongruously, there is a huge red-brick building, reminiscent of an Oxford college, except for the cupola that crowns it and the oversized Greek letters that circle the dome. This is the Greek Patriarchate's main lycée (the Great School of the Nation, *Megale tou Genous Schole*).

The Patriarchate itself is altogether more discrete. Just off the steep cobbled street, a quiet side road opens up under a canopy of trees. On the side of the hill there is a stairway leading to terraced gardens that climb up to the Byzantine wall. You enter between a church and a fountain into a little courtyard, and into the shade of a large tree. On your right there are several modest new buildings. On your left, there is a very simple church, in the form of a basilica with an apse, built in the seventeenth century, set in green grass that opens to a vista of pines, cypress, and roses. In the narthex is a beautiful Byzantine mosaic of the Mother of God, brought from an old church: the icon of the Presentation of Christ to the Temple—the Christ-Child, serious, and grave faced, in the arms of the Theotokos.

The service ends and the worshipers exit. It is summer and there are many tourists and pilgrims among them. A tall old man clothed in black comes out, wearing the tall black *kalimavkion* of an Orthodox monk. Everyone follows him—tourists and street people alike. He leads a crowd of fifty or more people toward the modern buildings. You cross the gardens on black and white pebbled paths. Passing by the jasmine, you climb a long set of steps. The old man invites everyone to sit down in the large room, and he himself sits at the desk. Large glasses of cold water are brought out, into which you place a spoon full of sugar. "Don't stir," he says. "First eat the sugar paste and then drink." Now he talks at length, in a quiet firm voice. He speaks about the world of today, in which we find ourselves, the world of the unity of the human race.

"All people are good, all races. I belong to all the people of the Earth. Christian unity should be the leaven of human unity. The unification of humanity is the expression of our perfect unity in Christ, in whom we are all members, one with the other. I belong to all the Churches, or rather, there is only one Church, the Church of Christ. There is only one theology—the announcement of the Resurrected Christ, who raises us from the dead and fills us with the power of love. Men may go to the moon but they no longer know the meaning of life. As Christians, we should fear nothing. We should ask for nothing. We should not insist on anything. We should be witnesses to a life that has meaning, a life that is boundless, a life that opens into eternity. Because God exists! God exists! and this unknown God is our friend."

As you have already realized, this old man is Patriarch Athenagoras, Archbishop of Constantinople, first in honor in the Orthodox Church.

2. Under the Snow

Aristocles Spyrou was born on March 25, 1886 in Tsaraplana, in the mountainous Epirus region of Greece, on the border of Albania. It was the day of the Annunciation. He was born under the sign of the Mother of God.

At that time, Epirus was in the Balkan part of the Ottoman Empire, and, under this benign rule, had a flourishing multi-national civilization. During the Byzantine period, Slavs had migrated into the region and become Hellenized. Nomadic Romanian-speaking shepherds, the Vlachs, roamed the mountains. Later, Turks settled in large numbers, followed by Albanians, converted to Islam in the wake of the conquerors. The Albanians were strangely Asiatic in their way of living: a coiled stone snake would sleep as a talisman among the glowing coals of the hearth.

Tsaraplana is a Slavonic name. After Greece annexed Epirus in 1913, the name was changed to Vassilikon, but the meaning is the same—a royal place. The Slavs had lived in this region for a long time and had left their trace in the place names and in the dialect. Most of the local words for trees and streams, for the woods and the springs, are of Slavonic origin.

"We lived like people of the steppes. There were no beds or chairs in the house. Cushions and sleeping mats were unrolled at night, the mat and covers, to be rolled up again in the morning. When evening came, everyone sat cross-legged around the hearth, by the light of the oil lamp."

The future patriarch's family was one of those dynamic solidly established families that were the backbone of Greek culture, first in the Byzantine Empire and then under the Ottoman Empire. His paternal grandfather was a sheep farmer. In 1822, when Athens became the capital of the new Kingdom of Greece, he went there and set up shop as a butcher. The business was successful, and his son Matthaios was able to study to become a doctor. In the Ottoman Empire almost all the doctors were Greek. The Turks trusted them. "In Istanbul, the Turks have always trusted their Greek doctors," the Patriarch said. "Often they prefer them, they are loyal to them." Medicine is a science that serves humanity. It is a deeply Christian profession. So it was the realization of the deep-seated and worthy ambition for an Ottoman Greek to see his son become a doctor. Matthaios set up his practice in Tsaraplana—he was the first doctor to come to the village.

"It was a village of about five hundred families on a windblown mountain plateau, snow-bound in winter. My father was a country doctor. I think he was a good doctor, esteemed as a good diagnostician. He was constantly on horseback, summoned to the neighboring villages."

The Patriarch's mother was the daughter of a leather craftsman, a shoemaker with several apprentices to help in the shop.

"My mother was from Konitsa, a much more important Epirotan town of some fifteen hundred families (and the regional capital). Konitsa was a very prosperous town, known for its *tsarouchi* shoes with their upturned tip, such as I then wore." Eleni Makarou had gone to school, to a private Greek school—the *Parthenagogion*—from which she received her diploma.

"Under the Ottoman Empire, the Church was the ark that kept the language and culture of the Greek people intact. Against all odds, the Church undertook a massive educational program. The first institution of higher education in Istanbul was founded by Patriarch Gennadios in 1454, one year after the Turkish conquest. Gennadios was himself a renowned professor. At the end of the sixteenth century, Patriarch Jeremias II mandated that all bishops should establish schools. In the following centuries, educated monks, their culture wedded to their prayer, devoted themselves to the education of the people. This was a Church that had no fear of science, that considered that educational progress would lead to a more conscious and more personal faith. The Church called on the solidarity of the Christian people. The wealthy should sponsor poor but talented children. The teachers—most often laypersons—developed primers and textbooks, to be distributed for free to the school children."

"When I was young, each parish had its own primary school and each town had its own secondary school. The Ioannina secondary school, where I studied before going to Halki, had a good reputation. Ioannina was an important center of Greek culture: a large and beautiful city, with a distinct character—its music, its dances, its legends—a uniquely Greek city where even the judges and the Turkish bureaucrats had to learn Greek to carry out their duties."

In the fifteenth century, when the Byzantine Empire, already weakened by 300 years of Western colonization and crusades, collapsed overnight, the new Turkish rulers set up a system of indirect rule over its conquered people. The Koran forbade the forced conversion of those "People of the Book" who accepted Muslim rule. Mehmet the Conqueror gave the Christian People, or *Millet*, full autonomy—following the theocratic model of the Umma-al-Islam. This had been the model for the Christians of the Middle East since the seventh century. Shortly after the conquest of Constantinople, Mehmet II told Patriarch Gennadios, on the day of his investiture: "Be patriarch, may our friendship be kept safe, receive all the privileges enjoyed by your predecessors." In fact, the patriarch received significantly more power. This included civil administration, as this was not separated from religious administration in Muslim law. The patriarch became the *millet-bachi*, the ethnarch, the leader of the 'Christian nation,' responsible to the Sultan for its conduct. This Christian nation, the *genos ton christianon*, was administered according to its own laws. Thanks to the robust parish system, each village managed its own affairs: a community of Christian families, symbolically set apart from the mountains and forests, and from the non-Christian world, by the chapels and icons that stood at its boundaries.

"There was a chapel dedicated to St. Elias (Prophet Elijah) on the hilltop overlooking the village, as so often is the case in the Orthodox world. The Prophet Elijah lived and prayed in the mountains. The mountains are themselves a prayer of nature. When you left the house in the morning, the chapel was the first thing you saw. You felt protected."

Nevertheless, until the end of the seventeenth century, the situation of Christians in the Ottoman Empire was humiliating and often tragic.

They were not allowed to carry weapons and had to wear distinctive clothing. Their churches could not be any higher than the surrounding houses. A Christian man was forbidden to marry a Muslim woman, but they could not prevent a Muslim man from marrying a Christian woman. There was a strong social pressure to convert to Islam—and conversions were the occasion of great festivities. By contrast, the baptism of a Muslim was punishable by the death of the convert, and of those who had introduced them to the Gospel. There was a heavy tax imposed on the community, for which the village was responsible. But the worst was the blood tax, the *devsirme*. Every year, officers of the Janissary—the elite Ottoman army—would visit the provinces and choose the most handsome boys, the strongest, those from the best families. Taken away, converted to Islam, they entered a fourteen-year military and quasi-monastic apprenticeship—the rules included celibacy—and became part of the knighthood of Holy War, the Janissary Corps.

Blood was also shed by those whom the Greek Church calls the "New Martyrs." The martyrdom of an apostate who proclaimed their return to the faith (having been driven by social ambition or the desire to protect his children); the martyrdom of a Muslim convert or of those responsible for his conversion; the martyrdom of one who refused to convert to Islam; and, in 1821, the martyrdom of Patriarch Gregory V, who was accused of leading the Greek insurrection in Istanbul, and who was hanged at the main gateway of the Patriarchate. Nicodemus the Hagiorite wrote: "if someone asks why God wanted new martyrs to appear in our time, I tell them that it is, above all, so that their blood renews the whole Orthodox Faith."

But the Ottoman Empire underwent a transformation over the course of the eighteenth century, just as it reached the peak of its cultural expression in the so-called tulip era, and just as it suffered its first military defeats, in Ukraine and on the Danube. The Turkish-born became the elite of the Janissary recruits and little by little the blood tax fell out of use. In the absence of apostates, the Empire had to turn to Greeks to fill the highest administrative offices of the state. This trend strengthened in the nineteenth century. Across the board, Greeks rose to become merchants, doctors, lawyers, engineers and university professors. When Aristocles Spyrou was a child, the Ottoman Empire's foreign ministers were Greek, first Savvas Pasha, then Alexander Karatheodori Pasha. There were a dozen Greek ambassadors and emissaries, including Moussourous

Bey, the grandfather of the Countess of Noailles. The private doctor of Sultan Abd ul-Hamid was Greek as was the learned professor of medicine that the Sultan sent to work with Louis Pasteur.

In the Kingdom of Greece there were some two and a half million Greeks, but overall in the Ottoman Empire there were more than eight million, mainly concentrated in certain regions, but to be found everywhere, especially in the towns and ports. After a series of grave constitutional crises, the Empire seemed to be moving towards giving equal status to all ethnic and religious groups. Many Greeks saw this, like the path chosen by the multi-national Hapsburg Empire, as the only solution that recognized their growing power and their role as a social and intellectual elite. But to fully understand them, and to understand the Patriarch, we should note that these Ottoman Greeks were not nationalists, in the modern sense of the word. Rather, they were Byzantines. From Byzantium, they had retained a sense of ecumenicity, of belonging, not so much by ethnic origin as by virtue of being Orthodox and of using Greek, if only as a second language.

"A whole diverse civilization was looking for a means of expression. The Turks had fallen onto us like snow: but under the snow, we felt warm. The region where I was born was occupied by the Turks a whole century before Constantinople. There were Christians and Muslims in Tsaraplana and everyone lived peacefully together. The one Turkish policeman—I remember his name, Ali Bey—had nothing to do. There were no quarrels, no fights, no lawsuits. Christian and Muslim children played together. The Christian family would invite their Muslim friends to a baptism, and the Muslims would invite us for their child's circumcision. In this biblical existence we all felt ourselves to be the children of Abraham. On the feast day of Ibrahim—that is to say, Abraham—the Muslims would roast a ram. The Christians would roast a lamb for their Paschal feast. On the great feast day of St. George—the church close to our house was dedicated to St. George and had an ancient icon of the saint—we would go up into the hills before dawn to see the sun rise, and then, after liturgy, there was dancing. But this same day was the Muslim feast day of Al Khidr, the servant of God and spiritual guide—in Jewish tradition he is identified with Elijah, and in Christian tradition with the forerunner, John the Baptist. That at least is what the Muslim holy men, the dervishes, told us. The children would play on the swings: If you played on the swings on this feast day, it would bring good luck for the whole year."

The Dervish fraternities played an important role in the Ottoman Empire. They were the guardians of Sufi mysticism. Each fraternity had its special way of invoking the divine name. There seems to be a hidden history of deep encounter between the hesychasts, the Christian practitioners of the Jesus prayer, and these masters of the holy name. Some of them gave special reverence to the breath of Jesus, the *nefes-Issa*. Muslim or non-Muslim, everyone would seek out the dervishes, for advice, for consolation, even for a cure.

"The dervishes were very good men, very open to Christianity, often true spiritual masters. Their communities were called *tekkes*. There were many dervishes in Epirus. They looked like Orthodox monks—the same long black robes, the same headgear—except that some of them cut their hair."

"There was a dervish in our village. His name was Iamil. He often came to our house and shared our meals. My mother and sister loved him and nothing was kept secret from him. He knew their secrets of the heart better than the village priest!"

The Patriarch's father, Matthaios Spyrou, was well-respected and even a little feared. He was very strict. The few remaining photographs show a stocky, severe, energetic man, with a trimmed beard, wearing a fez—the new fashion in the Ottoman Empire since the banning of turbans, an act of modernization. The Patriarch does not look much like his father. But from him, perhaps, the Patriarch inherited his self-discipline, and his complete lack of self-aggrandizement.

"My father was a believer, but in a very private way. He never spoke of those things. But he made the sign of the cross before eating and he went to church on Sunday. He was very strict with us, but not harsh. He was very fond of his daughter. As for us boys, he never hit us, except to swat at us with his handkerchief."

There were three children: Aristocles was the oldest, then a brother, two years younger, who died at the age of sixty, and then a sister, three years younger than the patriarch, who lived in Athens.

"My father was a doctor, but other relatives had farms and raised sheep, as my grandfather had before them. I liked to carve shepherd's crooks for them."

"I don't have a photograph of my mother. While she was alive there were no photographers in the villages. My father lived longer and I have one photograph of him, which I keep with the small folding icon that is always with me when I travel."

We know from contemporary accounts that Eleni Spyrou was very beautiful. She was nicknamed *Poulia*, the evening star. She was tall and slender and she walked "like a queen." The patriarch takes after her. He has her dignity and, when he wishes, her gentleness. He too "walks like a king." Eleni was loved. She is still spoken of today (in 1968) in Tsaraplana as a great benefactor. The children were very fond of their mother's home and family in Konitsa.

"Our maternal grandmother Euphrosine lived in Konitsa, as well as an uncle of whom we were very fond, and an aunt who would sing the *chansons de geste*, the epics of the indomitable bandits who lived freely in the mountains. We would go to Konitsa on vacation. And how we looked forward to those vacations!

"It was our mother who instructed us in the faith. Her own faith was intense and contagious. At night she would quietly sing hymns to rock us to sleep. She spoke to us of St. Kosmas Aitolos, who had come to Tsaraplana a century ago."

Kosmas grew up in a family of poor farmers. He worked in the fields. At the age of twenty he left for Mount Athos, in order to study, at one of those schools that served as a university for the Greek people. Then he became a monk, a man of prayer and silence, who wept for his sins. At the age of forty-five, he felt himself summoned by God to go out into the world to preach and teach. But was this really God's summons? Kosmas opened his Bible and read: "Let each of you look not only to his own salvation, but also to the salvation of others." (cf. Phil. 2:4) He sought out a spiritual father in the 'desert,' in the far reaches of the Holy Mountain. And the holy man confirmed Kosmas' inner call.

And so Kosmas went to Constantinople, where the patriarch blessed his new vocation. From that time on, until his martyrdom, Kosmas traveled the Greek world, on foot or on the back of a mule. When he came to a village, people would come running. He would erect a large cross in the village square and, standing at the foot of the cross, he would begin the discussion. "Is there someone here who loves his brothers and sisters? Let him come forward and tell me, and I will give him my blessing, and I will ask all Christians to grant him forgiveness. I am God's saint and I love God and my brothers and sisters.

Ah, very good, may my blessing be on you, my son. What is your name?—Kostas—What is your work?—I am a shepherd—When you sell cheese, do you weigh it?—I weigh it.—Ah, you have learned how to weigh cheese, and I have learned how to weigh love. Now I am going to weigh your love . . . .

How can we know that you love your brothers and sisters? When I travel from village to village, I can say over and over again that I love Kostas like my own eyes. But you will need proof in order to believe me. For example, I have some bread, and you have none. If I share my bread with you, that shows that I love you. But if I eat all my bread while you go hungry, that means that my love is false . . . . Do you love that little child over there?

Yes, I love her—If you loved her, you would buy her a gown, because she does not have one. Your love is false. If you want your love to be golden, clothe the poor children.

Because you must have 'the two loves,' the love of God and the love of your neighbor. 'Just as the swallow needs two wings to fly, so we need these two loves for our salvation.'

To gain the 'two loves' is also to have respect for women. The heart of a woman is more disposed to kindness. Our Savior was born of a woman, in order to bless all women. The woman is the equal of the man. She is worthy of our greatest respect, because, so often, what she accomplishes could not be done by a man.

To gain the 'two loves' is to provide teaching.—Do you have a school in your village so that your children can be taught?—No, holy father, we do not.—Then get together, all of you, and build a beautiful school, then set up a school council and find a teacher. All the children, rich and poor, should go to school. Only when your child has studied can they be called a man or a woman. And the school will bring churches, and the churches will bring monasteries."

We have quoted Kosmas at length because his message, in essence, is that of Athenagoras: the two loves that cannot be separated, the respect for women, the sense of social responsibility, the valued place of teaching and the conviction that with education comes a better understanding of the faith. Kosmas founded ten lycées and more than two hundred village schools, including the one in Tsaraplana. He showed a lively interest in technology and its new developments. He made some astonishing prophecies—remember that he died in 1779: "You will see horseless vehicles traveling faster than the hare. There will be a time when Constantinople and Moscow can talk to each other as if they were separated only by a thin partition. You will be able to see from one place to the other as if you were in the same room . . . ."

In the Patriarch we will find this same interest in human technological progress. We could say it is profoundly Greek, not in the Promethean sense of seizing power, but in the spirit of Sophocles, who knew that death and the meaning of life belong to the next world.

And so Aristocles Spyrou went to the village school in Tsaraplana that St. Kosmas had established a century before.

"One of my teachers was very beautiful. When I visited Greece seventy years later, I came back to my village and I saw her again: she was almost one hundred years old, blind and skeletal, but her mind was still sharp. I told her how I had found her so beautiful when I was a child. She was very moved by this belated confession."

After two years of elementary school in Tsaraplana, Aristocles went to the *Scholarchion* in Konitsa—the intermediate school—for five years. But in 1899 everything was disrupted—his schooling and his life.

"I was thirteen years old. My mother and I fell ill at almost the same time. I was seriously ill for several weeks, unaware of what was going on —everything was a jumble. When I recovered, I looked for my mother. She was not there. My father told me that he had sent her to her parent's house in Konitsa. 'We couldn't have two very sick people in the house at the same time.' I waited for my mother to come back. I was still convalescing and was very weak. I was just skin and bones. One winter day when I was sitting outside in the sunshine, a man came to the house: 'Is this where Matthaios Spyrou lives—the one whose wife just died?' And that is how I learned my mother was dead. She had already been dead for three months. She was thirty-seven years old. I have never recovered from this loss. I still miss her."

"My sister was ten years old when our mother died. And so, with the same great courage and fortitude that she displayed throughout her difficult life, she became the little mother, in charge of the household."

"But the three of us, brothers and sister, would often climb to the top of the hill and gaze towards Konitsa, just as the Muslims turn toward Mecca to pray. Konitsa, our mother's town."

The young Aristocles Spyrou only went back to school two years later, in 1901, to go to the Ioannina Secondary School. The following year he decided to enter the Halki Theological School, near Constantinople. The young boy had encountered death—his own near-death and the death of his mother, whom no-one would ever replace. And he discovered, through his faith and what he had been taught, a love that was stronger than death.

One August evening in Halki, Vespers is being served. I do not see the Patriarch. But he never misses a service and just as the bell rings he appears in time for the final blessing. "Have you seen my patriarchal throne?" He takes me into the narthex and shows me a modest monastic stall, beneath a sober and radiant icon of the Theotokos. "So close to the Mother of God," he says.

3. Halki

In September 1903, Aristocles Spyrou was admitted to the Halki Theological School, on the recommendation of the Bishop of Ioannina. There he would complete his secondary education and then study theology.

Halki is an island close to Constantinople, which was then a thriving cosmopolitan city. Nearly half-a-million Greeks lived in Constantinople, half of the city's population. To the north of the Golden Horn they had created a new, modern, European city, where the cultured people spoke French, where the women wore the latest Paris fashions and the men wore the latest London tailoring. Italian music played in the cafes. A string of Greek villages followed the banks of the Bosphorus, with rustic restaurants where you could sit in the summer, lazily watching the huge ships glide by.

"Many people from Epirus emigrated to Constantinople. They became butchers, grocers, and money-changers. Some returned home having made their fortune. Others stayed, their children becoming doctors or lawyers. The boldest were those who chose to leave in their youth. Others only came to Constantinople out of necessity, when there was no work in Epirus, often leaving their family behind. At home the children grew up not knowing their father, until one day they went to Constantinople to meet him."

"When someone left for the City[15] the whole village would accompany him for the start of his journey. They would sing haunting songs of farewell. 'The parting of those living is harder than the parting of the dead.'"

"But the return of someone still in his prime was a time of great celebration. The village matchmakers would count how many heavily laden

15 [Constantinople, Istanbul, is commonly referred to as "the City," or "the Polis."]

horses or mules he brought with him. They would hurry to tell the young women the good news."

"One of my uncles had established a grocery store in one of these villages along the bank of the Bosphorus, in *Megalon Rhevma*, the Great Stream—as it was called in Greek. The Turks called it *Arnavut Koÿ*, the Albanian village—there were many Albanians in Epirus and many Greeks in what was to become Albania. I spent my holidays there. In its way *Megalon Rhevma* is also my village."

Halki is a world away from the enormous sprawling city. It is a haven of peace, silence, and beauty. Imagine a cluster of little islands in the Sea of Marmara. They were first known as 'the Priests' Islands' because of their monasteries, then as 'the Princes' Islands', because many of the Byzantine ruling class had houses there, and these sometimes became their place of exile. On each island, there is a town that bears the name of the island, covering a whole hillside, or a wide valley, or the clifftops. The town lives off the sea, not by farming. The people are Greek, seafarers. When the future patriarch studied at Halki, the island population was almost all Greek.

The Master of the Theological College, himself from the islands, explained to me how the fisherman would spot shoals of fishes in the bays and in the channels between the islands, by watching where the seagulls were diving. Apart from a few gardens, none of the land is cultivated and there are no farms. Once you leave the town, you climb into scrubby, wild moorland. The soil is granular, made up of small grains, ochre in color. The island of Halki gets its name from the color of the soil, *chalkos*, meaning 'copper.' The pines growing in this loose, metallic soil are wide branching, and many limbed, with a reddish bark. The hidden red glow of the soil, of the trunks and branches is made more intensely vibrant by the omnipresence of the sea. This moorland, this 'desert', harbors monasteries and hermitages, such as the Monastery of St. George at Prinkipo, that are its spiritual axis. The islands are anchored both in the sea and in the heavens. At night, you can no longer tell which is the sea and which is the sky. The lights of the towns turn the islands into a vast constellation. From the heights of Halki, crowned by the Theological School, you feel as though you could sail through this star-filled space, where, as it says in the book of Job, the stars are singing in joy. (Job 38:7)

The small town of Halki is built in the valley around the church of St. Nicholas. There are large wooden Turkish style houses and gardens running wild with jasmine. At the pier, you are greeted by people selling sprays of perfumed, thin-stalked delicate jasmine flowers. All along the quay, the sea is so deep that the waves roll gently without breaking: endless, dark blue, silent waves.

The school is set apart on the hill and appears from the distance like a round navel. The white walls are barely taller than the surrounding pines. The theological school is also a monastery, dedicated to the Trinity, and, even if they intend to become married priests, the students live according to the rhythm of monastic life.[16] The monastery, founded by Patriarch Photius in the ninth century, is a thousand years older than the school, which dates only from 1844. At the end of the eighteenth century an earthquake destroyed all the old wooden buildings, but no one was hurt, because, as the Patriarch told me, everyone was in the refectory, and this was undamaged. And so were built the stone buildings that you see today. It is an elegant and spacious complex. The main block, with two perpendicular wings, faces towards the sea, and encloses the much older church, which dates perhaps from the seventeenth century. There are graves crowded against the east wall, including the graves of many patriarchs.

One approaches the magnificent portico and enters through the great hall. At the back of the hall under the two descending flights of the elegant staircase, you see a very simple open doorway. You glimpse the green and gold shade of a vaulted, barrel-roofed cloister. This leads to the church entrance. And in the distance, you can see the two candles burning on either side of the royal doors, one in front of the icon of Christ, the other in front of the icon of the Theotokos.

In this church, baroque art has been transformed into a sort of surrealistic enchanted world. The iconostasis, the pulpit, the patriarchal throne, the chandelier, the kandilia, are all gilded wood carved with delicate foliage through which winged animals fly. Above the choir stalls the lamps are supported by golden dragons. The great cross above the iconostasis seems to be carried in flight by wings of flame.

The Mother of God's quiet presence is felt everywhere. Some of the icons of the Theotokos rank among the supreme masterpieces of Orthodox art. In the narthex, the icon of the *Hodigitria*, the one who points the way, oversees everything: the consolation of all, the consoler of orphans,

16 [The seminary has been closed since 1971, by order of the Turkish Government.]

the Theotokos pointing to her son, who uniquely offers us the way. "You have touched my heart and it trembles at your call. The gaze of the heavenly Queen, who holds the pre-eternal Child, has entered my soul. This gaze contains the power of great purity, the prophetic sacrifice of self and the knowledge of suffering, and the same prophetic assent is seen in the gaze of the child, filled with a wisdom that is no longer child-like."[17] The dark tones of the faces and hands seem to emerge from a long and secret night-time vigil, while the almost violent white flashes that crisscross the flesh are like the flight of luminous birds that reveals the dawn of the endless day.

There is a grand garden around the church and the school, of cypress and pines, olive trees, oleander, and rose-colored laurel. And then roses and more jasmine. The monastic gardens of the Christian East are a symbol of the return to paradise, one of the major stages of spiritual growth. Contrary to our popular way of thinking, the Church and the world are not simply opposed to each other: the Church interpenetrates the world, and there are little corners of the world where prayer and the works of mankind have restored the earth to its true nature, to paradise. You must first rediscover the truth of the earth, where it unites to the heavens to build the temple of God. In Dostoevsky's *Brothers Karamazov,* Alyosha goes out into the monastery garden, after dreaming that his deceased spiritual master has invited him to the Wedding at Cana, to "drink the new wine, the wine of great joy."

> Over him the heavenly dome, full of quiet, shining stars, hung boundlessly . . . . Night, fresh and quiet, almost unstirring, enveloped the earth . . . . The luxuriant autumn flowers in the flowerbeds near the house had fallen asleep until morning. The silence of the earth seemed to merge with the silence of the heavens, the mystery of the earth touched the mystery of the stars . . . . Alyosha stood gazing and suddenly, as if he had been cut down, threw himself to the earth.
>
> He did not know why he was embracing it . . . but he was kissing it, weeping, sobbing, and watering it with his tears, and he ecstatically vowed to love it, to love it unto ages of ages. 'Water the earth with the tears of your joy, and love those tears,' rang in his soul . . . . He wept even for those stars that

17 Sergei Bulgakov, *La Lumière sans Déclin*, translated as *Unfading Light*, Wm.B. Eerdmans, 2012

> shone on him from the abyss . . . . It was as if threads from all those innumerable worlds . . . all came together in his soul, and it was trembling all over, 'touching other worlds.' [18]

"Yes, I began to read Dostoevsky here. He is one of the authors that made the greatest impression. What a great soul! And the way that he could see the lost child, the disintegration of illness, in the omnipotent claims of the atheist, to whose hell Christ comes, to seek him out and to save him from his imprisonment. And Christ brings him true freedom, in exchange for which Christ asks only for love."

"I also collected a whole library of French books; I had learned French while a student in Konitsa. There was a very cheap series called the *Bibliothèque Nationale*. Each volume cost only one piastre.[19] I had almost one hundred of them. Above all I loved Victor Hugo, and *Les Misérables*. The book opens with the portrait of a true bishop, one who knows that prayer and love are yoked together."

"There are two other books that made a great impression on me. One was Wagner's *Parsifal*. Many years later I saw it performed in the Greek Theater, in America. But I read it here first, in a French translation. *Parsifal* is the quest for the Holy Grail. That is, it is the ecumenical quest, the quest that is perhaps the most important event of the twentieth century, that in its essence is none other than the quest for the Holy Grail of the one cup, from which we can share communion in the Blood of Christ . . . . For the last several years I have had a dream, in which the Holy Grail appears over the hills that one sees from the Phanar, over the farther bank of the Golden Horn."

"The other book that was a revelation for me was a completely forgotten French novel by the Countess of Briancourt. I think it was called *The Two Ships*. The author had freely reimagined the Gospel miracle of the overflowing fishing nets. (Luke 5:1–11, John 21:4–14) The two ships are those of Peter and of John. Jesus appears on the shore and tells Peter to cast his nets. Peter replies that he has fished all night and has caught nothing. But he obeys all the same. And the catch that he hauls in is so great that it risks breaking the net. So Peter calls to John and Andrew, who are fishing in another boat. And they come to help him haul in the

---

18 Dostoevsky, Fyodor, *The Brothers Karamazov*, trans. Richard Pevear and Larissa Volokhonsky, NY Farrar, Strauss and Giroux, Kindle Edition, 2011, pp. 361–363, abridged to correspond to Clément's text.

19 [100 piastre = 1 lira, or $.58 in 1910]

miraculous catch. Today it is the same story: Peter calls out to John to help him, or else the net of the Church will break. Peter is Rome: John is the Orthodox East."

"These books were my awakening. Because our professors never spoke to us of the good that might be found in the other Churches, of the very rich Christian experience that they revealed, of everything that we, the Orthodox, had in common with them. Our professors spoke only of differences, of heresies, of what we were opposed to, not of what united us. It was the teaching of fear and fear breeds disdain and distrust."

"Not that Orthodoxy did not need to be protected. The Latin West had tried the patience of our people by seeking to profit from our weakness and the threat of Islam, by converting us, by rebaptizing us. When I was studying theology in Constantinople, a Catholic priest would turn away when he met an Orthodox priest in the street. He would look away; he would pointedly ignore him. I encountered the same thing again in the United States. For example, if a Catholic priest or bishop met me on a train, he would pass by without acknowledgment, or, if we were in the same compartment, he would emphatically ignore me. But I have felt, from the time that I was at Halki, that new times were coming, what I now call the third era of the Church, in which, after those times of hatred and ignorance, we are little by little rediscovering the undivided Church, deepened and enriched . . . ."

"At Halki we scarcely learned anything about the great tradition of the undivided Church, or the tradition of the Church Fathers. That is why I recently set up an Institute of Patristic Studies in Thessaloniki. We were taught an abstract and polemical theology. Now, of course, there was also the Gospel, which is inexhaustible, like the widow's cruse of oil. (1 Kings 18:8-16) This is when I formed the habit of reading a chapter of the Gospels every day. And I was lucky. Vassilios Antoniades, our professor of New Testament, knew how to make us love the Gospels . . . ."

"I spent seven years at Halki and that is why I am so fond of this place. When I come here to relax, I come not so much as patriarch but as a former student. In a way I am a monk of Halki . . . ."

"It is true the coffee was always terrible! I left school detesting coffee. Just recently, I have started drinking it again, but only on doctor's orders, as medicine!"

In 1906, Aristocles Spyrou learned that his father had arranged a marriage for his sister. She was sixteen years old. Too, too soon. This 'too soon' was a bitter portent: early widowhood, a ruined life, so the Patriarch recounted. The following winter, during the first semester of his theology studies, Aristocles fell seriously ill. It was an intestinal disorder that the doctor could not treat. He spent two weeks in the infirmary without getting better. He was wasting away and thought he would have to interrupt his studies. And then, he was suddenly healed from this new ordeal. Taking me to the infirmary, the Patriarch told me, with amusement, how he came to be healed. One day, he saw one of his classmates drinking a dark liquid. "Is it wine?" "How did you manage to get it?" "No, it's not wine, it's a syrup of prunes, a remedy." Aristocles bought prunes and gave them to the nurse who prepared the syrup, and so for six months he treated himself until he was fully cured. He only had to go back to the infirmary for four days in his third year and for one day in his fifth year.

In 1908, his father died. He was fifty-six years old and died suddenly, mostly likely from a heart attack. He was returning from visiting his patients and feeling ill, dismounted from his horse and sat on a rock on the side of the road. Then he fell on the ground. He was found lying there, dead.

Aristocles Spyrou decided to become a monk, not in order to live in a monastery, but to serve people, like his father, to become a monk and deacon, *diakonos*, one who serves.

He intended to serve the Christian people of the Ottoman Empire, whose future seemed, at that time, to be assured. On July 24, 1908, under pressure from the armed forces of the reformers in Salonica, Sultan Abd ul-Hamid had agreed to reinstate the Constitution of 1876 in full force. This guaranteed the equal rights of all the citizens and nationalities of the Empire. There was an explosion of joy in Istanbul. Everyone was in the streets: Muslims, Greeks, Armenians, Catholics, Jews, all together. People greeted each other with kisses, people wept for joy. People sang the *Marseillaise*. When, soon thereafter, the aged 'Red Sultan' tried to restore autocratic rule, he was deposed. The Empire seemed to be definitively committed to becoming a multinational state.

After his father died, Aristocles Spyrou had very little money, despite his prosperous uncle, the grocer. On Sundays, when his classmates went over to Istanbul, he had to stay in Halki. Thus, poverty became a discipline. Today, he says, those who serve the Church should know what it means to be poor. Completing his studies in March, 1910, Aristocles Spyrou took his monastic vows and was ordained a deacon.

He chose Athenagoras for his monastic name. Why Athenagoras?

"I greatly admired the Archdeacon of the Phanar, whose name was Athenagoras. I was also very interested in his namesake, the early Christian writer, one of the great witnesses of the early Church, who lived in Athens in the second century. This Athenagoras loved to reveal the presence of the Word in the work of the ancient philosophers, and even in the works of the poets. As I could not keep my baptismal name, I chose the name Athenagoras. I had got to know the archdeacon through mutual friends. He was very fond of me and became my spiritual guardian. He lived in constant hope of being named metropolitan, and he had promised me that I would then become his secretary. But nothing of the kind happened, and as I had waited a long time already, I agreed to become assistant to the Bishop of Monastir. In the end, the archdeacon did become metropolitan, but only thirteen years after me."

"There was one drawback to my new name. It was not in the Church calendar. The first Athenagoras was too much a friend of the poets to be a strict theologian—and so he was never canonized. So I found I had no name day. But when the archdeacon finally became metropolitan, he discovered a St. Athenagoras in the calendar of one of the old Eastern Churches—the Armenian Church, I think—and managed to get his name day added to the Orthodox calendar. But after his death, I discretely removed this innovation. And so I have no name day celebration." "He who has an ear, let him hear what the Spirit says to the Churches. To him who conquers I will give a white stone, with a new name written on the stone, which no one knows except him who receives it." (Rev. 2:17)

4. Monastir

In July 1910, the young deacon Athenagoras was assigned to serve the bishop of Monastir, Metropolitan Stephanos. The bishop placed him in charge of the schools, the schools that were the guardians of the language and culture of the Orthodox people. Athenagoras was passionate about this work. He embodied the lineage of the educated, teaching monks, who had formed the Greek Church's living Christian

Socratic tradition. This was the lineage of Kosmas Aitolos, who had just been canonized.

While overseeing and organizing the schools, Athenagoras was granted the title of archdeacon. On the death of Stephanos in 1912, the new bishop, Chrysostomos Cavouridis, placed the young archdeacon in charge of the chancellery. He was only twenty-six years old. His erudition and his diligence made him a natural leader. He worked methodically, verifying all the details. He still found time for extensive reading, especially at night. He was interested in everything. And now he was in daily contact with people, setting a pattern that has never changed. Every morning his door is open to everyone, even as patriarch. He loved to say "I am an old bureaucrat. I have spent my life in the service of people and I know them."

In 1910, Monastir exemplified the diversity of the Balkans. There were 30,000 Turks, 15,000 Greeks, two or three thousand Serbs. Here too, the doctors were Greek, and were trusted by everyone. This was a typical Balkan market town, a semi-rural trading center. Cobbled alleys, wide dusty main streets, a jumble of run-down shanties and elegantly carved wooden houses, and then the multicolored crowds on market day—a bustling but casual crowd, with mustachioed Albanians and the proud Vlachs from the mountains entering the narrow shops, with their deep interiors, men sitting at the café tables slowing fingering large prayer beads, an act not so much of prayer as of pure idleness, the rhythm of total leisure. In the distance there is a large mosque, with its interior space of pure emptiness. And there are many small churches, dug into the ground so as not to exceed the height of the surrounding houses, following the ancient edict of the conquerors. The Turks had planted poplars along the riverbanks, to remind them, in these green Balkans, of the dark flame of the cypress in Anatolia . . . .

At that time, Macedonia was a crossroads for the great mystics of the Abrahamic religions. On Mount Athos, hesychasts practiced the descent into the depths of the heart, in order to find the 'uncreated light' that shines from the face of the resurrected Christ. In Thessaloniki, the last of the cabbalists, whose ancestors had come from Spain, pored over the encoded secrets of the Bible, in order to set the divine Presence, the *Shekinah,* free from its exile. All around, the dervishes sought to lose themselves in the invocation of the Name, so that Allah alone would make himself known through them.

There were important *tekkes* of the Mevlevi and the Bektashi fraternities. Archdeacon Athenagoras befriended the dervishes. And in a very rare gesture, the Mevlevi invited him to take part in their spiritual observances. Was not Djedal-Eddin, the founder of the fraternity, surnamed Rumi, the Roman, that is to say, of Byzantium? Was he not a friend of Christians, whose spiritual brother was a Greek monk, near whom he wished to be buried at Konya?

The guests are seated on narrow couches around the walls of the prayer house. The musicians take their place on the stage. Some have tambourines, some have flutes. The bronze tambourines give the rhythm a dull, dark beat: the flutes have a plaintive nasal wail, that penetrates and awakens the soul. The *sheikh* chants a verse of the Mevlana, the words of the Master, Djedal-Eddini-i Rumi.

> O day, arise, the atoms dance
> The souls, struck by love, dance
> The vaulted heavens, because of Him, dance
> I will whisper in your ear
> Whither the dance will lead

And then the dervishes stand. The rhythm gets faster, and they each begin to turn on the spot, turning faster and faster. The bodies spin, the world turns, but the soul becomes the still point, the immobile axis. The soul is freed from thought and becomes anchored in silence and peace.

"They turn in a kind of ecstasy," the Patriarch told me, "and their faces! Their expressions! The face of inwardness, infinitely peaceful and filled with light."

This apprenticeship in the encounter of peoples and religions profoundly marked the future patriarch. Europe, alas, had lost track of this unity. The rise of violent ideologies, the destruction of traditional communities by industrialization and by individualism, the spiritual emptiness, all this had opened the door to buried collective animosities, to the resurgence of the old gods of blood and of the earth, in face of the world of technology and boredom. As the world stood at the threshold of the twentieth century, nationalism rose as a substitute religion. The tragic conflict in which Europe was thrown in 1914 had its beginnings in the Balkans in 1913. The Great War would destroy the multinational empires, including, notably, the Ottoman Empire.

While the liberalization of the Ottoman Empire appeared to have resolved the complex position of the Greek Christians, another tendency had been growing for the past century, inspired by the rise of nationalism in Europe. This was the ideal of a Greek national state based on a unity of language, and, it was imagined, of race.

From the time of its creation in 1822, the European powers had imposed a German monarchy on the embryonic Greek state. The monarchy had little awareness of the reality of the country's religious life and ways of living and wanted to 'civilize' the Greeks. They wanted to impose a bourgeois European ideal under the guise of supposed continuity with the 'lay humanism' of ancient Greece. A new centralized administrative structure destroyed the autonomy of the village community. Education was stripped of its Orthodox roots. The Church was forcibly torn away from the Patriarchate of Constantinople. In face of this destruction of the social and spiritual structures of Greek society, the bishops, many of whom were corrupt, remained on the sidelines. And then rough, lay prophets, such as Christoforos Panayiatopoulos, known as Papoulakos the butcher, emerged, preaching both insurrection and the Gospel. This movement was harshly put down and the armed prophets were thrown into prison. The only way forward, the only way to overcome the destruction and distress was to unite all the Greeks in the 'Great Idea' (*Megali Idea*)—that is to say, in the struggle to free all the Greeks, and unite them into one state, one homogeneous empire.

The Great Idea harnessed popular belief in the resurrection of a Christian Empire. It also appealed to Western-educated Greeks, who saw it as a humanist ideology rather than a religious-political movement. The Great Idea transposed everything into an ardent nationalism, drowning out the 'ecumenism' of Byzantium. Given the intertwining of religions and ethnicities in the Balkans, Asia Minor, and Istanbul, the Great Idea was fraught with extreme violence and extreme disaster, and it provoked the inevitable violent response. A Turkish nationalism also emerged from the ruins of the Ottoman Empire, and it too sought to unite against other races, and become homogeneous.

In 1912, Greece, Serbia, and Bulgaria declared war on the Ottoman Empire and seized all its European provinces. In 1913, the victors themselves clashed on how to divide the spoils. Monastir was first in the hands of the Serbs. But in 1915, Serbia collapsed and the Bulgarians occupied

Monastir. But, in the meantime, the French had landed in Thessaloniki and in order to hold them back, the Germans and the Austrians had marched into Macedonia. In 1918, Monastir, renamed Bitoli, was attached to the new state of Yugoslavia. Nationalism triumphed and there began the extended ordeal of the minorities.

These events revealed the courage of the young archdeacon. When Monastir was under Allied attack in 1916, and during the typhus epidemic in 1918, Athenagoras took care of those in pain, ignoring any danger. He went from house to house, treating wounds, helping, and bringing comfort. He was oblivious to the claims of nationalism. At this time when all the armies of Europe were fighting over one small town in Macedonia he was fearless. He was focused on practical needs. Much as he loves the universality of humanity, he is not in any way drawn to the abstract fusion of mankind. He is interested in the specifics, of every group, of every race.

"In Monastir I got to know the Slavs well," he says, "I got to know the Germans and Austrians. For two years, I lived with the French. All people are good. Every race deserves respect and admiration. I have seen how people suffer. Everyone needs to be loved. If they are mean, perhaps it is because they have not known real love, which is not contained in words, which makes light and life shine."

"I know that there are also dark, demonic forces that sometimes take hold of people and whole nations. But the love of Christ is stronger than hell. In Christ's love, we find the courage to love people, and we discover that, to live, we need all living people and all living races."

In 1918, Athenagoras was thirty-two years old. How well already he knew the human heart and soul! He told me that he heard the wounded soldiers in the military hospital singing a popular Parisian song. He couldn't remember the exact words. It went something like this. "What is life? A little bit of happiness, a little bit of pain, then a little bit of love, and good or bad luck, again." He repeats the words of the song, tenderly, rather than with sadness. Then he improvises, "What is life? Plenty of love, plenty of patience."

5. Athos

In the autumn of 1918, the Serbian army and bureaucracy arrived in Monastir. The new state of Yugoslavia was being formed. At the same time, the Serbian Orthodox Church assumed jurisdiction over the newly acquired regions. Metropolitan Chrysostomos was discretely requested to depart. During this transition, the Metropolitan withdrew to Mount Athos, accompanied by Athenagoras. For the next six months, Athenagoras shared the life of the small monastic community, the *kellion* of Mylopotamos, a metochion, or dependency, of the Great Lavra.

ΩΩΩ

To the east of Thessaloniki, the three fingers of the Chalkidiki Peninsula reach out into the Aegean Sea. At the tip of the easternmost finger, which is about sixty kilometers long and ten kilometers wide, stands Mount Athos, more than 2000 meters high. The Orthodox contemplative tradition originated on Mount Athos and continues to this day. Mount Athos was already a sacred place for the ancient Greeks: the huge boulder thrown by the giant Athos in defiance of Poseidon. Today, it defies the self-sufficiency of the world. It is the last remaining monastic colony, the last of those 'citadels of the spirit' that appeared in the Egyptian desert in the fourth century, just as the Christian Empire was taking shape, to remind the rulers of the world that the ultimate meaning of Christianity was not the organization of earthly affairs, but the taking of the kingdom of heaven by force. (Matt. 11:12)

It was in the tenth century that the first monasteries were established on the 'Holy Mountain', the 'Garden of the Theotokos,' where any female presence was barred. In this land, there is no physical birth-giving. Instead, there is the pursuit of a spiritual birth into eternal life. The ruling presence of the Theotokos, whose icon is venerated in every monastery, infuses this sought-for metamorphosis.

First came hermits, who pursued their radical adventure in close association with a monastic community. The first monastery, the Great Lavra, was founded in the year 963 by St. Athanasios the Athonite. This young Greek from Trebizond, a favorite of the warlord Nicephoros Phocas, had abruptly severed all ties with the world and had sought refuge among the hermits of Athos, escaping from his protector. But, says his hagiographer, the hermits refused to let him stay, he was too young, still smooth-cheeked, whereas the custom was that a novice's beard should 'hold a comb.' "If that is the only objection, then, look here, the comb holds"—and he plunged the comb into his cheek. And so he was accepted. When Nicephoros Phocas became emperor, he helped Athanasios to build a monastery, to bring the foundational disciplines of communal life and brotherly love to the spiritual life. From that time on, monks arrived from all over the Orthodox world—Greeks, Georgians, Southern Slavs, Russians, in the eleventh century, then Italian Benedictines, until the thirteenth century, then Romanians, in the fourteenth century. Twenty great monasteries rose across the peninsula, each effectively self-governing but organized into a federation, whose delegates from each monastery, the Council of *Epistates*, met in the small town of Karyes. From the time of the fourteenth century, Athos has recognized the supreme jurisdiction of the Ecumenical Patriarch, as a monastic state that has been an autonomous protectorate of Greece since 1912.

Every manner of spiritual life has flourished alongside the great monasteries, and under their care—small groups of disciples around a master, the hermit living in almost total silence. All live modestly by the labor of their own hands, growing vegetables, cutting wood, the work of the artisan whose rhythms are conducive to silent prayer.

And thus Athos has nurtured a multi-faceted contemplative life, that responds to the full range of personal vocations, and to the stages of a single monastic life: progressing from psalmody to 'pure prayer' which, in becoming the spontaneous 'prayer of the heart,' reveals the true nature of man, which alone can give voice and visage to creation's cry of universal praise.

"The New Testament says that man and all creation are subjected to vanity, and that all creation gasps and yearns for the freedom of the children of God. This mysterious movement of creation, this inner desire of the soul, this is inner prayer. It is in us and in all things."[20] Mankind is destined to become prayer, as the bird is destined to fly. And the man-become-prayer, even when he is completely unknown and hidden away in a cave, restores the great unity of the human and the divine, and makes living water flow secretly over the whole universe and the works of mankind.

On Athos, there is no monastic 'rule' in the Western sense, only suggestions and examples, shared experience, varying from community to community, but always allowing for the spiritual 'extremism' of solitary life. Side by side, sometimes as rivals, sometimes as co-workers, there are the great monasteries scattered among the forested northern hills of the peninsula—one of the few places where the original Mediterranean for-

---

20 *The Way of the Pilgrim*, no page reference in original

est survives, thanks in part to the absence of female herds of sheep and goats—and in the chalk massif of Southern Athos, a rocky 'desert' of hermitages and kellia, the huts where several monks, most often a master and his disciples, work and pray together.

And so the "art of arts and the science of sciences" is transmitted, through a living tradition of initiation into the path of silence that leads to prayer descending into the heart, "this land of the heart from which water flows, by which I mean the uncreated light that Adam lost through his disobedience . . . this living water fills the inner being with the Spirit and with the divine dew, while it turns the outwards person into fire."[21]

When Athenagoras came to Athos there were seven thousand monks, thanks in particular to the large number of Russian monks, not as yet affected by war and revolution. Among the Russian monks was one of the great mystics of the twentieth century, the Starets Silouan. He was a peasant who could barely write, a worker at the mill of the St. Panteleimon Monastery, who had lived one of the strangest and perhaps most meaningful spiritual journeys. In extreme humility, he found himself to be in hell, to be the only one worthy of damnation. And then, in the depths deeper than hell he discovered the Lord of Mercy. Christ had appeared to him and said, "Keep your mind in hell and despair not." And from this undespairing hell, he prayed with tears that all should be saved and that all should taste the infinite sweetness of the Spirit. This man who had known only Mount Athos and a remote corner of Russia carried all of humanity in his prayer, and, above all, the millions living in Asia. For Silouan, the greatest proof of a person's growth in the Holy Spirit was none other than their evangelical capacity to love their enemies.

Athos can be disconcerting to the Western observer. In the 1960s, the political captivity of Orthodoxy had made recruitment very hard, and what was superficially evident was the picturesque, and then, the darker aspects—the decay, the endless services, the hint of homosexuality. But perhaps this worker you meet at the mill is another Starets Silouan. Saintliness cannot be seen and yet certain places are filled with it. And the attentive soul will quickly discover that the silence of Athos is saturated with saintliness.

---

21 Callistus II, *On Prayer. The Century of Sts. Kallistos and Ignatius, Writings from the Philokalia*, ed. Kadloubovsky and Palmer, Faber, 1992. No page reference in original

ΩΩΩ

Archdeacon Athenagoras retreated to the *kellion* of Mylopotamos, not far from Karyes, on the east side of Athos. Mylopotamos stands at the very tip of a tall promontory, and you can see its watchtower from a distance. In the Middle Ages, all the monastic communities on Athos had to build fortifications in order to ward off the raiding Catalans and other 'Latin' plunderers. As a strange portent, this little monastery had twice given shelter to ecumenical patriarchs: St. Gregory V, who was martyred in Constantinople in 1821 and the great Patriarch Joachim III, who left Mylopotamos in 1901 to resume his patriarchal throne. The very next year, in 1902, he would issue an encyclical that called for the reconciliation of all Christians and for the orderly cooperation of all the Orthodox Churches. "We are seeking here," states the preamble, "the agreement of all the Orthodox Churches on an urgent subject, how to reconcile all those who believe in the true God of the Trinity, so that the day will come when, according to the judgment of God, beyond all understanding, all shall be one." In 1902 this declaration was prophetically new. It would guide all of Patriarch Athenagoras' work.

On one side of Mylopotamos there is a sweeping view over the sea. On the other side, there are the jagged hills, intersected by ravines, green with the foliage of the oak trees, whose leaves in the sun are light-colored underneath, but dark and almost metallic above. In the monastery garden there are lilacs and Judas trees. There are puddles of water everywhere from the autumn rains, that have also flooded the stone-flagged mule paths. A dozen monks work on the land, only celebrating the Divine Liturgy on Sundays and feast days. The measured chanting of the monks brings peacefulness, and harmony with the beauty of the world, to which Athenagoras is acutely attuned. "The beauty of the world," he says from time to time, "is creation's doxology, its hymn of praise." Time on Athos becomes relative. At Mylopotamos, the twelfth hour coincides with the sunset, following the Turkish custom. But at Iveron, founded by Iberians, the ancient Georgians from the Caucasus, the twelfth hour is at sunrise, as in Persia. The cycle of days and seasons is swallowed up by the immensity of the endless blue of the sky and the sea.

But after these six months of retreat, Athenagoras' search for the 'place of the heart' will be a long journey in the world, among the people. In the main church of the Great Lavra there is a fresco of the holy warriors, painted in the sixteenth century by Theophanes, the head of the school of artists on Crete from which El Greco also came. The holy warriors, wearing fantastical armor, are both solemnly dignified and engaged headlong in the most dramatic battle. "I always march ahead, I attack, I am fighting a war," the Patriarch says.

In March 1919 he was invited to serve in the administration of the Archdiocese of Athens. He accepted the invitation and left Athos. "No form of activity is a barrier to the love of God," said the Starets Silouan. "The Apostles loved the Lord, and the world could not quench this love, even though they never left the world behind, they worked in and for the world, and preached there."

ΩΩΩ

As archdeacon, Athenagoras spent six months on Athos, from October 1918 to March 1919. When he returned for a Pan-Orthodox conference held at the Vatopedi Monastery in 1930, he was a bishop. In 1963 he returned as Patriarch to commemorate the millennium of the founding of the Great Lavra in 963. He had planned this celebration, which was a great display of Orthodox unity and of friendship with the monks of the Christian West.

"Athos is a sacred place. Some part of me is an Athonite monk."

As Patriarch, Athenagoras campaigned for the return of monks from Romania and the Slavic countries to the Holy Mountain, and for the Holy Mountain's universal role—to serve all Christians. He ensured that American theology students, coming to Greece for part of their studies, would spend several months in one of the monasteries of Mount Athos.

The path chosen by the Patriarch was that chosen by Kosmas Aitolos, the path of active love, rather than that of the Kollyvades, the eighteenth century reformers who sought the path of pure prayer. But Athenagoras was aware that both paths are needed, and that love cannot transform life unless it is carried by and fed by silent prayer. Only the hidden presence of those who become columns of prayer linking heaven and earth can prevent the disintegration of the universe. Only this hidden presence can reveal the goal of all history, a history come to fruition in its ultimate passage into eternity, with whose fire these columns of prayer already burn.

The opposition that the Kollyvades encountered on Athos at the beginning of the nineteenth century proved to be providential. It led to their being scattered to every corner of the Greek world, to the islands and to the Peloponnese, where they became beacons of a renewed spiritual life. One of these beacons was on St. John the Evangelist's island of Patmos. On Patmos lived one of those spiritual fathers, in direct descent from the Kollyvades, who had received the grace of discernment and who, by the grace of the Holy Spirit, exercised a profound spiritual fatherhood. This was Father Amphilochios, now a saint, who had great influence throughout Greece and even in Western Europe. He had encouraged the establishment of women's monasteries, where contemplation and active love were practiced, where the Jesus prayer was joined to an active social mission. A frequent visitor to Constantinople, Saint Amphilochios was the friend and confidant of the Patriarch.

6. First Secretary

In March 1919, Archdeacon Athenagoras was named Chief Secretary of the Holy Synod of Athens, which oversaw the Greek Church, under the leadership of the Archbishop of Athens, the Greek primate. Athenagoras lived at the Petraki Monastery in Athens. His service to the Church has never separated him from the fundamental rhythms of monastic life.

He was however barred by his own inclinations and by his formative training from ever retreating inside a 'national' Church. The ecumenical movement had its first beginnings in 1919, with the support of Constantinople. In the spring of 1919, the 'Faith and Order Committee', the most doctrinally engaged section of what would become the World Council of Churches, sent a delegation to Athens to obtain the support of the Greek Church. The Archbishop and four other metropolitans signed an equivocally worded letter of support. However, Athenagoras took a great interest and so was asked to learn English—the language of the new ecumenical movement. This decision had momentous consequences. However, before he could exercise his world-wide vocation, the future patriarch would be called to plunge himself deeply into the tragic history of his people. Not in pursuit of a nationalistic dream, but in order to reveal, in the ordeal, the prophetic and diaconal vocation of the Church, a vocation that Orthodoxy sometimes seems to forget.

Greece had been a late entrant to the Great War and this only at the price of civil war. But the total collapse of the Ottoman Empire seemed to offer a real chance for the Great Idea. By the Treaty of Sèvres in 1920, Greece gained all of Eastern Thrace, right up to the outskirts of Constantinople (which was occupied by the Allies), and, most importantly, all of Greek Asia Minor in the region of Smyrna (Izmir), subject to a referendum in five years. Meanwhile, the enraged and humiliated Kemal Atatürk was intent on forming a Turkish nation from the ruins of the Ottoman past.

The Greeks underestimated their opponent, thinking they had hunted down the bands of the Kemalist 'rebellion' in their mountain hideaways. Delusions of power: the Greek 'reconquest' had no popular support: the Greek army was garrisoned in Muslim majority regions. The existentially threatened Turks launched a massive popular uprising. The Greek counter-offensive was overwhelmed. In August 1922, the Turkish army attacked. The major European powers stood on the sidelines and the Greek army was destroyed. Smyrna was set on fire. The Greeks of Asia Minor had two days to gather their belongings and leave the land of their ancestors, since time immemorial.

The Treaty of Lausanne of July 24, 1923 set the seal on this disaster. Greece abandoned Asia Minor and Eastern Thrace. The exile of two million Greeks was ratified under the title of an 'exchange of populations.' The Orthodox minority in Istanbul was permitted to stay, as was the Patriarchate, on condition that it become a purely spiritual entity. Abandoned by the Great Powers, Greece also had to give up any claim to other Greek populated regions that had been part of the sprawling Ottoman Empire. Cyprus was granted to Britain, Rhodes and the Dodecanese to Italy, Northern Epirus to Albania, at that time an Italian protectorate. The Great Idea had led to the worst catastrophe of Greek history, at least since the fall of Constantinople in 1453. Greek Asia Minor was no more. And this was the original Greece, the Greece of Homer and Heraclitus, of John the Evangelist and the Seven Churches of the Apocalypse.

Two million refugees flooded a country of five million people. In 1922, the Greek monarchy collapsed and a revolutionary committee, headed by Nikolaos Plastiras, redistributed the estates of the great landowners and the monasteries to poor peasants and refugees. The Greek Republic was proclaimed in 1924.

The future patriarch watched this unfold day by day. His sympathies were with the Liberals, with Eleftherios Venizelos and Nikolaos Plastiras, although he did not take sides. "Greece has been the homeland of democracy ever since Pericles," he told me. Under democracy he would assume new responsibilities—but before that, he would be blessed by St. Nektarios.

ΩΩΩ

St. Nektarios of Aegina is the most important figure in the Greek Church of the beginning of the twentieth century. A manual laborer in Istanbul, who became a school teacher and then a monk at Chios, Nektarios suddenly entered on a brilliant ecclesiastical career. A rich benefactor had taken notice of him and made it possible for him to study theology, at the age of thirty, and had him presented to the Patriarch of Alexandria. The old Patriarch was so struck by Nektarios that, in rapid succession, he ordained him priest, bishop, and then Metropolitan of Pentapolis and the Patriarch's designated successor. But everything came apart almost immediately. As a result of some never-explained palace intrigue, the Patriarch expelled Nektarios without a hearing.

And so here he was, back in Greece, snubbed and derided at every turn, a dethroned bishop whose ecclesiastical situation would never be made clear. He remained silent: he accepted whatever came to him. At the age of nearly fifty, he served in modest rural parishes. But word of his gifts percolated back from Alexandria. He was invited to head the Athens Theological School, which was then in great decay. He stamped it with his own brilliance, he sought out the best professors, and he gained the hearts of the students through his humility. He was himself a great pedagogue. He never punished his students: he only took the punishment on himself through severe fasting. He would preach in the churches of Athens and Piraeus. He was a spiritual father, a *pneumatikos,* who would read souls, prophesy, and sometimes cure. His practice of the Jesus Prayer became the 'spontaneous' prayer of the heart. "The love of God," the *eros,* he wrote, "is born in the purified heart where divine grace flows forth."

His adoptive son, Costi, who was still living in the 1960s, said that he had many times discovered St. Nektarios at night, deep in prayer and bathed in shining light. He gave away everything that he owned. He would look out of the window and bless those passing by. But he was also a man of thought and action, who understood the importance of taking action. He wrote very profoundly on the Bible and on the Church. He published his books at his own expense, sending them or giving them away to those he thought would learn most from them. He engaged in an active correspondence with Roman Catholics and Anglicans and advocated for the union of the Old Catholics with the Orthodox Church.

He tried to rid Greek political life of corruption and clan-based battles, laying out for his spiritual children the elements of an electoral ethics: "a good citizen makes his choice in the voting booth, by his secret and holy ballot . . . . Do not put your trust in princes, in sons of men, in whom there is no salvation. Choose the virtuous, with stable lives and stable behavior, firm in their speech, prudent in their actions. Do not choose those who are in conflict, worked up, self-interested, embroiled in the filth. Those who think of parliament as a business and not as service to the largest number of people are thieves and intruders. Keep them far away from the oversight of public affairs."

In 1904, he restored an ancient, ruined convent on the island of Aegina and installed several of his spiritual daughters there. Four years later, he gave up the leadership of the Theological School and retired to Aegina. He divided his time between church services, publishing his books, spiritual direction of the nuns and heavy manual labor. In the evenings, sitting under the pine trees in the courtyard, he would chat with his spiritual daughters. "One day we asked Father Nektarios to tell us how all of creation, that the psalmist calls on to praise the Lord, that has neither reason nor speech—sun, moon, stars, light, fire, sea, mountains, trees, all of creation—how could it praise the Lord?" St. Nektarios said nothing. Several days later at the same evening time, under the pines, he said: "You asked me how all creation praises the Lord. Well now, just listen." And we were transported into the transfigured world, where we could hear each distinct creature singing and praising the Lord in its own manner."

When Nektarios served the Liturgy he was assisted by nuns whom he permitted to serve as subdeacons. They wore the deacon's cuffs, the *epimanikia,* the deacon's robes, the *sticharion,* and the deacon's *orarion* or stole, worn crossed over behind the back. This was seen as a scandalous innovation that the Minister of Religion refused to recognize. Nektarios was unmoved. He was guided by clear signs. Sleep had been replaced by prayer. He no longer dreamed. He saw a reality that no longer blindly opposed the visible and the invisible.

The future patriarch met Nektarios in 1920, several months before the saint's death. He went to Aegina to see him. Nektarios was already ill and was being very lovingly cared for by the nuns. Among the Archbishop's entourage in Athens, only good things were said about Nektarios, so Athenagoras reported. Saints turn conventional wisdom and the status quo upside down. And yet, the Patriarch recalled, "I had the impression of a man of infinite goodness, of a man filled with prayer and peace."

Because of Nektarios' illness the meeting was very brief. And Nektarios blessed Athenagoras.

Nektarios died on September 20, 1920, in the indigent ward for the incurable of an Athens hospital. He died after several weeks of pain. His body was left in the ward for eleven hours, on his death bed. The ward was filled with the perfume of sanctity. To wash his body, the attendants took off his old woolen shirt and laid it on the neighboring bed, the bed of a paralyzed man, who stood up, started to walk, and praise the Lord. Since that time, Nektarios has continued to appear to those suffering, and to those who have never heard of him. "My name," he says, "is Nektarios of Aegina." He consoles and he cures. When his tomb collapsed, his body was found to be unchanged. He was placed in a new marble tomb where, three years later, his body was examined by a doctor. He found that the body was not only undecayed, but still flexible, not showing the slightest signs of *rigor mortis*. Miracle cures have occurred at this tomb.

On April 20, 1961, Patriarch Athenagoras canonized St. Nektarios, in recognition of his sainthood. "Shortly after my visit to Aegina a painter did a portrait of Nektarios. I had known this painter on Corfu and he gave me one of his preliminary sketches, a lively and penetrating study. I did not imagine then that I would come, as patriarch, to canonize Nektarios. But I placed this sketch on my desk, where it sits to this day."

ΩΩΩ

The Greek Church experienced a time of mission and renewal, thanks to the work of Father Eusebios Matthopoulos. This monk of *Mega Spelaion*,[22] one of the spiritual centers inspired by the Kollyvades, had managed to resist the evangelical overreach that had excluded the great Greek nineteenth century reformers from the Church. He patiently criss-crossed the country, organizing small groups of disciples that he brought together, in 1911, in a new brotherhood, *Zoe*—"the Life." Lay people and priests, under a vow of obedience, gathered for daily Bible reading, regular Communion and service to others. This became a movement of renewal.

It was only later that the limits of the movement became clear: a moralistic pietism, the formation of groups of 'the pure', set apart from

22 ["The Great Cave," a famous monastery near Kalavryta, in the Peloponnese]

the daily life of the Church. In the 1920s, *Zoe* was still in its youth. Strangely, its members had to undertake never to become bishops. Too many Greek bishops were seen as careerists, and the long period of Ottoman rule had left a pattern of corruption. This only made the split between the apostolic renovators and the bishops all the more marked.

Plastiras' reform government asked the Synod to name young bishops, who would be close to the people and above all suspicion (there was no separation of Church and State in the new Greece). And so Athenagoras was named Bishop of Corfu, Metropolitan of Kerkyra and Paxos. He was thirty-seven years old.

He arrived in Corfu to a scene of chaos. It was February, 1923. Thousands of refugees were camped wherever they could find space, in the schools, in the churches. The local government was overwhelmed. There had not been a bishop for several years. Athenagoras quickly took stock of what was needed. He used the available resources of the Church, and the support of the faithful, to build housing. He obtained the use of the enormous barracks, built by the English after 1815, to house refugees. He opened a medical center in his own house, where the care was free, and the doctors worked *pro bono* or were paid by the bishop. He also set up a job placement office—it wasn't enough to house the exiles, they also needed work. Since the women also worked—in fact they found work more easily—he set up childcare and kindergartens. He expanded the schools and set up new schools, so that soon all the refugee children were in school. There was only one secondary school on Corfu. Gaining the backing of the Minister of Education, himself, by chance, a native of Corfu, Athenagoras had a second school built, as well as a technical college. In 1924, he set up a seminary, to educate priests and theology teachers. He wanted an educated and engaged priesthood. And he wanted engaged parishes, not just random individuals assembled side-by-side as the 'clients of the priest', in Athenagoras' expression, where the priest becomes just the distributor of the holy gifts. In 1929, he set up an apprenticeship training center for the refugees from Northern Epirus.

And he not only gave material aid. He visited the refugees, listening to them and consoling them. Here again he was totally engaged. Rarely did he meet someone in the street without being stopped. And, displaying his horror of pharisaism, faced with the extent of poverty and deprivation, he lifted the Church's rules of fasting. "Someone who is dying of hunger does not need to fast."

In August 1923, Benito Mussolini decided to settle Greek claims to the Dodecanese, once and for all. As part of this campaign, on August 31, an Italian naval squadron opened fire on the old fortress of Corfu, and then landed troops to occupy the town. But the fortress was not a garrison. It held seven thousand refugees from Asia Minor and three hundred and fifty sick Armenian children. Armenians fleeing from the genocide of their people, during and after the First World War, had been swept up with the fleeing Greeks. The naval bombardment caused sixteen deaths and wounded fifty people. The people of Corfu took refuge. The local officials abandoned the town. Bishop Athenagoras went to the port and persuaded a fisherman to ferry him out to the naval squadron. He was met by Admiral Solari, who put on lordly airs and asked the bishop what he wanted. "I am not here to make a request but to lodge my protest. You have done wrong. Why are you shooting at women and children? They have done nothing. If you want someone to punish, here I am, the bishop."

Athenagoras' courage won him the respect of the Italians. The admiral came on shore the next day and brought compensation for the victims. The inhabitants of Corfu believed that their bishop had warded off disaster. When the Italians pulled back several weeks later, Athenagoras was feted as the 'savior of the island.'

However, in these formative years of the Greek Republic, partisan battles also raged on Corfu. The monarchists denounced the new bishop as the tool of the revolutionary government. Had he not just been offered a seat in the Synod? He had turned it down. Whatever his personal sympathies, he was not a supporter of the regime. He was the servant of all his people, above all political controversy.

His ecumenical vocation began to take shape. There were many Catholics on Corfu, which had, for many years, been inhabited by Venetians. Athenagoras established friendly relations with their bishop and could be seen walking with him in the streets—a gesture that was very meaningful in the Mediterranean, where the public street still retains the flavor of the *agora*, the market square.

In 1926, he took part in the worldwide assembly of the YMCA, in Helsinki. Although predominantly Protestant, the YMCA served all confessions, and in particular had offered great support to the Russian emigration, through its youth associations and its publications.[23] But, the Patriarch told me, the Greek Church distrusted the YMCA as a source of Protestant proselytizing. "But I had started supporting this movement when I was a deacon. Besides, in Helsinki I was more the representative of the Greek government than of the Church."

In fact, rather than succumbing to Protestant influence, through the YMCA Athenagoras discovered Russian religious philosophers such as Sergei Bulgakov and Nicolai Berdayev. Through their Orthodox understanding of the Holy Spirit, these thinkers were trying to understand how to engage contemporary culture, in the spirit not of rejection but of transfiguration.

Nevertheless, it was on Corfu itself, during the early, difficult months of his new ministry, that Athenagoras made his most important ecumenical gesture. The Armenian refugees, escaping from hell, had no priest of their own. Athenagoras himself gave them Holy Communion.

7. America, America

The oldest monument to Greek settlement in America, is, characteristically, a school. The oldest wooden school in the United States, is in St. Augustine, Florida, built in 1680, at a time when Florida was part of Spain. In 1767, a small group of immigrants founded New Smyrna, not far from St. Augustine. In 1864, the first Greek church is recorded, in New Orleans, home to a colony of Greek merchants. These were isolated episodes.

But from the end of the nineteenth century to the First World War, huge migrations brought millions of people to the New World from the Mediterranean regions and the Slavic speaking lands. This new wave of immigration made Protestant, Anglo-Saxon America into a multicultural, cosmopolitan nation, a microcosm of humanity. The Greeks were part of this wave, which peaked with the arrival of hundreds of thousands of refugees from Asia Minor after the First World War,

The industrial Northeast was the heartland of Greek immigration. The newcomers, not knowing a word of English, joined the underclass of casual laborers in factory towns such as Lowell, Massachusetts, tak-

---

23 [The YMCA Press and the Russian Student Christian Movement (ACER-MJO) were vital elements of the social and intellectual rebirth of Orthodoxy in France]

ing the hardest jobs. This wave of immigrants brought whole communities, who formed Greek speaking enclaves. The churches followed their arrival. By the end of the nineteenth century there were Greek churches in New York, Chicago, and Lowell.

This Greek population—very significant in comparison to the population of the mother country—formed an insignificant minority in America, at the very bottom of the social ladder. And, threatened by this invasion of other nationalities and other faiths, America clung to a model of nineteenth century Anglo-Saxon provincialism, a model of white Anglo-Saxon Protestant superiority. The social hierarchy was mirrored in the religious hierarchy, in which the Orthodox were at the very bottom—Carpatho-Russians from the Austro-Hungarian Empire, Russians, Syrians, Lebanese and Greeks. And what did this matter anyway to the mass of poor Greeks! They thought of themselves as temporary residents, above all glad to have a place to live, and convinced that they would soon return home.

But the boldest and most capable of them, and very soon the boldest of the new American-born generation, vigorously accepted the 'challenge' of America, to use the historian Arnold Toynbee's expression. These were people accustomed to a challenge, as the ascent of the Greeks in Ottoman society had already shown. Soon a similar pattern emerged, adapted to the American context. For these Greeks, becoming a good American citizen, speaking English, accepting the novel authority of the Supreme Court, joining the ferocious battle of free competition, becoming 'good neighbors' in the suburbs, did not require them to give up their ethnic and religious identity. This America was for everyone—at least if they were white—it was for those who knew how to seize the opportunity, where you could choose freely to have your community, your club, your church. Most Greek Americans maintained their Orthodox faith. More and more parishes were established. By 1925, two-thirds of all today's parishes had been established.

The first parishes were placed under the jurisdiction of the Ecumenical Patriarch, because Constantinople was the traditional center of the Greek-speaking Church, and because it had universal jurisdiction, beyond the limits of the established Orthodox nations. However, in 1908 the Greek Synod[24] obtained jurisdiction over the American parishes and this remained the case until 1918. During the First World War, America and Constantinople were on opposing sides. But the Greek Synod was weakened by the constant political strife in Greece and did not take any steps to organize parish life in America.

A proposed holistic solution took shape for all the Orthodox in America, within the framework of the Orthodox diocese that had been established by the Russian Church. Russian missionaries had evangelized the native people of Alaska, the Aleuts, and the Kodiak people, starting with a mission in 1794. After the purchase of Alaska from Russia in 1867, the diocesan seat was moved, first to San Francisco and then to New York, under the dynamic Bishop Tikhon (now St. Tikhon). It seemed that there would be one Orthodox Church in America, in which the Greeks would take their place, while retaining their autonomy.

But the Russian Revolution of 1917 split this 'Orthodox Diocese' into fiercely opposed factions. For the Greeks, in order to keep their historic language and not to be part of a distant 'national' Church, the only choice was to place themselves under the protection of the Ecumenical Patriarch.

With the end of the First World War, Constantinople sent Metropolitan Meletios (Metaxakis) on an exploratory mission to America. He drew up the basis for the local organization of the American diocese. In 1922, Meletios was elected Patriarch Meletios IV. He immediately decided to restore Constantinople's jurisdiction over the Greek parishes in America, grouping them in a new archdiocese, headed by his emissary, a patriarchal exarch.

These new arrangements muted the impact of the unfolding political crisis in Greece, from which the Greek diaspora in America was not, however, fully insulated. The new archdiocese was too weak to insist that all its parishes remained neutral. One by one, successive exarchs were powerless: schisms emerged, parishes separated, and factions formed within parishes. However, with the election of the Liberal government of Venizelos in 1928, which enjoyed broad popular support, and the election in the same year of a dynamic patriarch, Photios II, to the Ecumenical Throne, the ground was prepared for ending these disputes. On August

24 [On, March 8, 1908, the Ecumenical Patriarchate, under the leadership of Patriarch Joachim III, placed the churches in America under the jurisdiction of the Church of Greece.]

30, 1930, Photios II and the Synod of Constantinople designated Metropolitan Athenagoras as Archbishop of America. He arrived in New York on February 24, 1931.

Athenagoras forged an organic unity from a jumble of isolated and often hostile parishes, balancing the need for local autonomy and administrative coordination. As he had in Corfu, he displayed the visionary qualities of a statesman. Working tirelessly, he loved to talk to his coworkers, to his friends, to his guests. He asked endless questions. He would seek out advice, but once he had made his decision he was never swayed, and never second-guessed his decision. "I make war. I attack. I always charge ahead." In the evenings and late into the night he recharged himself by reading a vast range of literature. He set up a Greek Theater, where Sophocles, Euripides, Wagner, and Rimsky-Korsakov were staged. He read the principal works of Father Sergei Bulgakov, in French, and got to know Bulgakov personally when he came to the United States.

The early years were difficult. In addition to political tensions and personal disputes, he had to deal with parishes that had become accustomed to acting independently and irresponsibly, parishes that were geographically widely scattered, and that, particularly in the Northeast, were in competition with each other. Influenced by Protestant practice, the laity wanted complete control over the parish and had little understanding of the priest's or bishop's proper role. Athenagoras was, however, well prepared to understand the American way of thinking and the desire for local autonomy. He was a long-time member of the YMCA. He took part in the YMCA General Assembly in Cleveland in 1932, and here he was able to familiarize himself with Protestant ideas. He also had the experience of the self-governing parishes of the Ottoman Empire. In Corfu, he had already emphasized the importance of the life of the community and lay participation.

To begin with, he asserted the Archdiocese's independence from political events in Greece. This independence was critical when Ioannis Metaxas declared himself dictator, in 1936. Then, after stormy debates at the Clergy-Laity Congress, held in Chicago in 1933, Athenagoras achieved the adoption of a new balanced constitution, that clearly defined the mutual responsibilities of the clergy and the laity. The Archbishop was responsible for the pastoral and spiritual direction of the Church, working in close collaboration with a Council of Clergy and Laity. A biennial

Assembly, consisting of the archbishop, the bishops, and delegates from clergy and laity, had the ultimate authority to decide major issues.

But Athenagoras was particularly concerned with the organization of parish communities. "I organized four hundred parish communities in America, in a rigorously clear manner. Each parish was based on the cooperation of three elements: the spiritual authority of the priest, who was designated by the bishop after consultation with the faithful; the authority of the royal priesthood of the laity, which resided in a lay president, elected by the members of the parish; and the authority of culture and wisdom, represented by the teachers. Each parish community had its own school, its women's association (the Philoptochos), responsible for outreach and charitable assistance, and its youth group. Everyone should be responsible for the life of the parish. The priest should not turn the sacraments into a money-making venture. If you want to have your child baptized, or to marry in the Church, you should belong to the parish and actively support it financially, or, maybe, pay up all your arrears!"

"The life of the Church revolves around the great feasts of the liturgical calendar. But these feasts should not end. We need to make them the high points of life in this great family that is the parish community. So we decided that the Paschal season would be the time for the recognition of mothers, the forty days in which we chant "Christ is Risen," "*Christos Anesti*," during which there is a special focus on the Theotokos. And, starting with the feast day of St. Basil, January would be a month of celebration of the parish community, because St. Basil was, first and foremost, a pastor."

Thanks to St. Basil, Athenagoras was able to resolve the financial problems that had resulted from the *Megale Katastrophe*, the forced resettlement of hundreds of thousands of Greeks. The parish bank accounts were empty, the Archdiocese was in debt.

"I told them: 'I have found a benefactor who will deposit $80,000 a year for us into one of the most trustworthy banks.' And who was it? St. Basil. And what is the bank? The hearts of our people! The Feast of St. Basil today (1968) brings in more than $100,000 a year to the Greek Orthodox Archdiocese of America.[25]

Becoming an American citizen, Athenagoras was ready to adapt Greek Orthodoxy to American realities, just as long as dogmatic and sacramental integrity was not impacted. Not liking the Turkish-style music

25 [Today this would be worth nearly $1,000,000]

that had evolved in Constantinople, not yet familiar with the beauty of the original Byzantine chant—which he later actively worked on recovering and restoring at the Phanar—he introduced organs into the church and allowed Mendelssohn's "Wedding March" to be played at weddings.

In particular, Athenagoras addressed the economic and social standing of the priest. The poverty of priests in Greece, who were obliged to have long hair and beards and to wear a cassock, kept many young men away from the priesthood, even though they wanted to serve the Church. If this picture was carried over to America, there would be no possibility of attracting American priests. Athenagoras wanted young American Orthodox priests—from Greek families or converts. He decided that his priests should not wear the flowing black *exorason*, or cassock,—itself a Turkish innovation—or long hair and beards—the dress code imposed by the civil authorities of Byzantium and continued by the Ottoman Empire. The priests would be properly compensated by the parish. The priests would be educated, so they would be true pastors, not just servers of the liturgy. And so, in 1937, Athenagoras established Holy Cross Theological School as a two-year college in Pomfret, Connecticut, where the students would complete their studies in Athens or at Halki. In 1947, the college moved to Brookline, Massachusetts. Here the students could benefit from Boston's cultural resources and the presence of some of the best universities in the United States.

Going even further in his efforts to 'humanize' the status of the priest, Athenagoras drafted a reform proposal that would have allowed priests to marry after their ordination: the ordination of married men had been the practice of the Orthodox Church since the earliest days. Athenagoras had been planning to bring this reform to the Biennial Assembly. But before he could do this, he was elected Patriarch.

Athenagoras built a solid foundation for the future of Greek Orthodoxy in America. Under his leadership, his successors, Michael (1949–1958) and Iakovos (1959–1996) continued his work and obtained recognition for Orthodoxy as one of the 'major religions', alongside the Protestant confessions, Catholicism and Judaism.

Today there are five million Orthodox in the USA, of whom one million are Greek Orthodox. To address the problem of multiple Orthodox national jurisdictions in America, Archbishop Iakovos convened a series of reunions of all the Orthodox jurisdictions, and this resulted, in 1960, in the establishment of the Standing Conference of Orthodox Bishops (SCOBA), as a permanent consultative and coordinating entity.

The Orthodox were becoming more completely part of American society. At the inauguration of Richard Nixon, Archbishop Iakovos was invited to offer a prayer, after the Protestant pastor, the Catholic cardinal and Rabbi Edgar Magnin, but before Pastor Billy Graham. But this was also the beginning of the 1960s student rebellions and anti-war movements that challenged the establishment. At Selma, Archbishop Iakovos marched in his full clerical garb, alongside Martin Luther King. As Patriarch, Athenagoras watched these developments closely. Of all the Church leaders, Athenagoras was perhaps the most sympathetic to the counterculture and the 'underground church' movements in the United States.[26]

The other urgent problem was that of language. The Greek Orthodox Church had been reluctant to adopt the English language in its services. The Patriarch counseled flexibility: Greek in some cases, English in others. He had helped to create a miraculous 'New Greece' in America, an image of Byzantium, deeply Orthodox and fully engaged in the work of a multi-ethnic society. As Patriarch, Athenagoras would pursue this multiethnic ideal on the level of the whole planet and all religions.

As Archbishop, Athenagoras had personally known the two presidents who had held the office during his eighteen years in America: Franklin Delano Roosevelt and Harry Truman. The first time that he met Roosevelt was in the spring of 1931. Roosevelt was then Governor of New York. He was elected President eighteen months later.

"When I stood up to leave, Roosevelt also tried to stand but with difficulty (because of his paralysis, resulting from childhood polio). I went to him and kissed him on the forehead. And suddenly, these words came to me: 'The next time I see you it will be in the White House.' And that is what happened. The White House was always open to me and I met the President on many occasions. 'Your faith is your strength', I told him one day. At one of these meetings, I was able to plead the cause of the Russian Church. I think this was in 1935, when Soviet Foreign Minister Litvinov came to the USA, with the restoration of diplomatic relations with Soviet Russia, and for trade negotiations. I said to Roosevelt: 'You are a man of faith. You must defend the

26 [See *The Underground Church*, edited by Malcolm Boyd, New York, Sheed and Ward, 1968]

believers. I beg you to demand the improvement of the conditions of Russian Christians.'"

Several months later, the new Soviet constitution granted freedom of religion and restored the civil rights of members of the clergy.[27]

Athenagoras was even closer to Harry Truman, with whom he continued to correspond until his death. He perceived Truman to be a "great statesman and a person of great humility and simplicity." Truman had been one of the most self-effacing vice-presidents, a self-described shop keeper who had entered politics when his business failed. Roosevelt's sudden death in 1945 brought Truman to power at a critical moment in the Second World War. The war had to be ended, the economy converted back to civilian production, and his predecessor's ambitious social policy had to be continued or rejected. After the morally agonizing decision to bomb Hiroshima and Nagasaki, that brought the war to an end, Truman was hesitant to act in domestic politics. The war had increased the country's production capacity tenfold. Why should the state intervene when prosperity would resolve all problems? But the new president understood that the 'invisible hand' of the market economy was unseeing, and that, if politics did not address the common good, pockets of poverty would persist. And so, Truman adopted the broad outlines of Roosevelt's social program into a new plan for social justice—the Fair Deal.

Athenagoras was in favor of the Fair Deal, just as he had been in favor of the New Deal—he well understood the problems of the underclass, of day laborers, of urban and rural poverty. He spoke of slums where gangs of half-naked children played next to mounds of garbage that the city did not bother to collect. When Truman ran for reelection in 1948, the Archbishop for once abandoned his neutrality and came out strongly in favor of the president.

America left a profound mark on Athenagoras, not only from deep familiarity but also from deeper, more personal connections. Athenagoras found a successful multi-ethnic society in America. In drafting the Constitution, the founding fathers, among whom were great landowners and leading thinkers, took care to protect the rights of every minority [with the glaring exception of enslaved African-Americans]. This concern, this system of checks and balances, this respect for local freedom embedded in a federal structure, has allowed America

27 [This clause of the Soviet Constitution was largely not implemented]

to become a vast patchwork of minorities. Athenagoras' life may be understood in the context of the collapse of the multi-ethnic Ottoman Empire, and America's success as a multi-ethnic land of many religious faiths. Or again, in the contrast between the catastrophe of forced Greek emigration from Asia Minor and the miracle of the Greek communities in the New World.

At the Phanar, when so many visitors and pilgrims from this new Greece come to see the Patriarch, you can feel all the raw optimism of America. America is the land where penniless and devastated Greeks, carrying in their souls the images of Smyrna in flames, were welcomed and were able to establish themselves, become prosperous, build their churches and schools, and be proud of their heritage, without discrimination, because everyone, in America, is an immigrant, or the descendant of an immigrant.

At the Phanar, I talked to one of the Skouros brothers, the founders of what became 20th Century Fox. "He came to America aged twelve," the Patriarch explained to me. "He sold bunches of flowers to people as they left the theater." I talked to the Greek American Supreme Court Justice from Wisconsin, a state where the Greeks are a tiny minority. In this open and hard society, an energetic person, backed by a strong community, can choose their own path. But let me pause here on this married couple who have come to see the Patriarch. They are simple folk—not worldly, not intellectuals. He is a machinist in a tire factory, unshaven, with grime embedded in his fingernails. He is in a hurry to take off his jacket. She is more nervous. Her face is that of a true Greek—one of those women whom life does not destroy but only sculpts. Both of them are at ease in today's world yet deeply rooted in the faith. They respond warmly to the old Patriarch as he talks, not just about the meaning of life, but about their town, their neighborhood, as though he had walked there only yesterday.

There was a deeper, hidden, common feeling between Athenagoras and America: this ability to unite the mystical ideal and the practical solution, the spiritual vision and the day-to-day efficiency. On the Patriarch's desk at the Phanar, on one side you see the portrait of St. Nektarios, on the other side, the *Memoirs of Harry Truman* and three little volumes entitled *Mental Efficiency*.[28]

---

28 [A self-help book by the English novelist Arnold Bennett, in praise of American efficiency]

8. Byzantium—Constantinople—Istanbul

The election of Patriarch Athenagoras I came about in an unusual way. A new patriarch, Maximos, had been elected in 1946. He was fifty-two years old and was expected to serve for a long time. But he fell mentally ill. His illness caused him to be terrified of everything to do with the sacred, and he had to resign. And so Athenagoras was elected, on November 1, 1948.

"When I visit him, I am careful not to wear my official garb, so as not to cause him any resentment." I saw the Patriarch after one of these visits. He was sad and remained quiet for a long time. Then he explained to me what a remarkable person Maximos was, and that his agony was all the more terrible because Maximos experienced these crises with complete lucidity. I began to suggest that it was providential that this mental illness had made it possible for Athenagoras to become patriarch. He waved his hand to stop me. "Who can know," he said, "who can know."

Athenagoras arrived in Istanbul on January 26, 1949, on President Truman's official plane. In the unfolding Cold War, America was trying to obtain the support of Turkey and Greece, in order to contain the communists who had seized power in the Balkans. The split between Moscow and Yugoslavia, and the end of the Greek civil war seemed to create an opportunity for the American policy. Athenagoras was seen as the one person who perhaps could reconcile the Greeks and the Turks. More generally, it was hoped that his prestige would help the Ecumenical Patriarchate counterbalance the influence of Moscow in the Orthodox world.

The legal restoration of the Orthodox Church in the Soviet Union, as the Russians fought the Nazis in the battle for the Fatherland, had given the Russian Church a chance to reorganize, and now it was gathering the support of sister Churches inside and outside the Iron Curtain. The high regard in which the Russian Orthodox Church was held in the Arab world favored Russian efforts in the Middle East. The Pan-Orthodox Conference held in Moscow in 1948 was marked by pointed hostility to the West.

But things would develop very differently. The unforeseen twists of history and the visionary genius of Athenagoras would overturn any carefully made plans. Any hope of reconciliation between the Greeks and the Turks was destroyed by the Cyprus crisis of 1955. The new patriarch became the apostle of a Pan-Orthodox gathering, not in opposition to Moscow, but working with the Russian sister Church. [Greek independence fighters in Cyprus sought reunion with Greece, which Turkish partisans fiercely opposed—this led to Cyprus' independence and the partition of the island into Greek and Turkish enclaves. In Istanbul, violent mobs destroyed Greek businesses and houses, and as a result, many of the Greeks who had remained in Istanbul, now began to leave.]

"Constantinople is the world's crossroads. East and West meet here, Asia and Europe, the Slavic north and the African south." Queen of cities, Constantinople is also a world capital: its rivers are arms of the sea, one riverbank is in Asia, the other bank is in Europe. Emperor Justinian built the Hagia Sophia on the forelands of the hills, to show himself greater than Solomon and to make the city the symbol of the New Jerusalem. Suleiman built his mosque to show himself greater than Justinian, and Ahmed ringed his mosque with six minarets, so that his capital would become a new Mecca. Each wanted to give form to the vision in the Apocalypse, of the Holy City where "the glory and honor of the nations is crystallized," where the sea is no longer hostile chaos but the river of the water of life. (Rev. 16:1-14; Rev. 22:1) And the name itself of Istanbul, officially renamed by Atatürk, means "towards the town," *eis tin polin*, as the Greek peasants would say to the invaders, pointing them towards the town that reaches towards the eternal city.

Little remains in Istanbul of the terrestrial grandeur of Byzantium. The palaces and the statues have disappeared. Only the city walls remain, the form of the city, just as the soul is the form of the body. In the city square, the Maidan, formerly the hippodrome, still stand the serpent column, with its three-headed serpent broken off, and the Obelisk of Theodosius, brought in the year 357 from the Temple of Karnak, in Egypt.

The obelisk is a shaft of pure porphyry, the symbol of an impersonal eternity. The serpent column, with its three interwoven bronze serpents, was an offering to the Temple of Delphi from the Greek cities that had miraculously defeated the Persians at Salamis and Plataea. Here is the whole destiny of Byzantium: an encounter between East and West, between the celestial affirmation of eternity and the terrestrial struggle for the freedom of the individual and of the city. Its ultimate synthesis and its transcendence are perhaps found in the divino-humanity to which Byzantine spirituality witnesses, that becomes pure adoration.

The French theologian, Louis Bouyer, wrote that "the Byzantine liturgy is indeed a sacred festival, in which all the resources of Christian humanism are deployed in the glorification of God, not just as decorative notes but in their essence." In Byzantium, the true creators were not the refined, Socratic philosophers or the masters of the applied arts on whom almost all historians focus. They were the musicians, the poets, the iconographers, who, in their meditation on a total, liturgical form of art, created a heaven of timeless beauty here on earth.

When Mehmet II entered Byzantium, the city was only a shadow of its former glory. There had been one million inhabitants: now there were only one hundred and fifty thousand, and, as the Conqueror, the *Fatih*, nostalgically recalled, "the spider spun its web in the palaces of the Caesars."[29] Mehmet II, who knew the thinkers of ancient Greece, particularly admired the Stoics. He had his portrait painted many times by Italian artists. You can see two of these portraits in the Topkapi Museum. In the portrait by Gentile Bellini, you are struck by the fine-featured, melancholy face, with its long thin nose and sealed lips. The portrait by Costanzo de Ferrare emphasizes his massive neck and shoulders. In contrast to this solidity, the elegant face is that of an eagle at rest, an eagle lost in thought.

Topkapi Sarayi, the Imperial Palace Museum, with its gardens, its grand buildings overlooking the sea, its albums of illuminated Persian manuscripts and miniatures, evokes a sensibility that is different than that of Byzantium, a different type of beauty, no longer the transfiguration of *eros*, but the ultimate distillation of sensuality. There is an animal innocence, with a hint of cruelty, a hard-edged, severe sexuality lacking tenderness, yet steeped in nostalgia. The gardens, too, express this nostalgia . . . you feel a closeness to Persia, the land where the word for garden is *pardes*, paradise . . . . The gardens are delicate statements of space, without blocks of shrubs or massed plantings—each tree and each flower stands in its own quadrant. Softly incandescent roses punctuate the space, which overall is framed by pine trees—and everywhere there is the aroma of pines and the perfume of flowers. At the end of the seventeenth century, the Turks loved to make flower gardens of tulips, into which at night they would set tortoises loose, with candles stuck on their shells . . .

ΩΩΩ

The day that the Turks entered Constantinople, the Patriarch told me, was the feast day of the Church of St. Theodosius. The little church was all decorated with flowers. Seeing the flowers, the invaders left the church and its worshipers unharmed. They called it the 'Church of the Flowers.'

---

29 [A reference to the Persian author Firdausi, *The Book of Kings*]

There is a cruel innocence, of a certain 'East.' In the museum, the album that belonged to Suleiman the Magnificent is covered with intermingled peach trees, almonds in flower and cypresses, the symbols of life and death. With the same artistic precision, combat and suffering is portrayed in these miniatures in delicate arabesques, a severed arm appearing among the flowers, its blood yielding more flowers.

From the long nomadic past of the Turkish people, a life shared with animals, Turkish art has an acute sensitivity to wild animals. In the miniatures of Mehmet II's album, you see a precision in the rendering of the muscular mass, its knots. The animal is reduced to its muscular casing. It is portrayed as an embodiment of strength—unlike in Japanese art where everything becomes a wisp of eternity. One can feel the continuity with the art of the Hittites and of Mesopotamia, as Atatürk himself proclaimed. Sheltered by Islam and sheltered by God, Istanbul had given birth to a delicate and adamantine culture, that produced real beauty, marked by the love of flowers, a feral energy, the presence of death. Then came the collapse of the Ottoman Empire and the shock of Westernization.

The people, especially the poor, have a real nobility: the intense, pure love of their land, the love of the father for his children, the modesty of young lovers, and that ability to keep quiet, and to be present, without a false show of emotion, with those dark eyes, calm and profound in expression. Great fighters, great poets, great mystics—but not made for the modern world. The Greeks and the Armenians mastered the modern world, and became the professional classes, and for this reason, among others, they were hated.

And then came Atatürk, whose greatness the Patriarch explained to me. From the ruins of the Ottoman Empire and of Muslim culture, he gave birth surgically to a modern nation. He rejected the two temptations of the developing world—religious fanaticism and Communism. As a pseudo-religion, Communism turns modern rationalism into a form of religious fanaticism. Atatürk laid the basis for modern Turkey to be a tolerant nation, the inheritor of the Ottoman lands and their history. But he was a genius and his vision would not soon be realized.

In 1968, the Istanbul in which Athenagoras had lived since 1949 was a city where the civilizations were overlaid and juxtaposed, without yet becoming one. Beyoğlu, the Pera of the Greeks, a cosmopolitan district with Greek and Armenian merchants and dilapidated buildings from the turn of the nineteenth century, opened to the north to a sprawling modern city that climbs the hills overlooking the Bosphorus, the work of young Turkish architects. The Turkish old town, built on the Byzantine core, with several Greek neighborhoods and the old Jewish quarter on its western edge, has been cut through by modern roads, ringed around by highways and violently sliced apart by a giant multi-lane highway. When you reach the central railroad station, close to the Grand Bazaar, the outlying districts begin have the feel of the East, vulgarized by the tacky new buildings and highways, but still rich with a leisurely and lazy sense of being, that we have lost. Behind the modern storefronts of a street grid that has not changed since the fourth century are hidden old wooden buildings, with overhanging stories and sash windows, coming out from which can be seen occasional stove-pipes, held up by empty cans.

The city rumbles with sound—the sharp bark of an old American car used as a jitney, the deep honking of the boats.

Istanbul is in the form of an hourglass, with two narrow passages where the floating bridges across the Golden Horn are opened at night, so that ships can pass through. A commotion can be heard coming from the nearer Galata bridge. A fisherman has lit a grill right on his boat and is grilling the fish he has just caught, to sell to customers waiting on the quay.

The hills that define the old city are dotted with the large cupolas of mosques. They seem light and porous, as though made with hollow bricks, hollow like a bird-bone. The domes of the cupolas imitate the dome of the sky to which their minarets point upwards. The light of the damp sky descends in a very gentle mist.

ΩΩΩ

9. September 6

Only the Greeks of Istanbul were permitted to remain after the exchange of populations. The Treaty of Lausanne of 1923 guaranteed the Jewish and Christian minorities the same legal status as they had had under the Ottoman Empire, as self-governing *Millets*. However, when Atatürk began his reform program, at the end of 1925, the minorities were persuaded to give up their privileges, "in anticipation of the planned introduction of a Western legal code." Turkey adopted the Swiss Civil Code in February

1926, and this was followed several months later by the adoption of the Italian criminal code. At the same time, a law was passed making Turkish the language of instruction in all schools—with the result that the new generation of Greek Orthodox Turks spoke fluent Turkish, but did not always know their ancestral language.

In 1928, the minorities were rewarded for renouncing their special legal status by the elimination of all reference to religion, including Islam, from the Turkish constitution. Turkey officially became a secular republic. At the same time, Atatürk granted legal rights to women. His reform of the language and introduction of the Latin alphabet were intended to introduce a new era, in which Turkey would be guided not by Islam but by a sense of historical continuity not only with the Hittites, but also with Byzantium.

In December 1934, in a further symbolic step towards secularization, the wearing of clerical garb was forbidden, except inside places of worship. Exception was only made for the head of each religious community. That is why you would see Patriarch Athenagoras, in his full monastic robes, sitting comfortably surrounded by Turkish workers and day-trippers, on board the Halki ferry.

The Turkish Constitution of 1961 maintained the secular definition of the state. It granted "freedom of conscience, the freedom to choose religious beliefs, and freedom of expression." But the legacy of fear, hatred and ethnic pride would not disappear overnight.

As one born on Ottoman soil, the new Patriarch was able to obtain Turkish citizenship. He was warmly welcomed by a sympathetic press. And he further eased tensions and dispelled distrust through symbolic gestures, such as flying the Turkish flag over the Patriarchate on Sundays. In 1951 he established a weekly newspaper, *Apostolos Andreas*, as a gazette for the official calendar of the Patriarchate, and as a forum for lively religious discussion. On the Feast of Theophany, January 6, 1952, he blessed the waters of the Bosphorus, with the full support of the government.

> "What golden days those were! The relations between the Turks and the minorities were excellent. In the street, the Turks would kiss my hand and call me 'father.' The prime minister paid a visit to the Phanar for the very first time. I would visit schools, I would have lunch with our school children. At first, I had some problems in visiting schools.

> So I asked if I could visit a Turkish school—and the authorities quickly agreed—and from there, I went on to one of our schools . . . ."

The Patriarch also nurtured friendly relationships between Turkey and Greece. In 1953, Greece, Turkey, and Yugoslavia signed a treaty of friendship and cooperation, and in 1954 this was followed by the formation of a tri-country consultative body that would meet in turn in each capital.

> "I have been known to say that at that time the Turkish frontier was in Corfu, and the Greek frontier was in the Caucasus. There was a lively tourist trade between Greece and Turkey, as well as an active program of cultural exchange: Greek professors lecturing in Turkey, theater performances in Istanbul and even in Ankara. But these hopes were not fulfilled."

With the Cyprus crisis of 1955 everything collapsed. Archbishop Makarios, the Cypriot leader, is perhaps the only person about whom the Patriarch speaks with bitterness: "He failed to grasp his responsibility. He never should have played a political role."

The independence movement had begun with terrorist attacks against the British colonial powers in late 1954. In April 1955, with the full support of the Greek government, the Greek Cypriots, led by Archbishop Makarios, declared *Enosis*, or union with Greece.

Turkey watched these developments anxiously, concerned for the Turkish Cypriot minority and for Turkey's own national security. At that time, Turkey was firmly aligned against Russia, against the Soviet threat. But the extreme left was very active in both Greece and Cyprus. *Enosis* posed a threat to Turkey's security. "Cyprus sits right under Turkey's belly," the Patriarch said, "Turkey could never have accepted this risk."

The plots and schemes behind the riots in Istanbul in 1955 only became fully understood after the fall of the regime in 1960. In August 1955, Greek and Turkish delegations met in London to try to resolve the Cyprus problem. The Greek delegate said casually that the Turkish people had no real interest in Cyprus. Stung by this, the Turkish foreign minister sent a telegram to Ankara: we need street demonstrations. These were quickly organized. On September 5, a bomb exploded in Thessalonica, damaging the Turkish consulate and the adjacent house, in which Atatürk had been born. This was all the excuse needed. The following night, September 6, massive riots broke out simultaneously in all major Turkish cities. In Istanbul the riot turned into a pogrom against the Greeks. The organizers, armed with names and addresses, drove trucks from street to street. The crowds, infected by age-old animosities, rampaged out of control. 2500 homes and Greek shops were destroyed. The main street of Pera, the *Istiklal Cadesi*, was piled with rubble. One hundred churches were vandalized, ten were burned or demolished. Priests were attacked and one was killed. The police and the army were slow to respond. They only intervened to stop the rioters marching to the Phanar, intent on burning it to the ground. The Phanar was saved just in time.

For the Patriarch, this was the trial of Job. All his work to reconcile Greeks and Turks, in Istanbul and internationally, was destroyed. He found himself denounced in Greece as a traitor to Hellenism, because of his absolute loyalty to the Turkish State. And, in Turkey, his refusal to condemn Makarios caused the most extreme Turkish nationalists to call him a secret supporter of *Enosis*.

After September 6, he remained silent. He did not protest, he did not speak out about this day that had placed the future of his people in question. The government compensated the victims and gave grants for church reconstruction. But the Greek minority's trust had been destroyed. And with every new shift in the Cyprus tragedy there came new reprisals. The buildings of the Phanar were threatened with demolition for 'urban renewal.' In 1964, two members of the Synod were expelled from the country, for "activities against the security of the state." Both of them were close allies of the Patriarch. The Patriarchate printing-house was closed and its publications, including *Apostolos Andreas*, were compelled to cease. The Halki Theological School was requisitioned for use by the Naval Academy. After three years of patient negotiation, Halki was returned to the Patriarchate. Athenagoras restored its buildings, only to learn that foreign students would be barred from attending—thus stripping Halki of its Pan-Orthodox ecumenical mission.

Those Istanbul Greeks who had kept their Greek nationality were now expelled, and in their number were swept up many who had acquired Turkish citizenship.

The Patriarch endured this tragedy calmly and lucidly, but with great sadness. He continued to hope. The Greeks had left Constantinople many times before. In 1510, their number had been reduced to five thousand. Then they came back . . . . The Patriarch insisted that the Orthodox should be loyal Turkish citizens. He forbade the clergy of the Ecumenical Patriarchate to take political sides, anywhere in the world. Neutrality meant humility, stepping beyond worldly cares, openness to all. But this neutrality now earned him the hostility of the Greek military dictatorship, that had taken over the government in 1967. They wanted to make use of the Greek clergy of the diaspora. Faced with Athenagoras' refusal, the Greek government removed the remaining dioceses of Northern Greece from Constantinople's jurisdiction.

Did the Patriarch reach his full greatness through these ordeals? Stripped bare by tragedy, sometimes mocked, he irrevocably became the servant of Orthodox unity, of Christian unity, of the unity of all peoples, of humanity. Nevertheless, he was first and foremost a pastor who cared for his people and brought them comfort. And that is where we will now meet him, surrounded by his people.

10. The Bishop in the Church and the Church in the Bishop

As the head of the Church of Constantinople, the Church of New Rome, the Patriarch is the first among equals in the Holy Synod. This is composed of twelve metropolitans. In Athenagoras's time, only four of these represented actual dioceses. Under Turkish law, all bishops had to be Turkish citizens. Following the "exchange of populations" most of the metropolitan sees were purely nominal dioceses, now without any Orthodox presence.

The Patriarchal administration was made up of two main departments. The Vicar-General administered the Diocese of Constantinople; the Secretariat, headed by a Chief Secretary, administered the metropolitan dioceses and the autonomous Churches under the jurisdiction of Constantinople.

The Patriarch is elected by the Holy Synod and thus only by those metropolitans holding Turkish citizenship. The Patriarchate is jointly governed by the Patriarch and the Holy Synod, a fact that underlines the collegial nature of patriarchal primacy. All decisions are made by 'the Patriarch in his Synod." In Athenagoras' time, the Holy Synod met each week. Its work was supported by twenty-one committees, headed by both clergy and laity. The most important of these were the committees on Pan-Orthodox Relations, Ecumenical Relations, Canon Law, Finance and Social Service. The Patriarch himself headed a Central Ecclesiastical Committee, made up of two metropolitans, five bishops, and three archdeacons.

The election of Athenagoras brought a breath of fresh air to this cloistered world. The Holy Synod was inward-looking. Its concerns were purely local. By contrast, the new Patriarch had a sense of the universality of Orthodoxy, the search for ecumenical common ground and the common pulse of all humanity. After some initial resistance, Athenagoras established his authority over the Synod. Displaying a respectful tenacity, he knew where to concede and where to stand his ground. As his international standing grew, as for example his Pan-Orthodox outreach and dialogue with Rome began to bear fruit—the Holy Synod came to be solidly behind him. It was astonishing to see doors thrown open in the wider world at a time when the Patriarchate was experiencing acute challenges in Istanbul.

Athenagoras brought a group of younger bishops into the Holy Synod, with a strong sense of commitment and a solid intellectual and spiritual formation. These included Metropolitan Meliton, who became very active in the Patriarchate's ecumenical outreach, Metropolitan Cyril of Chaldia, who accompanied Athenagoras on his trip to Rome in 1967, and Metropolitan Chrysostomos of Myra, barely forty years old.

The Chief Secretariat was headed by Bishop Gabriel of Kolonia, one of the Patriarch's closest collaborators. But the Patriarch's inner circle was not only made up of bishops. One of Istanbul's leading lawyers had lunch with him almost every day, bringing him the local news. The same food was served to all who worked at the Phanar, from the Patriarch to the gardeners. The Phanar working day ended with Vespers at five o'clock.

Aside from his administrative duties, Athenagoras dedicated a large part of his day to meeting with his people. Every day, from ten o'clock until lunchtime, his door was open to all comers. All you had to do was place your name on the sign-in sheet and wait your turn. No-one was refused. As soon as one visitor left, the buzzer would sound and the deacon would escort the next visitor in. Except in the summer, when there were many tourists and pilgrims, most of these visitors were from Istanbul parishes. And the Patriarch knew these communities well and visited them often.

As he had in America, the Patriarch clarified the status and autonomy of each parish. This was based on the balance of authority between the priest; the laity, represented by a president, supported by a parish council that managed the parish finances; and the representatives of culture, the teachers. Each parish had its own school, in the same church complex. As in America, each parish had a youth group and a women's association. The latter was particularly important here in Istanbul. They provided free meals for all the students at midday. Here in Istanbul, the Patriarch had also introduced special observances: in March, dedicated to mothers; in October, to fathers; to students on the feast day of the Three Hierarchs (St. Basil, St. Gregory Nazianzus, and St. John Chrysostom); and in January, on the feast day of St. Basil, to the parish community. In addition to the parishes, the Patriarchate had six lycées, a hospital, and an orphanage.

This organization reflected the needs of a religious minority that was also an ethnic minority—(even though, as we shall see, Orthodoxy in Istanbul was not always synonymous with Greek identity). In its form, it revealed the possibility, *mutatis mutandis*, of creating the kernels of a free 'Christocracy,' in the midst of a secular society.

Athenagoras knew everyone. As you drove with him, he would point out a church here, a school there, a shop, the home of such and such a family. Whenever the car slowed down in traffic, people would run up to ask his blessing. It was also well known that he went incognito to visit those in the greatest difficulty, to help them and to offer them counsel. But of this, he would never speak.

He regularly visited parishes, to pray and to give talks. When I was in Istanbul, it was the time of the Dormition Fast, the two weeks of preparation before the Feast of the Dormition. Each afternoon, Athenagoras would visit a parish to take part in Vespers and the singing of the Paraklesis—the Canon to the Mother of God. Let me describe some of these parish visits, where he brought me with him to get to know his people.

On August 8, we are in Arnavut Koÿ, where the Patriarch's uncle lived while Athenagoras was studying at Halki. The town is set on the banks of the Bosphorus. "This is also, in a way, my village," the Patriarch says. As we have seen, "in a way" there are so many villages, so many monasteries, and so many countries that are close to the Patriarch's heart. It is a large church, where four patriarchs are buried as well as many of the Greeks who loyally served the Ottoman Empire.

Like so many of the modern churches in Istanbul, the church is a basilica, with a fine carved wooden iconostasis—in 1955 the rioters unsuccessfully tried to set this on fire. To the right of the royal doors there is a large icon of Christ, and on the left, of the Theotokos. Next to the icon of Christ is the icon of the Forerunner, John the Baptist, inclined towards Christ. The form of this *deisis* is very typical in Constantinople: on the one side of the Pantocrator is the Theotokos, on the other side, the friend of the Bridegroom, a representation of the intercession.

This *deisis* is found in various forms throughout the Orthodox world. According to the French theologian, Paul Evodikmov, the iconographic composition represents the Church. But it is also a commentary on the fullness of humanity recapitulated in Christ—with Mary as the archetype of the feminine, and John the Baptist, the new Elijah, the archetype of creative power.

The church is full. Wearing a plain black *exorason*, the Patriarch assists the priest in chanting the Canon. The congregation joins in the chanting, especially in the refrains:

> "It is truly right to bless you, Theotokos, ever blessed, most pure, and the Mother of our God. More honorable than the Cherubim, and beyond compare more glorious than the Seraphim, without corruption you gave birth to God the Logos. We magnify you, the true Theotokos."

At the end of the service, the Patriarch blesses the children and chats with the worshipers. Then everyone moves into the modern, well-lit meeting room. People get refreshments and sit down in a circle. Then the Patriarch stands up and begins to speak, without raising his voice, without any pomp, as if having a conversation.

He says how happy he is to be back in "his" village. He comments on the day's Gospel reading. On the way home, he tells me: "I so much prefer to talk about the Gospel in this kind of setting, where everyone can make themselves comfortable and get refreshments, rather than in the church where it is hot, and the faithful have to remain standing. They don't have any chairs, but I'm going to get them some. I don't like these pointless physical demands. I think about Jesus asking the crowd to sit down on the grass."

Today's Gospel is the story of Mary and Martha. "These are not opposite choices: the one completes the other. Together, they make up the full

Christian woman, who is both active and loyal like Martha, and is also aware of the "good portion"—Mary's choice—sometimes sitting silently at the Lord's feet, in church, or wherever she happens to be." (Luke 11:42)

As we leave, the worshipers follow the Patriarch to his car. On the other side of the street, young Turkish men are standing watching silently, arms crossed, hard faced. One of them makes a show of spitting at the Patriarch. The Patriarch looks at him gently and lifts his hand in greeting, in blessing.

On August 9, the Patriarch goes to the Church of Constantine and Helen, in the southwest of the Old Town, where the Sea of Marmara and the old Byzantine wall make an angle, close to the ruins of the Stoudios monastery. The church was destroyed in 1955 and then rebuilt on the same foundation. There are finely carved stones embedded in the walls, most often representing the cross lifted up from the ground, with the Emperor Constantine and his mother Helen on either side. According to legend, Helen found the place where the cross was buried thanks to the intense aroma of a clump of basil growing on the spot. In Greek, basil is the herb of the Empress, the basilissa.

In this working-class district, the worshipers are regular people. There are fewer men than yesterday. At the end of the service, the local bishop gives the blessing, and the Patriarch, surrounded by children like an old tree covered in spring flowers, leaves the church holding two tiny hands in each of his large hands. The children all hold hands and follow the Patriarch, like a large bunch of grapes. Then, reaching in his pockets, he finds candies for each child.

Today, the people gather in the courtyard beside the church—it is too hot to go indoors. The church has large buttresses against the wall, built on the hillside that descends towards the sea. Tables and chairs are set up under the trellis—as the Bible says, under the vine and the fig tree. As dusk falls the wind freshens and the swifts sweep through the sky, uttering their piercing cries, welcoming nightfall. To reassure this small congregation, which is isolated and unsure of its future, the Patriarch speaks of the greater time and space of the communion of saints. He talks about the universality of Orthodoxy, now represented on all five continents. He recalls the saints invisibly present in this corner of Constantinople—St. Symeon the New Theologian, who saw the light of Tabor everywhere, the "never sleeping" monks of Stoudios, who chanted psalms through the night, so that the psalmody was never interrupted (it was the community as a whole that never slept). Their prayer, the Patriarch said, has woven heaven and earth together, for eternity.

Finally, the Patriarch takes a taxi to return to the Phanar. He has sent his car to the airport to meet an arriving guest.

On August 13 we go to Blachernae, where there is a holy spring, a *hagiasma*. The gardens are bright and the earth smells richly from the recent rains. There is a square of pines and fig trees surrounded by masses of flowers. At the center, there is a pool. The form is that of the archetypal Semitic garden, a garden of annunciation. The church is small and simple, decorated with beautiful frescoes, recently painted in the traditional style. But your gaze does not stop at the church. It is drawn to a vaulted opening across from the entrance, deep into the womb of the earth. A vaulted crypt, flowing with water, leads to a barrel roofed pool dug out of the cave: the crystal water on the white stone . . . the sculpted facets revealing the virginal fecundity of the earth . . . .

"The water never stops flowing. It is an inexhaustible spring, even in the driest summer," the Patriarch says. On the side of the spring there are tumblers, for drinking. At the end of the service we take a long drink from the spring that never dries up.

Our sinfulness has obscured this original transparency of matter, the transparency of the symbolic water offered to the Holy Spirit. But here the transparency is revealed once more in the Virgin Mother, who offers the flesh of the world to the Word, the Logos. Today, science tells us that matter is light, a light that wants to be revealed and not fragmented. In the frescoes of the church, the Virgin is pure whiteness. I am reminded of a friend who spent ten years on Patmos as the cell attendant to a hermit. In his translations of the Byzantine Liturgy he calls the Virgin "the all-white."[30] The frescoes remind you that the Great Church of Blachernae was built to house the precious robe of the Mother of God. This was where Andrew the Fool-for-Christ saw the Theotokos reach out in prayer to cover the whole city with her mantle of tears. How similar this vision of the Virgin is to that of two young shepherds at La Salette, one thousand years later.

This district is industrial where it meets the Golden Horn, becoming rural as one climbs the hills, entering a confusing maze of unmade

30 [Clément is referring to the French translator and editor of the *Philokalia*, Jacques Touraille]

roads. The worshipers are poor. There is a group of brown-skinned children. The Patriarch gives them handfuls of small candles to light in front of the icons in the narthex. They place the candles in the trays filled with sand.

In this modest church, the Patriarch serves and also chants. Age has freed his voice of any personal emotion. The age-old prayers run through him like a river. And in his chanting, he raises up a hymn of timeless praise.

The president of this parish community is Bulgarian, a young, slim, elegant man. "I was glad for him to become president. As for the brown-skinned children, they are Arab Christians, from Antakia, the Antioch of old. There is a community there, led by a layperson, a doctor, that is like one of the early Christian communities. The rural families there are very poor. To help them educate their children we have brought them to Istanbul, where we have more than enough room."

Here we have assembled a Bulgarian, a Frenchman, some Arabs—the whole Orthodox spectrum. After we have shared *loukoumades* and drunk fresh water, I tell this to the Patriarch and he expands on the theme. He explains the preparations for the Pan-Orthodox Council, and how important this is for Orthodoxy's presence on the world stage. He is frequently interrupted by questions to which he responds, engaging one woman in a long dialogue.

Sitting close to us in the visitors' place of honor is a man in his prime, with a wide, calm face. "He is a Turkish Muslim," the Patriarch explains. "He likes to come here. I know him well. I am very fond of him." The Patriarch repeats this in Turkish. The man looks at him warmly.

The faces of the Arab children have the same calm expression, and they are wide-eyed with eagerness. The Patriarch envelopes each little face with his caress of his large hand.

In the celebration of the Eucharist, the bishop embodies the fullness of his apostolic mission, which is to integrate the Eucharistic community into the body of the Resurrected Christ. "According to the custom of the Church of Constantinople, the Patriarch serves Liturgy seven times a year. Four of these are in the Patriarchal Cathedral, at Christmas, for the feast day of the Triumph of Orthodoxy, at Easter, and for the feast day of St. Andrew. Three are outside the Cathedral: in one of the great churches of Beyoğlu, in a monastery, at Halki. On other Sundays and feast days, the Patriarch takes part, staying on his throne. Seven times a year—it's very little. I would have liked to serve liturgy more often, but the Synod was not in agreement, because of this ancient custom. I accepted it. Why pick a fight when it is not completely necessary?

For the Feast of the Dormition, the Patriarch takes part in the service 'on his throne', but he also receives Communion. The evening before, after a frugal supper, Athenagoras had entered the small chapel next to his study. Two deacons and a metropolitan were chanting. The Patriarch stood in front of the altar, and remained there, completely still, for the whole service. He had gathered in the flowing sleeves of his *exorason* and his silhouette formed a vertical shaft. In the half-light of evening, the prayers of preparation for communion filled the air, prayers of repentance, prayers of trust.

> "O Christ, grant me tears to wash my heart clean so that I may dare to draw near in trust and reverence to the communion of your holy gifts . . . ."
> "Receive me, today, O Christ, the friend of mankind, as you received the prostitute, the thief, the tax-collector and the prodigal son . . . ."
>
> "You, O Master, said 'He who eats my flesh and drinks my blood abides in me and I in him. The word of my Lord and Master is the very truth."
>
> "He who partakes of these sacred and heavenly gifts is no longer alone, but is with you, O my Christ, the light of the Triple Sun that illuminates the world."
>
> "So that I may no longer be alone and separated from you, the giver of life, from you, my breath, my joy, the salvation of the world, I draw near to you, as you can see, with tears and a broken and humbled heart . . . ."
>
> "Trembling with joy, I receive the fire, who am but straw; and, strange miracle, I am filled with a fire beyond words like the burning bush of old, that burned and was not consumed. I give thanks with my whole spirit, I give thanks with my whole heart, I give thanks with my whole body, with body and soul filled with gratitude. I adore you, O my God, I magnify you, I glorify you, who are blessed now and forever, and unto the ages of ages. Amen."

"You will take Communion tomorrow," the Patriarch says to me. "You are much more worthy than me: be glad that you are not the patriarch."

Now it is night time. To end the day, the Patriarch takes me to the narthex of the Church of St. George. On the way he pauses in the garden and breathes in the night air. "How good it is!" "How beautiful the world is!" In the narthex, he lights a candle in front of the icon of the Theotokos, and another in front of the icon of the Prophet Elijah. He wants to chat. "Elijah," he tells me, "is the patron saint of the furriers. In Kastoria, in the time of the Ottoman Empire, their guild was especially wealthy. These furriers were amazingly skillful. They could use even the smallest pieces of fur. This was a real Byzantine town in the heart of Macedonia, with seventy churches all richly decorated with frescoes. The town was built on an isthmus that reached out into a lake. On the hill above the town stood the Church of St. Nicholas. From there you could see the whole lake, and the harbor, with its boats moored in pairs . . . ."

On August 15, the Feast of the Dormition, the Patriarch sits on his carved wooden throne in the packed Cathedral. He is wearing his dark purple *mantiya*, decorated with bands of gold. He holds his episcopal staff: the top is carved with the image of two serpents subdued by the Cross. The Patriarch looks pale and tired. No doubt, from the long fast . . . . He is totally concentrated in prayer, his gaze turned inwards. The service is lively. The Byzantine chant is a pure, modulated song of praise, austerely free of pathos. At the Great Entrance, when the priest carrying the Holy Gifts processes around the nave, the Patriarch stands up from his throne, takes off his *kalimavkion* and bows very low to venerate the chalice.

Before Communion, the Patriarch stands facing the worshipers in front of the royal doors, and again bows very low, asking their forgiveness.

While the faithful take Communion in an eager throng, the Patriarch himself comes to hand out the *antidoron*, the blessed bread. The Patriarch takes great handfuls, so that each worshiper receives at least two large pieces of this dense, leavened bread, gently scented with anise.

Outside the church, the Patriarch greets people and chats with them, agreeing to be photographed with anyone who asks. Then he takes a group of fifty or more people into his study: the street-person and the diplomat, the beggar and the college professor.

A teaspoon of sugar in a glass of water. And once more he speaks tirelessly of the Word that brings peace, of the unity of all people.

11. The Poor Lover of Mankind

In summer, the Phanar is an extraordinary meeting place, a crossroads of churches and nations. The Patriarch greets each person in turn, in Greek, French, or English—all of which he speaks fluently—or with a few phrases of Italian, German, or Spanish. The atmosphere is warm and friendly. Glasses of cold water, or little cups of richly scented coffee, are passed around. People sing the Lord's Prayer together, or, if they are French, the *Marseillaise.* The Patriarch suggests a new ecumenical version:

> Forward, you children of the Church,
> The day of unity is here

Athenagoras invites distinguished guests and any Orthodox visitors from the diaspora, or from sister churches, to join him for lunch. According to monastic tradition, "the Patriarch cannot have any flowers at his table," and men and women sit separately. A simple lunch is quickly served. Afterwards, everyone returns to the Patriarch's study. There are babies sleeping in their mothers' laps—the Greek mothers have a selfless dignity—and the shouts of children at play. The Patriarch talks warmly to the Pope's informal representative at the Phanar, Father Berghato, the priest of the main Catholic parish of Beyoğlu. He is an elegant, slim, distinguished man, with the air of an important diplomat. But the Patriarch's attention is elsewhere. He loves children, even more than he loves Father Berghato.

Suddenly the Patriarch's face lights up. He has found what he was looking for. He reaches behind his desk for a small angel carved in gilded wood, an Italianate cherub with its trumpet, and then he rifles through the papers on his desk to find a large envelope, in which he carefully wraps the angel. He gives it to the brown-haired girl who had been pirouetting around the room and is now sitting on his lap. Her father is a distinguished physician from America. The Patriarch shows the doctor the pills he is taking: "Maybe you have a cure for old age . . . ."

All of a sudden, the Patriarch stands up and hurries to greet a young Lebanese couple with a small son, who have just arrived. They belong to the Orthodox Youth Movement, that has brought new life to the Patriarchate of Antioch. They know the Patriarch well, and have stopped in Istanbul to see him, on their way back from Europe. They are a handsome young couple. The Patriarch looks at them with the warm affection of an old man, who is not jealous of youth but rather blesses it. The Patriarch says to the little boy: "your father is so strong and handsome—you must be proud of him."

In the midst of this typically Orthodox hustle and bustle, there are Catholic and Protestant visitors trying to observe the proper decorum. The mini-skirted wives of the Anglican clergymen sit with their knees tightly together. The Patriarch greets them with a broad smile. He tells the wife of Dr. Ramsey, the Archbishop of Canterbury, that she is the first lady of the Anglican Communion. The room reverberates with the heat. A baby is sleeping in her mother's lap, the wife of a sea captain. Across the Golden Horn, the reddish hills shimmer in the heat.

The Patriarch says: "Let us return to the undivided Church." Out of the window you see the spark of the welding torch against the hull of a ship, and a wall painting of General Sunay, the president of the Republic, who has the distinguished air of an old soldier, and, on another wall, a painting of Kemal Atatürk as a heroic gray wolf in the foothills of the Tien-Chan Mountains. You hear fragments of conversation: "There are squirrels in Central Park;" "We have a beautiful new Greek church in Milwaukee;" "We have been here in Istanbul for three thousand years." The icon of the Mother of God over the Patriarch's desk, with unusual gloved hands, watches over the scene with a pure, distant detached gaze—and thus also the hidden face of the Patriarch—"separated from all and united to all."

"I am a citizen of the world," he says. "I am a man of the East, but I have become a citizen of the world." From Epirus to Macedonia, from the Balkans to the United States, from the taste of the American Dream, to this cosmopolitan celebration that occurs every summer at the Phanar, he has nurtured a vision of the universal republic in which Christians are the leaven, in which all people find their home. This is the great brotherhood of all people in Christ, of which Dostoevsky spoke at Pushkin's tomb.

Coming to Halki to relax after the Dormition Feast, the Patriarch likes to watch Austrian newsreels and documentaries, projected on the wall of the adjoined reception rooms. Here was a society that had modernized without losing its refinement, without marginalizing the role of the Church. A country that no longer was burdened by the 'will to power,' but had maintained the heritage of a great multinational empire. There is a short film extolling the happy situation of Austria's Hungarian and Slovene minorities. Here is a world in which people live without fear. The Patriarch had dreamed that the planned Pan-Orthodox Council would meet in Vienna, in 1967. The Austrian government had invited him to come to Vienna when he visited Bulgaria and Romania. But the Turkish government had a problem with the invitation of a religious leader by another country, rather than by another church. And so the Patriarch never went to Vienna.

Suddenly the scene on the screen shifts to Russia. An Austrian orchestra on tour. The endless snow-covered plains. The atmosphere is suddenly heavy, muffled and serious, but also uncertain and incomplete. Austria is a fully formed work: Russia is a work in progress. Orthodoxy is secretly fermenting in the heavy dough of Soviet life. This, the Patriarch knows. Athenagoras has a great love for "Holy Russia." He is a Greek from the Balkans, where many Greeks are of Slavic descent, and a Byzantine who knows to what extent the great Russian thinkers created a "Byzantium after Byzantium."[31]

The great tree of the Orthodox Church forms a cross on the world map. Its roots are in Jerusalem. The Patriarch has been there twice, the second time to meet the Pope. Its lower branches are in Alexandria and Antioch, with the Egyptian awareness of the eternal soul and the Semitic sense of history. At the heart, Constantinople is the providential crucible, in which the best of Asia, Africa and Europe are joined to form a vessel that holds the Light. The path of the legendary journey of St. Andrew from the Holy Land to Byzantium, and from Byzantium into the Scythian north, forms the northern arm of the cross. Russia to the east and the diaspora of Europe and America to the West form the horizontal cross bars.

"All people are good. I belong to all people. Christian unity should be the leaven of the unity of mankind."

The Patriarch follows a strict schedule. Eight o'clock Matins is preceded by an hour of work or meditation. After Matins, he meets with his staff for updates and discussion. From ten to one, his door is open to visitors. After lunch, and, in summer, a brief siesta, he works in his office. He reviews all outgoing correspondence and all the accounts. He is meticulous and in total control. At five o'clock there is Vespers. Then he signs letters and official documents for an hour. He shares a quick supper with one or two of his closest confidants. Then an evening of reading.

Nowadays, the Patriarch does not read many books. He quickly scans the books he has been sent, pausing only when he finds something thought-provoking. But, more and more, he is drawn to magazines of

---

31 [The phrase is from Basil Tatakis, *Byzantine Philosophy*, Hackett, London, 1949, reissued 2003]

every genre, religious, political, scientific. More and more, he wants to understand the people of today, to be able to speak to them, in their own language, about the joyful news of God's existence.

This passionate desire to know people almost explodes when his mail is delivered after dinner. He opens it himself, with eager fingers, all the while continuing to talk to his guests. "For fifty-eight years I have opened the mail with the same excitement, with, dare I say, the same joy. Isn't 'correspondence' a wonderful word! All these messages prove that, in their heart of hearts, each person yearns to love and to be loved."

He delights at being with people in the evenings, as he slowly drives through the streets of Istanbul. The day's work done, people have given themselves over to idle pleasures, to the simple act of watching the world. "Enjoyment is a person's first right," the Patriarch says, lending a spiritual overtone to the language of the Declaration of Independence, "Delight is one of the names of God."

You sense an enormous appetite for action. Sometimes, he seems to want to do everything at once. During a conversation, he will be opening his mail, someone will bring him a report, which he scans and adds to the growing pile on the armchair to his right. There is a letter or an official document to sign. And, all the while, he is engaged in a probing conversation, attentive to those around him, wrapping a present for a child, reaching for the money needed for his aged assistant to send a telegram.

> "For me, one word sums it up, I attack. I always attack—not the people but the goal. Once I have made my choice I know I will have to agree to some compromises. I know that I will have to be patient. I am patient. But I always go forward. If I lose a battle, I don't slow down. Why try to work out who is to blame? I never say 'unfortunately.' I always attack."

But he also breathes in the scent of the jasmine, observing the seabirds flying back over the open sea at evening, and pausing in his conversation in the garden to watch the intricate movements of the ants. At Halki, he has managed to buy some land close to the school, with a spring that never dries up. This has let him irrigate the grounds around the school and make them even more beautiful. He can be found lovingly gardening, bare headed, with his *exorason* tucked in.

He also has a way of accentuating everything he says, by way of completely engaging with the person he greets. "He exaggerates in everything," one of his inner circle tells me with a smile. The Patriarch does not so much exaggerate, as stretch language to its furthest limits, amplified by those oriental gestures that we have so completely lost. He comes straight up to a friend, he hugs him, he presses his friend's head against his chest, he takes him firmly by the hand. Suddenly, one senses how good it is to have a father, or dare I say, a father and a mother. The Patriarch displays not just a masculine vigor but also a maternal tenderness, that the Bible calls racham, the womb of compassion.

Above all, he knows how to look the other in the eye, to meet them, or rediscover them, to seek the other's gaze, their inner self. To live in the knowledge and joy that here is another person, and that both persons, the one and the other, are made one, in God.

Although he always advances, he has a great sense of the mystery. Everything is astonishing and miraculous, from the smallest things to the human face, the human presence. He steps forward to meet the miraculous. And the miracle happens. God continues his great works. "Our God is the God of wonders."

"And when you are completely at a loss, you place yourself completely in the hands of God, in his mercy. Then there is no more fear. Only trust."

He reads a chapter of the Gospel every day. The Gospel has taught him that the unknowable God is the hidden friend. Nothing matters except love. But, in the words of the Apostle, "all things are lawful but not all things are helpful." (1 Cor. 10:23) The Patriarch strictly follows the monastic rule. "I am in part a monk of Athos, a monk of Halki, a monk of Moni Petraki." During the fifteen days of the Dormition Fast, I saw him eat only a bowl of vegetable soup and a few olives at dinner, while the Phanar menu included tomatoes, potatoes, and fruit. And he drank only water. On Wednesdays and Fridays he drank nothing. Ascetics understand the meaning and the importance of fasting and thirst. "The only difficult thing for me," he told me, "is no olive oil."

Through his calm acceptance of the strict monastic rule, he has become a free, whole person. But he does not impose this rule on others.

After his childhood illnesses, he has become stronger and stronger. The older he becomes, the stronger he feels, he told me. "But now I am too old."

Now he is always ready for sleep. "I fall asleep as soon as my head touches the pillow." But he is a light sleeper, waking frequently. At night he will walk alone in the Phanar gardens. He goes to the narthex of the church. "I light two candles in front of the icon of the Mother of God, one for all the living and one for all the dead." And he prays. "What I say to the Mother of God, what she replies—no words can describe."

The long ascetic practice, the sober and moderate asceticism of the typikon, the sustained prayer of the long Byzantine services, the trust and wonderment, have unified him. In his sleep, he is visited by dreams that have been purified of any hostile forces, that are images and messages from God. "I dream a lot," he says. "Every time there is a difficult problem, the solution comes to me in a dream." Sometimes he has premonitions. In August 1968, the Patriarch was passionately hoping to be able to visit Russia, to complete the grand pilgrimage of Orthodox unity that he had planned for that autumn. But the promised invitation never came.

He told me one morning, "Now I know that I shall never go to Russia. I dreamed that I had been invited and I was beginning to write my words of greeting to Patriarch Alexis. But suddenly everything got completely jumbled up, and I understood that this would never happen." He also has vast, prophetic images come to him in his dreams. So, for example, he saw himself and the Pope painfully climbing a mountain, at the summit of which stood the Holy Grail, the one Eucharistic chalice.

The Greek popular tradition greatly values dreams, and in this regard, the Patriarch is profoundly Greek. The pagan tradition of dream interpretation was also incorporated into Byzantine Christianity. But we should also pay attention to the biblical tradition. In the Septuagint, the Hebrew word for Adam's "sleep" is translated by "ecstasy" or "trance"—the trance from which the Creator brings forth woman. The ancient monastic chronicles frequently refer to visions received "in a trance," in a purified form of sleep, sleep that has been penetrated through and through by prayer, exorcised and made a vehicle of light. "I sleep, but my heart watches."

There is something of the *starets*, in Athenagoras, of the *geronta*. He has no pomp or affectation. He has a simplicity of person that reminds one of Pope John XXIII, combined with an elegance and nobility that expresses all the glory of Byzantium. The Patriarch is friendly, animated, and quick to laugh. In his wisdom, which is both childlike in its simplicity and profound in its sagacity, everything is sign and correspondence. Or rather, it is the wisdom of one who knows that God is revealed in everything.

To John XXIII, he applied the words of the Gospel that introduce John the Baptist: "There was a man sent from God, whose name was John." And immediately you think of how John came "to bear witness to the light." He calls Pope Paul VI "Paul the Second." "Today," he says, "there is no time for speculation. We must just tell people about Christ, crucified and glorified. What the Apostle Paul said in his first letter to the Corinthians, this is what Paul the Second must tell the people of today."

When he introduces me to the Metropolitan of Halki and the Princes Islands, a beaming old man, the Patriarch adds, "and he too is a prince, a prince of the heart and the spirit, a true poet." The old Metropolitan replies, "the Patriarch too is a poet. To which the Patriarch responds: "If you are not a poet, how can you talk to people?" One day, he began a long explanation of my name, Olivier Clément, the Olive Tree and the Merciful, and when he introduced me, he would add "a clement and merciful theologian, which few theologians are!"

His humor softens each profound word, that darts out like an arrow. He picks up the refrain of the old French song, that the French troops sang in Monastir in 1918:

> What is life? A little bit of happiness. A little bit of pain . . .

The Patriarch is very tall and lean. There is a certain resolved alacrity in his gestures; there is no time wasted; everything is action and presence. The lively spareness, the tawny skin (the color of the faces of icons), the youthful expression coupled with the whiteness of his hair and beard, all witness to his victory over his trials by fire. You have only to compare the photographs of him in Corfu or in America to grasp how he has been purified by experience, becoming at once unity and transparency. When he relaxes, he sometimes betrays a certain heaviness, that of tiredness and passion, of a dignity more regal than monastic. But, at the slightest hint, he comes together again with a sort of quiver of his being, in which he both arms himself and disarms himself completely. And old age has given his shoulders the fragility of those of a child.

His eyes are very dark, serious, deep, reaching into space. Occasionally, he squints and creases up his eyes in disgust. His beard is less ample than his photographs suggest—it resembles the long white strands of the bearded old men of the Byzantine frescoes and the prophets in the medieval sculptures of the western cathedrals. His gestures, his demeanor, the way he wraps his *exorason* around his legs when he sits, lend him a Byzantine, or even Roman, appearance. The straight, thin symmetrical nose and the regal nostrils lend his face a classical beauty. His high forehead, the crystallized deposit of prayer and meditation, is typical of the great Orthodox ascetics, whose face has been purified and condensed into a gaze, that is held between the sky of the forehead and the earth of the mouth. The mouth itself is transfigured by the whiteness of his beard.

Recounting his trip to Sofia, where the crowd had greeted him with fervor and veneration, he was careful, like the Apostle Paul, not to take credit. "I do not speak of myself. As for myself, I do not matter. Let us say: "There was a man, whose name was Athenagoras." And shortly before we took our leave, he asked "and what will you say about me? What does it matter? There was a man whose name was Athenagoras. He lived to be very old. He had done nothing of his own doing. He had tried to love mankind, as one who was just one grain of sand among the millions."

Saint Symeon the New Theologian said that the *ptochos philadelphos*, the poor man who loves mankind, is one with Christ.

Part Two: Words

1. Christos Anesti! Christ Is Risen!

Patriarch People are unsettled. Nothing can satisfy them. Nothing that has been made—not even the whole universe and the distant stars. The more people get, the more restless they become. They find no place to rest. A person's heart is made for the infinite, for limitless love. So many of our contemporary ills can be explained by the repression of this desire for the infinite.

Professor This makes me think of young Western intellectuals. They have been especially protected. They have everything they need and every day they get more. So they stumble around all the old ideologies, or they blow them up, refusing to doze off comfortably, refusing the "alienation" of bourgeois comfort. But how can they no longer be alienated from themselves, if they do not rediscover their beginning and their end in God? One of the Church Fathers said: "Man is an animal whose vocation is to become God."

Patriarch The young people are so much abandoned, their cry is the cry of orphans, their very rebellion is a cry for help. What do we do for them? In trying to understand them, are we only trying to overcome the fear that keeps generations apart? We talk and talk, but we do not know how to turn words into deeds. And so the young have no trust, they have no trust in the words we speak, and the young are very demanding. Some say we must take care of the earth and of society—and if we do only this, mankind will be so happy that we will forget about God. How untrue this is. The more the raw hunger of mankind is satisfied—and it must be satisfied, in all places, for all people—the more the hunger for God will grow, openly or in secret, in adoration or in idol-worship. And this, above all, because we all will die.

Professor And death is not just the end of life, an end that we put off further and further. It is a manner of living without living, of living unaware, apart, in a state of constant envy.

Patriarch Death is also what gives life its gravity and transforms life into an enigma. Despite everything, death is what opens life to the presence of the infinite. People need God, even when society is at peace, because, together, life and death reach for eternity. Life in its fullness, and death in its gravity, unite to reveal the unknown.

As for the others—I am thinking of those Christians who are satisfied with themselves and frightened by what is happening in the world—they tell the young that Christianity is opposed to humanism. This is not true either. Mankind finds its true humanity, a creative inspiration that must transform life, in God.

Professor Not God against man or man against God, but the mystery of the God-man, that is the essential mystery of Christ. This is who we must witness to.

Patriarch And we should bear witness by our lives, by lives freed of fear. First we should try to live our Christianity. All the rest will follow naturally.

Professor It seems to me that people don't know anymore what Christianity is. For me, and I chose Christianity when I was already an adult, after a long exploration of atheism, it is an ever-deepening sense of wonder. But most often, people refuse to find out, because they think they already know what Christianity is—when in fact they don't. They confuse the God who turns everything upside down with the centerpiece of social order and worn-out morality. They think of Christianity as a sort of humanism for the religiously-minded. What is worse, many of those born into the Church have almost nothing to do with it and are tired of being Christian.

Patriarch You have to become the prodigal son to discover the love that the Father has for us! Alas, as you say, so many Christians have only a vague notion of becoming more virtuous or becoming a better person. They think they are Christians, but in fact they have not encountered Christ. First and foremost, Christianity is Christ. It is a face, the face of the

Resurrected Christ. Only by meeting Christ in a personal encounter can we become participants in his life and rediscover our lost resemblance to the Creator. God is close to us in Christ, and so we become close to people. In Christ, we discover that God is love, that love is the animating force of the universe, and that love is what gives a person's gaze its transparency.

Professor For the man or woman of today we must retranslate the fundamental language of life, the language of death, the language of love that is stronger than death. If God exists, nothing is without meaning, we are no longer alone.

Patriarch Retranslate, yes, but let's not get stuck on the words we use. If we are alive, the Spirit of life will breathe into us the words we need. It has happened to me, on Christmas Eve, that I feel I am simply one of the shepherds on watch in the darkness, guarding their flock, who suddenly discovers Emmanuel—God with us.

Professor The Fathers say that God is the Unknown, the Inaccessible, beyond our images and ideas, beyond even the word 'God' . . . and yet if we fall down in fear and trembling before his mystery, we will meet Emmanuel.

Patriarch The Savior born in Bethlehem, not a distant and nameless God but God-with-us, who counts each hair of our heads. He leads us each, from all time, and enters with us into total communion.

Professor And yet so much evil persists.

Patriarch So much ill-doing . . . but God is not a supreme ruler, a heavenly supercomputer controlling all creatures like objects. His all-powerfulness is that of love. And love does not constrain in any way. We must turn toward Him freely and open ourselves to Him so that He can shine in us. God is the fundamental energy in the history of the world, but this energy is in the form of love: and love imposed by force is not love.

But there are demonic forces at work under the surface, as people's lives and history show us. This is what gives historical tragedies their unexpected depth. They are like a fault-line through which a dark lava bubbles up. Then people are swept away like so many pieces of straw. I have seen this so many times.

Professor But love is stronger than death . . . .

Patriarch In its own way, which is the way of love. When God became man, he conquered death by death.

Professor The Cross is the only silent answer to the long trial on the nature of evil, prosecuted by today's atheistic world against God. God descends into the hell and death of our tragic freedom, he descends into my inner hell, this inner wall of anguish and darkness, or of fever-bright light.

Patriarch And he destroys them by his Resurrection. God so loved mankind that he came into our lives in total communion freeing our energy, our power, that had been skewed by evil, to be freely deployed in the harmony of holiness, that resonates even to death.

Professor And in all the death-tarnished moments of our lives,

Patriarch Which, if we have faith in the Resurrected One, are opened to the light. We have no greater joy than the joy of Pascha.

ΩΩΩ

Ever since the earliest times of the Church, the faithful have spent Easter night in the church. This is usually decorated with flowers, and soon it will glow with the light of many candles, lit to celebrate the abolition of the 'night', the abolition of the 'nocturnal', infernal mode of our existence.

When the service begins, all is silence, darkness, and expectation. At midnight, Matins begins with a procession around the outside of the church that stops at the front doors of the church. Then the worshipers sing the Resurrection Troparion:

> Christ is risen from the dead,
> by death trampling down upon death,
> and to those in the tombs
> He has granted life.

At the end of the Paschal Liturgy, the priest blesses the food that the faithful have brought for the Paschal agape feast. In Greece, each family celebrates the agape feast at home and then, for the whole following week, the table is set for guests. People go from house to house. They kiss. They greet each other with "*Christos Anesti*". They share food. They share life and they share their Paschal joy.

ΩΩΩ

Patriarch Everything is straining toward the universal Resurrection, in ways in which we cannot know. Everything is oriented toward the Resurrection. The Resurrection is the only total event in history, one that contains all human reality and all cosmic reality. The Resurrection gives history its meaning and direction, like a universal force of gravity.

Professor And so, all will be transfigured?

Patriarch Everything. Everything that we have loved, everything that we have created, all the joy and all the beauty, all will take its place in the Kingdom.

Professor And evil?

Patriarch Evil will be defeated and rooted out, death will be put to a final death. But our experience of evil, our sense of repentance in which we fall down at the feet of Christ, the knowledge that nothing except for limitless love can satisfy our desire—all this will find its place in the Kingdom. Christian joy is a tragic joy; it is a resurrection by way of death. The Resurrected Christ bears the marks of the nails in his hands and feet. The water of baptism and the blood of the Eucharist flow from the opening in his side made by the spear. And resurrected humanity will also bear the marks of its suffering and its battles.

Professor Dostoevsky said that awareness comes from suffering,

Patriarch We must always keep our eyes on the Resurrection of Christ, so that we can welcome everything in his light. Pascha means 'passage.' If we are rooted in the Resurrected Christ, the world and its history will begin its passage into eternity. Our lives should be illuminated by hope and by our peaceful expectation of the One who will judge the living and the dead at the end of time.

Professor In your Christmas and Easter messages, you have often said that the Kingdom of God will be created here on Earth.

Patriarch We prepare it on Earth and it is the Earth that will be transfigured. All that is human is a preparation for the Kingdom. Our culture is a preliminary sketch, an evocation . . . .

Professor But culture can also be a closed chamber in which you suffocate, or a caricature of religion, a collective effort to forget death and to find an unattainable sense of security. We build a Tower of Babel, that is to say we want to become god-like through our own efforts and devices.

Patriarch Everything is all mixed together. Our role is precisely to discern the possibility of life and prepare the path. When Christ returns —and we can hasten his return through prayer and the act of love—death and deception will disappear, and the Earth and our culture will be transfigured.

ΩΩΩ

Professor One thing that has struck me in recent months is the extent to which the Resurrection seems to trouble some Western theologians. This is not the case for the simple believer, with a modicum of faith. I heard one such theologian say that Christ's earthly body was subject to decomposition like any other body, while his glorified body had come from above. Mostly these theologians limit themselves to saying that Christ is still alive. They reduce the resurrection appearances to subjective visions on the part of the apostles. They attribute them to the religious fervor of the early Christian community. They deny any real transformation of matter, as a historical fact. For them, the earth is not transformed into a spiritual substance, in Christ. It is as though they are afraid, or ashamed of the miracle.

Patriarch I cannot understand this fear. For those who know how to see, everything is a miracle, everything is steeped in mystery, in the infinite. The least object is a miracle, as is every encounter. I have had the real experience that our God is the God of wonders, the author of all miracles. I experienced my meetings with Pope Paul VI as miracles, in Jerusalem and in Istanbul. But, on a day-to-day basis, the mere fact that something exists, as opposed to nothing, the fact that someone exists, and that they are not a mere bundle of atoms but a face—is this not also a miracle?

Professor That may be true, but people will say that this sense of the miraculous is just a subjective sense of wonder that alters nothing in reality, and that the miracles described in the Gospels are something else—that they are the mythological representations of this sense of wonder, that we need to declutter our faith . . . .

Patriarch This is the intellect at work as always, dividing and opposing! But if you separate the miracle and the reality in this way, how can you still believe in Christ? He is the greatest miracle and the greatest reality. To declare Christ as true God and true man, and to confess his Resurrection, is one and the same thing. In Christ, divine light penetrates and transforms life and everything that we call matter. In Christ, creation is revealed in its inner truth, and is transparent to the glory of God. The Resurrection is not the reanimation of a body: it is the beginning of the transfiguration, the metamorphosis of the Earth.[32]

32 [See Olivier Clément, *On Human Being*, Ch. 7 Human Beings and the Cosmos and *The Roots of Christian Mysticism*, Pt. 3, Ch. 2, The Glory of God Hidden in His Creatures]

Professor You could say that the Resurrection is the true essence of all being and things, whereas the fallen world is, as the Fathers say, buried in death and partly contrary to nature . . . .

Patriarch In Christ's Resurrection, a person finds not only true life, but the ability to communicate this life. This is the miracle: to become one of the living, through union with God. This can be expressed in the confidence of a person's gaze.

Professor In the heart of stone that becomes a heart of flesh,

Patriarch Or if by some miracle, "the light of life," in St. John's words, fills the heart to overflowing.

Professor "The light of life" that is nothing less than the appearance of the real world, a prefigurement of the Kingdom. If I understand you correctly, there is nothing more natural than a miracle—children and poets are the first to understand this.

Patriarch The miracle is that God exists. And so, everything is possible. Because He exists! He exists and He comes to us and makes us His friends. We were dead and in Christ we became alive.

Professor And the living person brings life to everything around her.

Patriarch You have only to consider the lives of the saints to see that the life and love that we receive in the communion cup can transform history and the natural world. It is the saints and the prophets, the warriors of the Spirit, who have made history possible, who have protected us, and who at times have illuminated all of history and the universe. If we no longer understand this, and if we no longer are capable of this, it is because our faith and our love have grown cold.

ΩΩΩ

Professor How do you relate the tragic problems faced by humanity today to the miracle of the Resurrection?

Patriarch One third of the world goes hungry. To this bodily hunger we can add spiritual hunger. Two-thirds of the people in the world have never really heard Jesus' name. In the countries that call themselves Christian, there is a massive disconnect between the Gospel, on the one hand, and the way Christians live, and the underlying thrust of social policy and research, on the other.

How do you relate all of that to the Resurrection? Well, it's very obvious—these so-called Christians don't live out the Resurrection. They are not resurrected! They have lost the Spirit of the Gospel. They have made the Church a machine, they have made theology a pseudo-science, and they have made Christianity a vague moral creed. Let's rediscover and relive St. Paul's incandescent theology: "Just as Christ was raised from the dead by the glory of the Father, we too, who have been baptized, might walk in the newness of life." (Romans 6:4) If those who believe in the Resurrected Christ convey this living force, we will be able to find solutions for the problems that people are agonizing over . . . .

First, you must give shape to the inward person, so that they can experience creative adoration. We need people who have experienced the illumination of history and the cosmos, in the light of the Holy Spirit and the Resurrection. From their inner strength will emerge a force that will reorient human values and social ideals. This is the whole thing! Inaugurate the new life inwardly and clothe your soul in festive garments. Then we will come to our brothers and sisters who are hungry, with arms filled with gifts for the nourishment of the body and soul.

ΩΩΩ

Professor Where can you find the Resurrected Christ, to enter into communion with Him, so that, as the Gospel says, "the water that I shall give you will become in you a spring of water welling up to eternal life" (John 4:14)?

Patriarch Christ is everywhere. Ever since the Resurrection, all of history has unfolded in Christ, seeking Him, celebrating Him, fighting Him, denying Him, rediscovering Him. His secret presence, His revelation of the person and love, have become the leaven of all of human life. If you remember the Gospel of Matthew, Chapter 25, it says: "I was hungry and you gave me food . . . as you did it to the least of these my brethren, you did it to me." Commenting on this text, St. John Chrysostom says that the poor are the sacrament of Christ, that Christ is made flesh in the poor. Christ is present every time that there is a real encounter, every time that a little bit of love is shown, every time that unbiased justice or learning are displayed, every time that a person's heart is touched by beauty . . . .

Professor But people know nothing of this. Our task is to help them recognize Christ in the heart of their lives.

Patriarch They know more than you may imagine. The Christians do not have a monopoly over the Gospels. Think about Gandhi's work, or even some aspects of what Kemal Atatürk accomplished. What we can say is that, in these cases, Christ's presence is partially concealed. These are Christian values, but they are detached from the person of Christ. The fear of death and collective pride get in the way; the possibility of full sanctification is blocked. Only the person of Christ can give life its full meaning.

Professor "God became man so that man could become God." For the Fathers, this is the ultimate meaning of Christianity.

Patriarch That is true, and to attain this fulfillment, you have to be able to be in total communion with Christ—not just to subscribe to the values of the Gospel but to be grafted onto the one tree so that Jesus' life flows in you, like the sap flows into the grafted branch. And where do you find this total communion, if not in the Eucharistic chalice, in the heart of the Church? Christ is at the center of everything. The communion cup is at the center of everything. Here and here only Christ gives Himself totally. How is this possible? How can it not burn my lips, unworthy as I am?

In the Eucharist, we are united with our brothers and sisters, but only because we have first been united with Christ. And we are united with Him in the most realistic way. In Him, we become one life, one blood, one body. And so we become members with one another, without the least separation.

This is what the Church is, in its truest reality. In the Eucharist, it is no longer this sad and self-deceiving society from which we have driven out the Spirit of Christ. It is Christ Himself, the Resurrected Body of Christ, through which the divine energies pour out into humanity, and into the universe.

Professor And so, what is the point of asking the "how" of this total presence. What is the point of the "how" over which the Christian West has torn itself up?

Patriarch What is the point, yes! We do not have answers to this "how." The Fathers never claimed to know the answer. This is where real theology becomes adoration, not explanation. Like the Resurrection, it is a miracle made present by the Holy Spirit. By His love, the Word of God, in whom everything lives and has its being, in whom everything is recreated through his Incarnation, becomes contained and becomes our food. We confess his total presence.

Professor We do not see this because we are blind. But the saints have seen it. They have seen a boundless ocean of light flowing from the Eucharistic cup. Scientific instruments and the eyes of the body can never reveal this spiritualization of matter, this transformation of matter, by and in the Holy Spirit. No one will ever invent a spirit-meter. Or perhaps, the only possible measure of the Holy Spirit is the sanctified human heart.

Patriarch We confess the miracle, in adoration: This is truly your own Body, and this is truly your own Blood, the Blood of the Resurrected Christ. Christ gives Himself in the bread and the wine. And in the Communion host—I am certain of it.

ΩΩΩ

Patriarch Christianity is life in Christ. And Christ never denies us or refuses us. We are the ones who have burdened people! Christ never says: don't do it, you must not. Christianity is not built on what is forbidden. It is life, it is fire, it is creation, it is illumination. As trust grows, the heart changes. And so, little by little, the life of the Resurrected Christ begins to flow in us.

Professor Nicholas Cabasilas wrote that for a person to love God, they must first know that they are loved by God. Love summons love and renews life. Because this love becomes our being.

Patriarch If you remember, Jesus is invited to a pharisee's house and a prostitute comes in, carrying a jar of oil. She throws herself down at Jesus' feet, washes them with her tears, dries them with her hair, kisses them and anoints them with oil. The Pharisee thinks that Jesus cannot be a prophet, or he would have known that this woman was a sinner. And so Jesus tells him the story of the two debtors. One of them owed five hundred denarii, the other fifty. The creditor forgave both of their debts. Which one did he love more? Jesus asked. And the Pharisee could only answer, the one to whom he forgave more. And then Jesus reminded him of all the woman's acts of love—the tears, the hair, the kisses, the oil. And he concluded "Therefore, I tell you, her sins, which are many, are forgiven, for she loved much." (Luke 7:36–47)

> "*Oti igapisen poli*"
> for she loved much,
> for He loved much.

All of Christianity is there. And the woman caught in the act of adultery . . . Jesus wrote in the sand . . . and no one dared throw the first stone. "Go, and do not sin again." (John 8:3–11) When someone discovers how much they are loved, they begin to come out of their negative solitude and their separation. They stop hating themselves. A person accepts that they are loved, that they have a friend who shares this secret. They enter the light of the Resurrection and, little by little, their life is rebuilt in trust and humility. It is not built from the hammerings of 'thou shalt not'—these only impact the surface, they just push the bad from one place to another, and they don't touch the heart or the center of being. Repentance—*metanoia*—is the movement of returning to the center of being, returning to the heart. The heart that has been oriented toward nonbeing suddenly turns toward God, in a great exclamation of faith . . . .

Professor This is the cry of the thief on the Cross. Christianity does not so much contrast virtue and vice, good and evil, as the two bandits crucified with Christ. The one blasphemes, wanting to see a demonstration of Christ's power: "Save yourself and save us too." The other implores Christ: "Remember me when you come into your Kingdom." And Christ replies to him: "Today, you will be with me in Paradise." (Luke 23:42-43)

Patriarch And what have we made of Christianity? A religion of laws and self-satisfaction! Think for a moment about the pathological fear of women and of love that are so deeply ingrained in Christian psychology. And yet Jesus never said anything against women, not once. Nor does he say anything against the human being. He loves people. He lets them rediscover the resemblance that unites them with the Creator. He only accuses the pharisees and the hypocrites, and He does that harshly: those who are self-satisfied, those who judge and exclude others.

Because she loved so much, *oti igapisen poli*, what other reason is needed!

ΩΩΩ

Patriarch The mystery of Christ is inexhaustible. It is greater than any formula that seeks to grasp it. The mystery cannot be circumscribed or possessed. We can only be filled with wonder, a wonder that is always new.

Professor This is why the Fathers only approached this mystery by antimony, by the joining of opposites. You cannot take hold of a person, of the Person Supreme. Christ, the second Person of the Trinity, is the One about whom, when all has been said, nothing has yet been said. You must die to yourself, be reborn in love, and worship him.[33]

Patriarch Something that the Fathers perhaps missed is Jesus' very simple humanity. Remember yesterday's Gospel reading, of Martha and Mary. "And Jesus loved Martha, and her sister, and Lazarus." (John 11:5) He liked to relax close to his friends. He wanted to see them again as he went to his Passion. He went voluntarily to the Cross, to fight and win a cosmic drama—the Fathers have written admirable words about this. But at the same time, this was precisely the time when he needed to be with his friends, and to taste that human love once more . . .

Professor I have always been struck by how Jesus, the lover of mankind, is sensitive to how different each friend is. The Russian thinker Rosanov said that the universal love of the ascetics was an abstract, impersonal "glass love." Jesus' love is nothing like that. It resonates with all the power and warmth of human tenderness and friendship. Martha, Lazarus, and above all Mary . . . and John, the beloved disciple, who rested his head on Jesus' breast.

Patriarch St. John is the foundation of our most profound spiritual knowledge. The hesychasts [those who practice silent prayer] know about this mysterious exchange of hearts. They invoke the name and the presence of Jesus, and their hearts are on fire, just like the pilgrims on the road to Emmaus, who said: "Did not our hearts burn within us?" (Luke 24:32)

Professor No doubt that is why you chose Emmaus as the symbol for the historic journey that you have been making with Pope Paul VI ever since your meeting in Jerusalem.

Patriarch When we discover Christ's love for us, we discover that we are all brothers and sisters. The fact that Jesus had friends, that he was sensitive to their differences, does not mean that he has less love for anyone else. He has a secret preference for each individual person. And from this we can draw a fundamental principle of spiritual life—do not compare. Every person is beyond compare. How can you take the measure of a person except by love, which itself is beyond measure? Each person is incomparable. Christ does not compare. He loves each of us without limits. Let us remember that when we go out to meet people.

---

33 [See Olivier Clément, *On Human Being*, Ch. 2, The Person in the Image of God, and *The Roots of Christian Mysticism*, Pt. 1, Ch. 4, God: Unity and Difference]

Professor I have noticed that when you greet a person, you give yourself to them completely. You seem to take no notice of whether or not they are 'important.'

Patriarch I don't know. I am one human atom among millions of others. I know that everyone is infinitely important. But enough of that. Let's return to the simplicity of Jesus—which is more profound than the most profound theology. All of the Gospel and all of Christianity can be found in the parables. I especially love the Parable of the Good Shepherd. When I was a boy, I used to carve shepherds' crooks, for fun.

Professor And you became a shepherd, the pastor of men.

Patriarch In order to serve and to intercede. He is the only shepherd. Only he knows the doorway to the sheepfold. He calls his sheep by name. He is the shepherd and he is also the door. We enter by Him and he knows the secret name of each person. (John 10:1–18)

Professor Which is written on the white stone of which the Book of Revelation speaks. In giving us a name, he gives us life. (Rev. 2:17)

Patriarch And we enter and we leave, and we find green pastures. We enter by Christ and we find the communion cup. We leave in Christ and we discover our brothers and sisters.

What a miracle! The unattainable God has become our friend. He said, you are my friends. What unlimited joy!

> Because he loved much.
> *Oti igapisen poli.*

ΩΩΩ

2. The Church and Christianity

One evening at the Phanar the Patriarch motioned to me to come and sit next to him at his desk. His head in his hands, he seemed to be deep in sad thought. And the exchange that followed was like a cry of pain.

Patriarch What have we done? What have we done? Christ has abandoned us. We have chased him away. We have mocked the spirit of the Gospels by our hatred, by our pride, by our pharisaical self-sufficiency. And Christ has left. Christ has left.

Where is he now? Where is he? He is walking like a pilgrim with the poor, the downtrodden, with those who have been mistreated and abused. Where is he? Perhaps in India, perhaps in Africa? Somewhere in the huge urban crowds? But we cannot live without him. We have to find him again.

ΩΩΩ

I think about Mother Maria Skobstova, who died in the gas chamber at Ravensbrück because she saved the lives of many Jews. After a tumultuous political and personal life, this young Russian revolutionary became a nun in Paris, the Paris of the Russian emigration. She did not wall herself off in a convent. She placed herself at the service of the downtrodden: dockers in Marseilles, miners in the Pyrenees, drug addicts and alcoholics whom she consoled in their squalid crash pads. She worked to save Jews who had been compelled to wear the yellow star. She comforted her companions in Ravensbrück. On her train journeys to serve the poor and the sick, she would write poems. One of these describes Christ's departure:

He lived among us.
Twenty centuries have borne his mark.
In him was everything.
He was the reflection of the universe.
Not so long ago, on a calm, gray day
He left the temples
And the houses,
Alone, barefoot, carrying only a satchel,
And the cross, and fire . . .
And the world has become poor
Beyond all measure.

ΩΩΩ

Professor Traveling the world incognito . . . But he remains faithful to his Church, despite the hardness of our hearts . . . .

Patriarch That is the tragedy. We drive him out of the very place where he gives himself, totally, in the communion cup. The divided Church has torn its Savior apart, when it ought to be the one whole living communion chalice from which divine energy overflows for all mankind.

Oh, we are so pleased with ourselves! We are the pure ones, we have the truth, we condemn the others. But life and history are knocking at the door of the Church to ask the ultimate questions. Everything is changing. The unfolding scientific revolution does not only alter the dimensions of human life. It changes men and women, their upbringing and education, the relations between men and women, their psychology. Tomorrow, perhaps, it will modify us genetically, and change our whole character. Not that the world constructed by science and technology necessarily excludes God—as is sometimes suggested. But scientific and technological change compels us to ask where this all leads, what does it mean, and what do our own lives mean. Atheism is also changing, becoming a generalized indifference in which people are trapped. Communism is changing: while it continues as a pseudo-religion, new hopes are emerging. In some ways, Communism is just the mask of a new ruling class, in other ways it claims to be a new rational model of social organization.

Professor And now in the West we are beginning to see a new "mystical atheism," which seeks to recreate the feeling-state of religion through drugs, trances, and hallucination, through eroticism, through the "game of revolution." But this is always based on the refusal of a personal God, and the systematic dismantling of the human person. This "mystical atheism" finds common ground with a somewhat distorted version of Indian spirituality.

Patriarch I have seen the same tendencies in contemporary Greek thought. It is always the same tragedy. If so many seekers of the unknown turn towards yoga and eastern spirituality—towards what the Greek poet Sikelianos calls 'Holy Asia'—this is because we seem to be missing a Christian spirituality. Christianity does not know how to speak to the person of today's industrialized world. But we cannot avoid the major questions. What is the meaning of these scientific and technical discoveries and the emergence of a planetary humanity? Humankind studies the secrets of the universe and collides with the mystery that is the gateway to God. It has a choice: to find God or to find desolation. The disintegration of matter, and the dismantling of the soul, reveal both non-being and the infinite. And where, at this solemn moment, is the Church? What is the Church doing? What face does the Church present us? We say—the Church: but we are the ones people see. And what do they see? What do they see?

ΩΩΩ

Several days later, at Halki, the Patriarch again picks up this sad meditation, and, as so often, without any preamble.

Patriarch What the men of the Church are most lacking is the Spirit of Christ: humility, the stripping bare of self, the universal welcome, the ability to see the best in the other person. We are frightened. We want to keep hold of everything that is worn out, because it is familiar. We want to be right and for the others to be wrong. We conceal our pride and lust for power with over-used humble words. We are playing outside the arena of life.

He stands up and paces the room. His voice hardens. At the end, he seems to be almost shouting.

Patriarch We have made the Church one institution among all the others. It took all of our efforts to build it and now, it takes all our effort to keep it going. And it works, more or less, less rather than more, but it works. Only—and he is shouting, the only time I heard him shout—it works like a machine and not like life.

ΩΩΩ

Professor One of the themes that you return to frequently in your messages is the difference between Christianity and the Church.

Patriarch As I have told you, Christ and Christianity are everywhere. We need Christ, we are nothing without him. But he does not need us to act within history. Since the Resurrection, even since the creation, all of human history is a sort of pan-Christianity.

Professor Since the beginning . . . the Fathers say that the non-Christian religions present so many facets of an 'evangelic preparation' (not that they ignored the need to purify these religions). Today we could say that non-Christian religions are a preparation for the final outpouring of the Spirit, that will reveal the glorious face of Christ to mankind.

Patriarch The ancient covenant is in reality a whole series of covenants, and all of them continue today, one beside the other.

Professor In the second century, St. Irenaeus of Lyons explains this very clearly. And when St. Gregory Palamas was a prisoner of the Turks—a well-treated prisoner, who was free to debate with Muslim scholars—he said that the vocation of Islam was to have brought the God of Abraham to the Arabs.

Patriarch And the covenant of Adam, or rather, the covenant of Noah, continues in ancient religions, especially those of India, with their cosmic symbolism . . . .

Professor Which see the whole world as a theophany—seeing the world, one might say, as a rainbow, the sign of the covenant of Noah. In a certain way paganism prefigures the final transfiguration of all life in the Holy Spirit.

Patriarch But paganism is unaware of—or has forgotten—the living God. We know now that the divine light radiates from a face. The covenant of Abraham was necessary as was, no doubt, its renewal in Islam. The covenant of Moses continues in Judaism. And everything is recapitulated in Christ. The Logos of the Incarnation is the Word that created the universe, which the universe makes visible. The Word is also what takes hold of the prophets and shapes history. This is why I consider Christianity to be the religion of religions, and why I can say that I belong to all religions.

Professor And as for modern, so-called secular humanism, its driving force comes from the fundamental biblical truths. The unacknowledged biblical revelation is what structures our modern, European perception of the world. . . . Whereas for traditional India, the material world is an appearance, an illusion that must be reabsorbed into the inner world, and all knowledge and all spiritual techniques of any significance concern this inner world.

For the spiritual thinkers of Ancient Greece, the material world was a tomb—Plato called it soma-sema—from which one had to become free. (And I haven't yet mentioned the Manicheans . . .)[34]

Patriarch The biblical revelation made science and technology possible. But above all, it opens history to the hidden driving force of the last two millennia, that of the human person and of freedom. In the Orthodox tradition, the person is precisely defined by freedom and responsibility.

Professor The search for a free and responsible existence is certainly what animates all of modern history, in Europe, in America, and in the Third World.

Patriarch All of Atatürk's work points to this. Look at what he did for the liberation of women in this country, my country.

Professor How strange that this search for freedom should so often collide with the hesitations and mandates of the Church.

Patriarch The Churches are afraid of the Gospel—even though the Gospel is why they exist. And so, Christ has gone out among the people, and has inspired their history, without the help of the Churches and sometimes in opposition to them . . . . The same can be said about social-

---

34 [See Olivier Clément, *Transfiguring Time,* Introduction and Pt. 1 Cyclical Time]

ism. Insofar as it tries to create more justice and more community for mankind, it takes its power from the Gospel . . . . The poor are the incarnation of Christ.

Professor Some historians of medieval France have recently discovered that the religious movements of radical evangelical poverty in Europe were inspired by what the Greek Fathers had written about the incarnation of Christ in the poor. We find the same movements in the Byzantine world, for example, the 'zealots' of Thessaloniki. The same thing probably occurred at the time of the Russian Revolution, at least on a popular level. And every time the split between the Church and the world is overcome —between the Church as the guardian of the Eucharistic mystery, and this evangelical alter ego of the Church, the world driven by the desire for liberty and communion: every time this split is overcome, there occurs one of the great Christian renewals.

In the Middle Ages, there is St. Francis of Assisi, who, in a very public act, designed to challenge the city merchants, marries Dame Poverty. There is St. Gregory Palamas, who, as Bishop of Thessaloniki takes up the themes of the 'zealots,' calling for social justice. And in our century, there are the great French and Russian religious philosophers. And then there is Pope John XXIII.

Patriarch And do not forget Pope Paul VI. In my opinion, his encyclical *Populorum Progressio* is of vital cosmic-historical importance.[35] Christianity and the Church need to come back together to inaugurate a new period in the history of Christianity, a glorious but humble period. Science is knocking at the door of the unknown, but science will not give the unknown its meaning. Its meaning is the Resurrection, which is revealed in the Eucharist. Humankind is becoming one. But this unification will only avoid violence and drab uniformity if it respects and encourages the uniqueness of each person, and the unique contribution of each race and culture. In the image of the Trinity, in the image of unity in diversity, the Church can be the leaven of this unity. Modern man is seeking freedom and responsibility, but this freedom must be based on love, and if it is to conquer death, love must be fed by the Eucharist . . . .

Professor Dostoevsky predicted that socialism would be much more susceptible to the three temptations that Christ overcame in the desert . . . . Because socialism wants to turn stones into bread, but people cannot live from bread alone. And what is true of socialism, is true of our indus-

35 *On the Development of Peoples*, 1967

trial society. And who, if not the Church, can exorcize these temptations, so long as it returns to the One who said: "for what does it profit a man, to gain the whole world and to lose his soul." (cf. Mark 8:36)

Patriarch The Apostle said, in all things, hold on to that which is good. (1 Thess 5:21) Everything should be secretly oriented to the Resurrection: the search for freedom, the search for justice, the search for fraternal cooperation and peace; the slow rebuilding of the world, through technology by human intelligence; a more equitable sharing of the earth's resources; the rebirth of oppressed cultures and races; the liberation of women; the recognition of the value of labor—everything secretly points to the Resurrection, everything should converge toward the final transfiguration.

Professor But how can we encourage this re-encounter of the Gospel and the Church, of the poor and the Eucharist?

Patriarch We need a renewal, of which there are signs all around the Christian world. But, the first fundamental requirement must be the unity of Christians, who are called to go out into the world together, to serve mankind. Christ prayed that we all might be one, so that the world may believe. Even now, trust has begun to replace the fear and distrust that has for so long gripped the Churches: or rather, that has ruled inside the Church, because there is only one Church. These summer months, Christians of every confession come to see me, from all over. We talk like brothers and sisters. We pray together. Love descends on the face of the Church and transfigures it. Christianity and the Church begin to be one, with one common source, the Gospel, and the Eucharist.

ΩΩΩ

That same day, with these words still ringing in my ears, I take a walk in the Old City, where Byzantium lies hidden beneath Istanbul. Suddenly you come upon a church that is undergoing renovations and that seems, despite its age, to have just been built and not yet finished. In the doorway, three Turkish archeologists are carefully cleaning broken pieces of sculpture. They explain to me that the church, which has long been used as a mosque, will become a museum of Christian art, and that is why it is being restored. The contemporary secularization of Istanbul is bringing us holy spaces, in which the silence is witness to the Transfiguration. It is freeing the human face of God, the divine face of the human, from the white chalk of its Muslim coating. What can this discovery mean for someone who knows nothing of Christianity? I think of the Patriarch's words about Christ traveling through history. And I recall what he said about Hagia Sophia, how it was turned into a Christian museum, and how its mosaics were restored, thanks to Atatürk and Roosevelt—for both of whom he has huge admiration.

And what about these young archeologists? They grew up in a non-Christian world, that was either Muslim or overtly secular. Now they are applying their scientific curiosity—perhaps, even, their love—to these superb testimonials to Christian faith. This is the fruit of the Western scientific tradition, whose roots are in Christianity, a secularized tradition that belongs to all mankind. What can these young archeologists feel?

One possible answer emerges a few days later. A young woman approaches the Patriarch in the narthex of St. George's Church, as people leave Vespers. She has a beautiful, strong, animated, sensitive face, with large dark eyes. She too is an archeologist. She wants the Patriarch's permission to photograph the Byzantine mosaics that have been re-installed in the Phanar. The Patriarch at once agrees. But as always, he enters into conversation. The young woman is from a Muslim family, but grew up in a completely secular environment, like so many of the country's intellectuals since the time of Atatürk. She became an archeologist out of love for her country and her people, a love for every part of its history. She has become enthralled by Byzantine mosaics. And through the mosaics, she has discovered Christ. Now she considers herself a Christian.

"Without belonging to the Church?"

"Without belonging to the Church. Christianity is not bounded by the Church. Besides, the weight of historical tradition, and ethnic problems, would make conversion difficult. We do not allow any proselytizing. Even so, there were two adult baptisms recently."

Secularization has opened a door. Christ steps in, still incognito for a while. On the main shopping street of Pera, young street vendors—probably students—have piled books on the sidewalk. There are the great revolutionary texts of the nineteenth and twentieth centuries. But also Dostoevsky. As Albert Camus said, we believed this would be the century of Marx, but we find out that it is the century of Dostoevsky. What if it is the century of both? With a renewed Christianity on the horizon.

ΩΩΩ

Professor What I like most in your thinking, is that you do not create opposites. At one and the same time, you have the sense of Christ's presence in all of human history, and a completely realistic sense of his presence in the Eucharist. Very often in the West, those Christians who see the work of Christ in the upheavals of history end up forgetting or rejecting the unseen power, and they turn the Eucharist into a simple shared meal. And those who feel the pull of the interior life and the sense of holiness tend to see only threats, excesses, and the dark shadow of the Antichrist in the life of the world.

Patriarch We have to tell those who reduce the Eucharist to a shared meal that, even if shared with love, this meal will not save them from death. The Eucharist is first and foremost union with the Risen Christ, in whom we are resurrected. The bread of immortality brings us eternal life, here on Earth. And that is why the Eucharist is at the same time a completely fraternal meal, shared between brothers and sisters—and is more than fraternal, because we become one body in the mystical body of Christ.

As for those who are afraid of history, we should remind them that Christ has conquered hell, and that the fullness of life overflows from the chalice, for all mankind. They should not reject life, because the wheat and the tares are intermingled. They should discern the work of Christ that is leading everything towards his Resurrection . . . There is only one Christ . . . we must unite the Christ of history with the Christ of the Communion cup.

ΩΩΩ

Patriarch Our pain at seeing so many Christians turning the Church into a machine, our feelings of being torn apart before the divided body of our Lord, these should not mask our love for our Mother, the Church, the vessel of divine life, the axis of history and the heart of the world. The Church is the body of Christ. It is brought together, not as an institution, but by the Eucharist, the mystery of Christ.

Professor And the body of Christ is the place of an ever-renewed Pentecost. The tongues of fire set the blood of the Communion cup aflame.

Patriarch The unity of the Church is in the image of the mystical unity of God the Trinity. We enter into the love of the Father, the source of the divine, by the Son, through the Holy Spirit. By our communion with the holy gifts, the mystery of the Trinity becomes part of our own living being. Our life becomes infinitely open to the Trinity. Every time that I discover that the face of my neighbor is both transparent and unique, I take part in the mystery of the Trinity. This is why the Church's existence on Earth can have no other symbol than unity in love, thus accomplishing the 'new commandment' that the Lord gave us.

Professor The paradox is that the Lord is always faithful to his Church, but his Church is not always faithful to him.

Patriarch We chase Christ out of the Church, but he always gives himself in the chalice.

Professor Some of the Fathers have said that the Church is a prostitute that Christ washes with his blood, so that it can become his spotless bride.

Patriarch That is why the Church lives by repentance and the action of grace. As we were reminded at the first Pan-Orthodox Conference at Rhodes, "our Church is not made up of bricks and mortar; it is made of faith and life." Wisdom is the discovery that you are responsible for everyone who lives on the face of the Earth, for all mankind, for all who are created of the same flesh and blood. When I celebrate the Divine Liturgy —especially at Christmas or Pascha—I not only mystically concelebrate with the heads of all sister Churches, I pray with the Pope and with the heads of all the Christian confessions. And then I can offer this bloodless sacrifice "for the prosperity of the holy Churches of God and for the union of all," for the salvation of the world, for all the earth, for which we, the Church, should invoke Christ's mercy and peace.

Professor "For those who love us and those who hate us," as we pray in the Liturgy.

Patriarch "But I say to you, love your enemies and pray for those who persecute you, so that you may be sons of your Father who is in heaven; for he makes his sun rise on the evil and on the good, and sends rain on the just and the unjust." (Mt. 5:44–45)

Patriarch If the Church and Christianity are to become one, the Church must first show itself to be poor and humble in the face it presents to the world. Of course, Churches need sufficient financial resources, and these must be well-managed. When I reorganized our parish communities, especially in America, I insisted on financial discipline. And people gave what was needed and more besides. But the leaders of the Church must learn to bare themselves, to set an example of simplicity. In this regard we can learn a lot from the Pope and from certain Catholic bishops. The person of today only understands simplicity and spontaneous acts of love—at least, outside of the Church. Inside the Church, it should be a great feast of beauty of every kind, whether we are talking about the decor or the manner of celebration.

ΩΩΩ

I think about the Patriarch himself, who sometimes takes a tightly packed jitney or public bus—the Phanar has only one car. Inside the church, he scrupulously observes all the ritual gestures and accepts the veneration traditionally offered to the bishop—people kiss his hand and then bow down until their forehead touches his hand. But outside the church, he spontaneously and lovingly engages with everyone whom he talks to.

ΩΩΩ

Patriarch There must be close collaboration between the ministers and the rest of the people in the Church. Because these are God's people.

Professor I have seen how simple and direct you are with people when you visit their parish: how you engage them in a real dialogue.

Patriarch There is nothing more important for the head of a Church than to know how to hear the mysterious voice of the people. It is the people, joined in love and faith, who guard the truth. In the Church, ministry is a form of service, the ministry of love, unity, and peace. The leader draws his strength from his sense of responsibility. He brings all together in communion. His authority depends on how far he embodies the evangelical overturning of values: if anyone would be first, he must be last of all and servant of all. (Mk. 9:35)

Professor And how do you achieve this collaboration in the daily life of the Church?

Patriarch Take a look at our parish communities. Their smooth functioning depends on the day-to-day collaboration of the priest and the lay council president, who is elected every two years by the parish faithful. In America, we had an archdiocesan assembly every two years, in which there were as many lay delegates as clergy, which was responsible for all important decisions. We the clergy can do nothing without the laity. We would run the risk of becoming closed off in our own little circle, removed from life. The lay people know life and we should listen to them.

If I know a little about people, if sometimes I have a sense of the destiny of the Church and the future of Christianity, it is because I have been in direct contact with people for fifty-nine years. I am an old bureaucrat who serves people, day after day.

ΩΩΩ

Professor In this close collaboration between the laity and the ordained clergy, what role do they each play in solving the great ethical, social, and political problems of the world?

Patriarch May the lay people act responsibly! My role is not to impose rules on them. And anyhow, how would that be possible? Our Orthodox Churches live under such different conditions—in the East, in the West, in the developing world. My task is to remind people about the meaning of life and to help them become responsible citizens.

Professor In this respect, what are your thoughts about the Papal Encyclical, *Humanae Vitae,* which there is so much talk about right now?

Patriarch Everyone criticizes this encyclical. But listen to me carefully. The Pope had no choice to say or do differently. On this question, the Vatican has its own traditions and its own language. The Pope cannot ignore these or throw them aside. You must understand what the Pope is saying through this language that, in part, is not his language. You have to understand the values that he wants to defend: the sanctity of human love; the mystery of the child. Remember the joy of a person's coming into the world, of which the Gospel speaks. Pleasure sought for itself brings disintegration, if it is not mastered and transformed, sanctified by shared tenderness; if pleasure seeking is not also an opening to the immensity of life, the immensity of love in all its richness. The Pope also is defending the rights of the family against new forms of chemical and biological totalitarianism.

If you take a look, the encyclical was thirty-one pages long . . . . How sad that he needs to convince people and prove his case. Could he have said it all in just a few words? But these few words should be on the question of birth control, at a time so many millions of people would like a clear answer . . . .

Professor And the Orthodox?

Patriarch Happily, this is not a problem for us. We leave this question to each person's conscience, to the secrecy of the confessional, to the relationship with their spiritual father. Not that we have nothing to say—far from it! We need to help people become fully responsible, especially in this aspect of life. We need to remind them of the meaning of love. The love of a man and a woman is one of the magnificent features of Christian love. It expresses the love of Christ for his Church. “This is a great mystery,” the Apostle Paul said. It is both the slow discovery of the other and the discovery of the immensity of life.

Professor There is this ascetic ideal of wholeness, *sophrosyne*. Sometimes it is translated as chastity, but it is the chastity of the soul, the unification of one’s being. This can so well apply to human love. There is a wholeness, or true chastity, when all the immensity of life is contained within an authentic encounter; when passion is contained within tenderness. The miracle of the wedding at Cana is evoked in the Orthodox marriage ceremony. There is a wedding and Christ turns the water into wine. The sacrament of marriage seals human love with the sign of Eucharistic delight.

Patriarch This is why, today more than ever, we need to remind people, especially the young, that love is possible, that this sober and noble love between two people is possible, and that it is infinite: an infinity of faithfulness and eternity.

Professor Love like this, by definition, is creative and fruitful—whether it brings forth children, or hospitality, or shared service, or the mutual creation of life.

Patriarch My role is to remind people of the meaning of love. To help each person be attentive to the other, to be attentive to life, to become a person filled with respect and wonder. And I have only respect for each person. The nuptial chamber is sacrosanct. I do not enter. If there is true love between a man and a woman, that love is completely holy.

But people attack the Pope. He is alone. He suffers. He is a very sensitive person. He is not an old bureaucrat like me. So I need to stand by his side. He just sent me a telegram for the anniversary of his visit to Istanbul. I have sent one in reply to say that I am in agreement with him. I agree with his fundamental intentions. And, above all, I love him.

Several days later, the Italian ambassador to Turkey visited the Patriarch.

Patriarch I expressed my support for the Pope and told him how much I had felt at home in Rome. After all, Constantinople is the New Rome and the Byzantines called themselves Romans. So I am also Roman! The ambassador thanked me for the support I had given the Pope around the *Humanae Vitae* encyclical. “But what about you, the Orthodox?” he asked. “It is a question for the next Pan-Orthodox Council.” “And for now?” “We leave it to each person’s conscience and to the wisdom of their father confessor. We do not want to lay down rules. I am not going to issue a decree: I only want to remind people of the value of life.”

Professor I sometimes wonder if the Catholic requirement of a celibate priesthood has not in some way skewed the understanding of human love—whether it hasn’t created a sense that the Christian mystery and human sexuality are incompatible.

Patriarch That’s quite possible. In any case, I think there is a great benefit to having married priests in the Orthodox Church.

Professor At the First Ecumenical Council, it was St. Paphnutius, one of the great Egyptian ascetics, who spoke against obligatory celibacy for priests. He said that spiritual chastity could illuminate married life just as it does monastic celibacy. Celibacy is a monastic vocation . . . .

Patriarch Or perhaps, it is one of the modes of the monastic vocation, like fasting and other ascetic practices. It is about bringing one’s life force to a higher level, about giving love its supreme expression . . . .

Professor Evagrius wrote that the true monk is both separated from all and united with all. The person of today so badly needs these examples, and these lessons of the deep study of spiritual rebirth.

Patriarch But this can only be the result of a free calling, to love God directly, with no intermediary, that leads to internalizing and transforming one’s whole being, in this love, so that it becomes prayer, prayer that encompasses all of humanity and the universe. And this center, radiating goodness and kindness, can also be a couple . . . and hence the potential and the exemplary character of the married priest . . . .

Professor And his wife, because she exercises a real ministry in which her maternal tenderness is not enclosed within the family but is offered to all, in a self-offering . . . . Some of the best priests that I have known became priests at a late age, influenced by their wife.

Patriarch Believe me, sooner or later there will be married priests in the Catholic Church. But you should neither require priests to be married, nor forbid them. It should be a free choice. Clerical celibacy can also have a great, apostolic value, signifying the total gift of oneself to God . . . .

Professor Our merciful mother, the Church, represents the love of Christ, who came not to call the righteous, but the sinners, and who did not reject the Samaritan woman, despite her many husbands. The Orthodox Church venerates the great ascetics who became transparent to the divine light. It magnifies the sanctity of married life and ordains married men to the priesthood. The ideal of human love is the marriage of one man with one woman. And the apostle likewise desires this of the bishop, and so today, the Church demands this of its priests.

That is why our Church does not encourage remarriage (and only celebrates a second marriage penitentially). And yet, in its great mercy, the Church recognizes that sometimes a man and a woman cannot achieve this model of unity in Christ that marriage has offered them. So the Church accepts divorce and the remarriage of divorced persons. She welcomes these battered existences into her communion. But there is nothing legalistic about this. Divorce and remarriage are not by right but are granted out of the mercy of the Church, in recognition of the failings of the world. To fully explore the mystery of marriage, you need all time and all of eternity. The Church teaches nothing less. But here, too, the Church points the way, animates life, and lights the path—without rejecting those who hesitate or lose their way.

Patriarch The real concerns of the Church are not legal, but pastoral. The canons are therapeutic suggestions that the bishop or the father confessor should adapt to each person, according to the principle of 'economy.' But be careful, your vision of the Orthodox Church is too optimistic! We too have weighed people down with unnecessary burdens, that have no justification in the Gospel. We will ordain a married man, but we forbid an unmarried priest to get married. Why?

Professor There are some Orthodox circles that are very attached to tradition.

Patriarch But this is not Tradition. It is a custom, a discipline that the Church instituted, quite recently, and that the Church is free to alter.

Professor True. But in certain traditionalist circles I have heard the following justifications. Human love can expand into the deep love that unites a priest, and his wife with him, to the parish. But it would be unthinkable for a celibate priest, united with his parish in this deep love, suddenly to place this love 'in parentheses' and redirect his attention to a single person.

Patriarch But why are we trying to measure love? If a woman marries a priest, it is because she loves him as he is, and wants to consciously join him in his service, not to diminish it. My belief is that a priest should be able to marry after ordination. It is absurd that when a man decides his priestly vocation, he should be compelled to find a wife, quickly, almost impersonally. After all, you don't marry just to get married; you marry because you have met someone—and you can't dictate when this will occur—because you love someone deeply and personally. This should all happen, peacefully and maturely, in the fullness of time.

Patriarch If a priest is celibate, not by vocation but because he did not meet the person who was destined to become his wife before his ordination, he should be able to marry, after ordination, if he meets her. Otherwise, there is no justice in the Church. If people are to discover that Christianity and the Church have been reconciled, there must be real justice in the Church.

When I was Archbishop of America, I was ready to propose this reform to the archdiocesan convention. That was the moment that I was elected Patriarch, so everything was left hanging. But I am hoping that the Synod will adopt this for consideration at the next Pan-Orthodox Council.

Professor In the early Church, the bishops themselves were married. One of the most remarkable Church Fathers, St. Gregory of Nyssa, was a married bishop. When his wife died, after many years of marriage, one of his colleagues acclaimed her as "a saint, and the true wife of a priest." St. Gregory Nazianzus was the son of a bishop. In the West, St. Hilary of Poitiers was also a married bishop. There are many such examples. It was only in the seventh century, I think, that the Eastern Church decided to select its bishops exclusively from the monks. The Church had become to look like an arm of the Empire and the morale of the clergy was affected by this confusion of the Kingdom of God and the Kingdom of Caesar. The monks alone, these prophets of the world to come, seemed to be the guardians of the spiritual independence of the Church. Hence the decision to choose the leaders of the Church exclusively from among the monks. Probably also, they hoped to bring the Church hierarchy and the prophetic monastic tradition together. Even today, the positive changes we have seen in the Church over the past ten years are due, in large part, to the prophetic figures who are at the top of the hierarchy. I'm thinking of John XXIII and yourself.

Patriarch This is certainly true of Pope John XXIII. For myself, I don't know. But the historical conditions under which bishops are recruited have changed significantly. The Pan-Orthodox Council will need to consider this question. The Church is no longer the Church of the Byzantine Empire. Monasticism is no longer such a strong force, and no longer plays quite the same role. Meanwhile, there are some remarkable married priests who cannot become bishops. Young men are set apart and become celibate, so that they can make a career as a bishop. Why shouldn't we have married bishops? There were married bishops for many centuries, at a time when Christians were a persecuted minority. In fact, the conditions then were much closer to the conditions of today than to those of the Imperial Church. St. Paul tells us that Peter and the other apostles each had their partner . . . . A man who dedicates himself to the service of the Church should be able to choose freely whether or not to marry.

Professor In the early Church, the bishop's house was where services were most often held. At the heart of the Christian community, you find either monastic intercession for the world, or the radiance of true love. Nicholas Berdyaev said that this love also inaugurates the transfiguration of the world.

Patriarch The Church must be a place of justice. Then people will discover the face of the one "who loves mankind," as we say in the Liturgy, the face of God who loves mankind.

ΩΩΩ

3. Islam

Istanbul has immense mosques whose architecture seeks to imitate and even surpass Hagia Sophia. Under the cupolas, you find a tranquil, refreshing space, bathed in the light reflected from the blue and green tiles that cover the walls. These are pure and empty spaces, neither of incarnation nor of transfiguration. The lettering and the arabesques of the tiles transform the space into an illuminated manuscript, seemingly no longer architecture but a two-dimensional plane. Everything points to the unattainable divine.

Here and there, a man kneeling, sitting on his heels, swaying forward gently in prayer, close to tears and chanting in a nasal tone. Some women are praying with a prayer bracelet. Every evening, the mosque fills with rows of men at prayer. The chant rises, a swelling sound, and each person bows forward deeply to touch the ground. The unceasing invocation of the One God elevates the soul into the pure and empty space, suspended between the nothingness of the Inaccessible and the nothingness of the contingent created world, of which every instant comes from God, which may, at any instant, be reduced to nothing by God.

A religion without a face, the only true religion of the Word, not of the word made flesh, but of the Word made word, in this spare, molten Arabic, the created flesh of the Inaccessible. The soul does not only hear the well-beloved: the soul must become extinguished so that God alone is proclaimed. In the proclamation of God, the soul becomes consumed. Religion of He, rather than of He and Thou, of Him that is beyond all definition and indication, an arc intersecting with another arc, whose center remains concealed. In the mosque, there is no apse—that recess in which the Word becomes flesh – only a flat wall, with a small niche where a lamp is lit each evening, shedding a green light. This is the sign pointing towards Mecca, the *qibla*—a sign without symbol.

The tour guides leading the Western tourists carefully point out the social equality of the mosque. They try to assimilate the heritage of Islam to the values of today's secular society. But Islam did not generate this secular society. In the lands of Islam, secular society is introduced from the outside, by force. And then all things fall apart.

On the one hand, there is the material world to be mastered, and individual people who want to 'live their own lives,' in tune with the times and with the earth. On the other hand, there is this pure, empty space, the never-to-be-crossed frontier of the Inaccessible. On the one hand, total immanence, on the other hand, total transcendence. The realm of the divino-human is absent. And yet, at the Topkapi Palace Museum, you can see Mohammed's relics: his sword, his sandals. The Prophet wanted to be no more than the insignificant conduit of the eternal Koran. And yet, he is loved. People hope to meet him in their dreams, they venerate his relics. Is this a sign of a forlorn search for the human presence of the living God?

ΩΩΩ

Patriarch We have co-existed with Islam for thirteen hundred years, ever since the Muslims conquered Syria, Palestine, and Egypt, in the seventh century. There are many points of contact, but it is hard to assess their impact. The intellectual interactions are the least interesting—even though real debates took place, especially towards the end of the Byzantine era. Each side tried to convince, or rather overwhelm, the other side, without any real attempt at understanding. But in the life of the people, in that Old Testament atmosphere that I knew as a child, there was a real interchange. At the spiritual level, one can discern even deeper relationships. There is a remarkable convergence in the practice of the invocation of the divine name, and some of the dervishes had a real respect for the name of Jesus. There was an encounter. But it's not that someone copied someone else—people of prayer have their own way of communicating and it leaves no trace behind.

Professor The scholars of comparative religion have labored long and hard to show that the hesychast 'method' is borrowed from the Muslim *dhikr*. But the 'method' existed long before the birth of Islam! If you consider the respect that the early Muslims had for the Christian monks, it is more likely that the borrowing was in the opposite direction. The truth is that the invocation of the divine name, using the rhythms of breathing and the heart, can be found everywhere—in India and in Japan. From the beginning, the human body was created to become the temple of the Holy Spirit.

Patriarch The holy fool in Islam and the fool for Christ in our tradition show the same feigned madness and self-abasement. They become the object of people's derision in order to free themselves. And we find they have the same gift of prophecy, the same spiritual clairvoyance, to which they bear witness, abruptly.

Professor Today, first of all, we want to understand. And the mystery of Islam causes us to stumble: this revelation that comes many centuries after the fullness of the Christian revelation, that acknowledges both the covenant of Moses and the covenant of Jesus. We cannot simply resolve this by calling Islam a Christian heresy, as St. John of Damascus did. But in that case, what is Islam?

Patriarch Perhaps we can say that Mohammed is a prophet of the Old Covenant. He himself refers to Abraham as "the first Muslim." Islam is like a rebirth of the faith of the forefathers and patriarchs—it not only precedes the Incarnation, it precedes the Law of Moses. For many peoples, Islam made possible the passage, from a worn-out, idolatrous paganism, to the faith of Abraham.

Professor And Islam also encountered Judaism and Christianity. The Koran recognizes both Moses and Jesus.

Patriarch And many Muslims live in expectation of Jesus. He will come at the end of time as *Mahdi* and judge. Islam criticizes Judaism for waiting for a messiah born of the tribe of David, in the paternal line of succession. Islam affirms that Jesus was already born, of a virgin birth. Jesus is the "seal of holiness," just as Mohammed is the "seal of prophecy."

Professor Nevertheless, the Jesus of Islam is only one prophet who takes his place in the ranks of the other prophets. And because of his ultimate holiness, Islam considers that he could not have died on the Cross. For Christians, the two arms of the Cross symbolize the union of history and the transcendent. On the parapet of Hagia Sophia each marble block was marked with a cross. But the Muslims erased the horizontal arm. God alone is God and he only is God!

Patriarch That may be true, but since the Muslims love and venerate Jesus, as well as all the patriarchs of the Old Covenant, and since the old distrust and animosities between them and us are dissipating more and more, we will be able to present our own witness of the Bible and the Gospels to the Muslims. But for this to happen, we must take their witness seriously!

Here in Turkey, one difficulty is that there are too few intellectually trained leaders of Islam. But I am ready to join any initiative in this arena, whether it comes from the Vatican or the World Council of Churches. And you should not forget the important role that the Arab Orthodox of the Middle East, living in the heart of Islam, are already playing in this dialogue.

A real dialogue will clarify many things. You were just talking about the Muslim horror of the Cross. And yet, the mystery of the Cross is well-known to Islamic mysticism. Al-Hallaj was crucified because he proclaimed his union with the living God. He wished for his death by the cross, not just to die to himself and be reborn in God, but to become identified with Jesus. I remember a very striking Sufi saying: “How will you know God in the beyond if you have not known him in this life?” We are not talking about an egotistical mysticism. The one who is consumed by God becomes a powerful intercessor, one of the *Abdal,* one of the ten just men who, thanks to the prayers of Abraham, could have saved even the city of Sodom.

Professor The mystery of the Cross reaches far beyond the visible boundaries of Christianity. How strange it is that the Jewish people, who rejected the crucified Messiah, have suffered so many experiences of total crucifixion. The Jewish mystics have seen the Jewish people as a collective messiah, who carry the sins of the world by their suffering! They also invoke the memory of the ten just men.

But in Islam and in Judaism we do not find divino-humanity. Mankind is either separated from God or the person is totally consumed in God. There is no transfiguration.

Certainly, when Christendom attempted to realize this transfiguration through a whole society, not just through the efforts of personal sanctity, this was not without risk. Perhaps the Byzantine Empire was too confident that it had already created the New Jerusalem. Perhaps it was too quick to claim ownership of the divino-human presence, beneath its many domes and in its many icons, when in fact, especially at the end, it was ridden with superstition, hints of paganism and social injustice.

Islam came and shattered the images. Islam wrote the name of the Inaccessible on the cupola and reminded people of the time of judgment to come. Islam reproached the Christians for not achieving the monastic perfection, *rabbaniya,* of which Jesus is the sign. If Islam is a rebirth of the faith of the patriarchs, it also has something of the ultimate—as though it has come to clear the way for the End. Thanks to Islam, the space inside the great churches of Constantinople, and of Hagia Sophia above all, has become the space of the Apocalypse, the image of the heavenly Jerusalem, in which there is no longer an altar, because God will be all in all . . . .

Patriarch We pray facing the east, in expectation of the dawn of the unending day. The Church is a pilgrimage towards the heavenly Jerusalem, of which the earthly Jerusalem is the symbol . . . .

Professor That is why your meeting with the Pope in Jerusalem was so important. As is your appeal for the leaders of all the Churches to meet on Calvary, with tears of hope and penitence. If this should one day happen, it would be a momentous event, not only for the unity of Christians, but also for peace between all the sons and daughters of Abraham. Israel and Ishmael are hostile brothers. If they are still fighting for Jerusalem, the City of Peace, perhaps this is because the Christians have not yet fully realized how much they owe to their Abrahamic brothers and sisters. For too long, the Christians have forgotten to pray toward Jerusalem for the coming of the Lord. Whereas the Muslims have always prayed toward Mecca and toward Jerusalem. Just as the Jews have prayed ceaselessly for the end of their exile. And they have returned, but only at the price of chasing Ishmael once more into the desert.

Patriarch Palestine has become the center of the world once again, the place in which empires and ideologies collide. The Holy Land is fouled with blood like the face of Christ. We must fight and pray for Jerusalem to become a place of encounter and peace, in which we can together prepare for the return of Jesus, the *mahdi* of Islam, for Israel's messiah, for our God.

4. The Science of Life

Patriarch There is no basis for a new life other than the Resurrection. The Resurrection forms in us "the man of God . . . complete, equipped for every good work." (2 Tim 3:17) The inner person, the hidden person of the heart: this is the slow maturing of our conscience, of our whole being, by our resurrection in the Risen Christ.

Professor St. Gregory Palamas said, enigmatically, that the heart is "the innermost body of the body." The whole problem is to unite the mind to the heart, so that the mind is no longer volatile and prone to dissociation, and the heart is no longer blind. Unified through grace, the person acquires an 'intelligent heart' and sees the divine light emerging in the depths of their body, the body that was grafted by baptism onto the luminous body of Christ.

Patriarch You might say that 'the intelligent heart' is the heart that has a loving intelligence. Love is the only force: it is divine energy penetrating and impelling everything, the whole universe, as far as the most distant nebulae. To have a loving intelligence is to welcome the mystery in every being. At the end of his life, St. John had only one thought: "Love is of God, and he who loves is born of God and knows God. He who does not love does not know God: for God is love." (1 John 4:7–8)

I need the other person in order to become aware of God's existence and of my own existence. My awareness of my own existence arises from the other, and I receive it from God at the same time as my awareness of my neighbor. We seek to meet each other and together we discover "the center in which the rays converge."

Professor Perhaps the secret of Christianity is this inexhaustible reciprocity between the one and the other, without separation or confusion. Ultimately, all in India is fusion, while, in Islam and Judaism, all is separation. By contrast, in Christianity, the more I find common ground with the other, the more this person seems endlessly new, as if we are meeting for the first time.

Patriarch It is the same with God—the same infinite expansion of the soul.

Professor St. Gregory of Nyssa celebrated the flight into infinity of the soul-dove—"Oh, for the wings of a dove"—into a light that is, at the same time, darkness. Because God hides himself as he reveals himself. In his presence he is inaccessible. The more the soul is filled with God, the more the soul hungers for God. The more the soul is filled with the light of God, the more it becomes aware of the darkness of the unfathomable light.

Patriarch The other only becomes close through self-revelation, through the self-giving of the always-yet-to-be-grasped person.

Professor In Uppsala, Metropolitan Ignatius Hazim said that "the object is the exile of the person." A person is never an object, not even an object of knowledge.

Patriarch We must know how to pay attention. What a joy it is when a face lights up. We are greedy for love. We wait until our neighbor is dead to offer them flowers. Give them a flower right now—a word, a glance, a smile. Let them know that you need them. What a joy it is that the other is there, that they exist. That they exist and are totally real, with the same interiority as mine. Because God exists, my neighbor exists. They are God's miracle. Above all, the gaze is a miracle. What a joy to plunge deep into the other's gaze, into the inner ocean of their eyes.

Professor When I hear these words, I feel as though I am the one who is speaking. Did you know that I became a Christian because Christianity was revealed to me as the religion of faces? During my childhood, I was raised in an atheist family where no one ever spoke of God or of Christ. I asked: "What happens when you die?" And they told me: "There is nothing." And yet faces haunted me . . . . Where did they come from, where did the light that dwelled in them come from, occasionally lighting up a glance? In a face, in a glance, I sensed something immensely significant breaking through the physical matter. Were faces and glances no more than earthly flowers? What sun has caused them to blossom?[36]

Patriarch Love makes everything understood: both God and life. It makes life the revelation of God. Christ, that is to say the face of God, is the life of all. The Mother of God turns her gaze toward us with infinite compassion.

Professor Christianity is the religion of faces, of the revelation of the face. In a Church filled with icons, the sky has become our friend and the faces of the icons are the stars.

Patriarch And Christ is the "sun of righteousness" who makes shine the faces of the just. (Malachi 4:2)

---

36 [See Olivier Clément, *The Other Sun—A Spiritual Autobiography*, p.82: "Faces . . . where do they come from? This flesh that is at times permeated with a light not that of the sun"]

Professor This reminds me of another time when I was in Greece. The blue sky covered everything as if in blessing. I went into an old church. Immediately I was struck by the dome of the cupola. It had the same fullness and gave the same blessing as the blue sky. But at its center was the face of Christ, from which the light flowed and towards which it flowed back.

ΩΩΩ

Patriarch Love sustains prayer and prayer sustains love. If you intercede or give thanks, you water the universe with the blood of the communion cup. "Give thanks in all things" says the apostle. (1 Thess. 5:18) Be amazed that God exists, then you will discover that everything is alive. Prayer becomes life, the life of those who refuse to close themselves up in their self, and who open themselves up to all that is simple and immense. The pure of heart will see God and the merciful will inherit the earth.

Professor And the poor in spirit?

Patriarch They are those who no longer see their ego as the center of the world. They find the center of the world in God and their neighbor. They strip themselves of everything, at the limit, even of their self. And at that moment they receive their being from God, as a gift of grace.

Or, to go further, let me use the language of war. I like this language: I make war, I attack—this is how I try to live. But I also make war against myself, to disarm myself.

To fight effectively against war and against evil, you must know how to wage inner warfare, to conquer the evil that is in you. You must wage the most difficult war, which is the war against yourself. You must reach the point of being disarmed.

I have waged this war, for years and years. It was terrible. But now, I am disarmed. I am no longer frightened of anything, because "love casts out fear." (1 John 4:18) I no longer need to be right, to be justified by proving the others wrong. I am no longer on guard, jealously clinging to my wealth. I am not stuck on my own ideas and my own projects—if someone suggests something better, I accept it without any regrets. Or rather, not better, simply something good. I have given up comparisons. Whatever is good, and true, and real, whatever it is, that is what is the better for me, always. That is why I have no more fear. When you no longer have anything, you are no longer frightened. "Who can separate us from the love of Christ?" (Rom. 8:39)

Professor This makes me think of the instruction given in the Cherubic Hymn, that we sing during the Liturgy, as the Eucharistic gifts are being consecrated—"set aside all the cares of life." Most people live in a state of worry, perhaps so that they can forget death. For them, time is woven from cares and worry, and becomes a thick fabric that lets no light pass through.

Patriarch Time is cruel. But if a person is secretly wounded, this is because they know they will die, and they know that they need God. With their worldly cares, they escape their horror of death and their hunger for God. It is both an escape and a betrayal.

Professor And the disarmed person? Shouldn't they also rid themselves of their doubts and cares and lay bare this fear of death?—to turn it into trust in Christ, who conquered death. I love the way that, in our tradition, we ask to receive the 'memory of death' by grace, and that it should become the 'memory of God.'

Patriarch Time is cruel. But every passing instant, which, in passing, dies, can become the instant of Resurrection, if only we receive it, not from time, but from God. Worry ties us to the past and to the future. It prevents us from living in the present. The past lives in us. The bad past persists within us, full of separation and violence, feeding fear and hate.

That is why we must let God wipe away the bad past. The good is transfigured and takes its place in the Kingdom. This is the communion of saints that illuminates and protects our present moment.

Professor Human memory itself is transformed. We forget the pain. We remember only the experience of suffering, how it deepened our understanding and our ability to show sympathy. In memory, joys and beauty are, as it were, filtered, to become part of the eternity from which they sprung. In history, also, we forget human suffering and cruelty. All that remains is a picture, a symphony, the ruins of a building. We forget the cruelty of the Roman circus. And the building, like Hagia Sophia, rejoins its archetype, the New Jerusalem.

Patriarch But you do not forget the bad things that you have done and the bad things that you have experienced, especially when they were done by people or organizations that are still there. You do not forget. And you cannot force yourself to forget. But if you disarm, if you strip yourself bare, if you open yourself to the God-man who makes all things new, then He will wash the bad past clean and will give you a new time, in which all is possible.

The God who takes flesh, dies on the cross and is resurrected. He forgives us and allows us to forgive, because he has renewed time, even time past. This is the mystery of repentance. And this mystery can come to pass between people, but above all, between the Churches. Because the Church only exists because of God's forgiveness. That is why the Pope and I—with the support of the Synod—asked God to wipe away from the Church's memory all the bad past that has separated us—this saga of the year 1054 from which hatred is still bubbling up.

"And so, let us go forward."

We cannot choose the future. This is in God's hands. We know only that in our lives and in our history, the Resurrection will have the last word. That is why we have no fear. We turn our gaze toward God, placing our complete trust in him for whatever is to come.

And so, we will be able to welcome the present and to live it to its full intensity. Every day, I wake up grateful for being alive. The new day comes to me as a blessing. And the promise of life, that we have heard in the past, that points to our future in God, that is what I seek to nurture today, in living the fullness of every moment.

Professor But the moment can also be a time of crucifixion—the ordeal of Job.

Patriarch Nothing bothers me. Nothing can bother me. I am in the hands of God. In suffering, in difficulty, we still have the fundamental assurance that God loves us with a limitless love. We still have the blood of Christ and the compassion of the All-Holy Theotokos. Do you remember the icons of the Theotokos—especially those where she leans her face gently against the face of her Son. Think of her icon surrounded by flowers, in the church where we were yesterday. Her presence is multiplied by the icons. When we no longer understand, her faith comes to rescue ours. Her gentleness wipes away our bitterness.

I know how it is when the situation is out of our control, when there is nothing more we can do. Then I hand myself over completely, I go forward in trust, with the full force of my own powerlessness. And I become at peace, that peace the Lord gives us, the peace that surpasses all understanding.

ΩΩΩ

That evening, on leaving the church after Vespers, the Patriarch stops for a long time in front of the jasmine bush. He breathes in the scent, first of one flower and then another. He takes his time, in a gesture of detachment and gratitude that is like an offering. "Your own of your own, we offer to you, in all and for all."

Professor When I see your love for nature it makes me think of the 'contemplation of nature' of which the great masters of the Christian East spoke: the offering of the essence of things, of the whisper of creation, to God. In the Church, in which the created world is restored to its Eucharistic vocation, we become able to discern and to celebrate the cosmic liturgy. Each person can become the priest of the world, on the altar of their own heart . . . .

Patriarch God gives us nature, as a source of consolation, like a memory of Paradise. The peace and strength of nature, the wisdom that orders it, comfort the soul at times of uncertainty, especially during troubled and tragic episodes of history. At these times, mankind is in a mad fever, but nature still teaches us that God is faithful and that the laws of fruitfulness are patience, slowness, and silence.

Professor I remember how, one year, at the start of a painful separation, I was comforted by the buds that were already formed on the trees in autumn. I was reassured and found peace. Each bud was a condensation of the time to come, witnessing, even before winter began, to the coming spring and summer.

Patriarch "While the earth remains, seed time and harvest, cold and heat, summer and winter, day and night, shall not cease." (Gen. 8:22) The great cycles of nature remind us of God's promise and blessing. The Church blesses the earth. Remember the grapes that were blessed at the Feast of the Transfiguration. The Church sings hymns to the maternity of the earth.

Professor I remember Boris Pasternak's great novel *Doctor Zhivago*. During those apocalyptic years of the Russian Revolution, that wished to remake man by decree, the chaos became more and more nihilistic, and innumerable lives were destroyed. Zhivago found his footing, returned to earth, one might say, in contemplating the great cycles of nature. He particularly loved trees, which grow so imperceptibly that one can only track their growth over long intervals of time . . . this is how real historical growth occurs, he says. It seems to me that today we need people who will be like trees. We have destroyed the trees under the illusion that they serve no purpose, and now we realize that, without the trees, the earth is no longer fruitful. The saints are the people who are like trees, and, in truth, the Church is perhaps a silent forest that grows in the breath of the

Holy Spirit, without anyone noticing. By its very presence, it calms and protects humankind. Every day, there are monks who march towards this forest and enter its silent shade, in their turn becoming trees that will heal and will foster new life.

You must forgive me, I have got tangled up in my metaphors . . . .[37]

Patriarch Not at all. When people are tired, they rest in the shade of the trees and the birds of the sky rest in the branches. And only their leaves let us hear the sighing of the wind and the Spirit. The Cross is the new tree of life that joins heaven and earth, the living and the dead, men, and angels. Scripture uses many symbols from the plant world. This is not an accident. This is the real essence of things. Christ is the true vine and we are all shoots of the vine. Israel is the original olive tree to which the gentiles are grafted. Ilias Venezis—a writer whom I greatly admire, both as an artist and as a man—has wonderfully described the exchange of life that occurs in grafting . . . .

I found the text the Patriarch was referring to. Father Joseph is an old peasant, talking to the author and his sister when they are still children.

> "Here we are." Father Joseph laid the bundle of shoots on the ground. He could no longer see very well. So he felt around the trunk of the wild olive tree to find the right place. His expression became more and more serious: his whole being was concentrated in the touch of his hands. When finally he found the right spot, he looked up to the skies. He made the sign of the cross three times and his lips moved gently in a silent prayer. After a moment of contemplation, he turned his gaze back to the tree to be grafted. Now he became calm and assured. With a firm hand he cut the shoot, taking the cutting, a sliver of bark shaped like a ring. With the same knife he cut a notch in the bark of the wild olive, and taking out the piece of bark, replaced it with the new slip. Then he bound the cutting very tightly to the trunk of the tree.
>
> He was finished. The old man's face became very pale. He looked up at the sky again and began to pray, trembling: "I thank you, God, for the gift of this year to once more graft the wild olive."
>
> Then, calmly turning toward me, he said: "There you are, my son, I give you your tree. Love it as a gift from God."

37 [Note: See Olivier Clément, *On Human Being*, p. 23]

At that moment, the old man had something of a profoundly religious expression, that, unconsciously, we also shared. But we did not understand why. What had happened? A piece of bark from a scion had been tied onto a wild tree. Nothing else happened!

We looked at the old man with amazement. As if he knew what we were thinking, he turned to me and said: "Hold your ear against the tree trunk."

I pressed my head against the trunk as he told me. He did the same and listened. Our faces were close, almost touching. Little by little his eyes began to close, as if he was falling into a trance. Then they closed completely.

"Do you hear anything?" he murmured. "Nothing. I can't hear anything."

"But I can hear it!" he said in a murmur.
And his calm voice was full of joy.
"But I can hear it" he repeated.

Then he explained to me that he could hear the sap of the tree from which he had taken the scion, and he could hear it gently flowing into the sap of the trunk and mixing together, and that this was the beginning of the miracle, the transformation of the wild olive.
"When you have grown to love trees, then you too will hear this."[38]

ΩΩΩ

Professor Sadly, people say that those living in the big city are no longer aware of these cosmic symbols.

Patriarch People in the big cities get out to the country as soon as they can. In America, many people live in houses built of wood, surrounded by trees. Technology has freed us from our dependence on nature. Now we can encounter nature more freely. Now nature is not so much the mother, on which we depend for everything, as our fiancée for whom we are responsible, whom we shall guide, with respect, to the eternal wedding feast. This is one of our great challenges: to place technology in the service of the great cycles of life.

---

38 Ilias Venezis, *Terre Eolienne*, Paris, Gallimard, 1946, pp. 60–62

Professor There is a hidden connection between the mystery of marriage and our relationship with nature . . . . The greatness of Pasternak in *Dr. Zhivago* is precisely how clearly he shows this. Zhivago deciphers the mystery of nature through the face of the woman he loves . . . .

Patriarch Love makes everything known. Perhaps I can decipher the mystery of nature in the face of the Theotokos . . . .

Professor In our earliest religious intuitions, the grain died in the earth and God brings forth the young plant. It is a miracle, a form of death-and-resurrection.

Patriarch It is a miracle. Science has defined the workings of these sequences—or more precisely the statistical probability of these sequences—and yet every birth, and every development that occurs within the defined limits of the natural order, is marked by the seal of God's wisdom.

ΩΩΩ

We are sitting in the garden. It is evening. The light becomes motionless, like a flame that becomes a glowing coal. The sky is an immense blue glow.

Patriarch We were talking about birds. Look at the seagulls. They come inland in daytime to scavenge for food. Now they are going back out to sea.

Dozens of birds are swirling high in the sky. They circle around in a vortex and then fly south, towards the Sea of Marmara.

They are saying goodbye to the day
Their wings are broad and strong
They fly in pairs, always,
They know the way,
A long way, sometimes, across the sea.
One bird gives the signal and away they fly

He also points to the small, gray pigeons perched for the night on the cornices and parapets of the Phanar.

Patriarch I have been here for almost twenty years and there has always been the same number of pigeons. There is great wisdom in the natural balance of things.

Night has come. The Patriarch takes me to the narthex of the church. He stops on the steps for a long time and gazes into the night. "Everything is peaceful. Oh, how I love this." He enters the church and lights two candles, which he places in the round basin of sand in front of the icon of the Theotokos—the stars on her protecting veil echo the stars emerging in the dark blue sky. "I light two candles, one for all the living, and one for all the dead."

ΩΩΩ

After his visit to (former) Patriarch Maximus, the Patriarch starts to talk about flowers, as if to shake off his sadness.

Patriarch There was a large bouquet of flowers on the table in Maximus' study. I never have flowers in my office. I don't like to see them picked and killed. They have their own life. They are there for all the world. When I see the living flowers, it is as though I am talking to them, it is as though they talk to me. Sometimes my eyes are filled with tears.

There is one shrub that is the first to flower in the Phanar, in February. I go to see it and I greet it, "Welcome!" There are also a lot of birds at the Phanar. And cats. One of the cats waits for me every night. I talk to him and stroke him and he walks with me to the top of the stairs.

ΩΩΩ

On Halki, our conversations often took place on a garden bench, behind the church. From there you can see across the water to the coast of Anatolia. At our feet, ants are scurrying along the stone ledge. Some already have wings for their nuptial flight. As always, when the natural world draws his attention, the Patriarch pauses to watch at length. Where someone else might glance hurriedly and distractedly, the child and the man of prayer gaze for a long time.

Patriarch I am always amazed to see the collective intelligence of the ants, their organization, their language, their endless activity carried out in complete forgetfulness or ignorance of self. And how proudly the one who has found a trophy carries it in!

I read the Patriarch the quotation from a French physicist on the 'search for God' that I have found in one of the magazines. "The idea that the world and the material universe should have created itself seems absurd to me . . . . For a physicist, a simple atom is so complicated and so full of information that the materialist conception of the universe makes no sense. Science is very modest. It cannot claim to explain everything."

Patriarch We need to turn the question back around to the atheists. They ask, "How can there be a God?" Perhaps instead we should ask, "How can the world exist?" "How can it be intelligible?"

ΩΩΩ

One evening, the Patriarch spoke about death. I listened without interrupting. I did not try to take the conversation any further. I simply listened.

Patriarch Death is this formidable event. A whole generation approaches it together. First one falls and then another. I am still marching, almost alone. Most of my childhood companions are dead. Most of my friends from my student days, too. When I went back to my native village, four years ago, I found only the young. Of the old people I had known, there were very, very few.

I was thirteen when my mother died and eighteen when my father died. An old man is more and more rooted in the unseen world, by all those he has loved who have died, whom he still loves. To disarm—this is also to become acquainted with death. When you have disarmed, when you have no more fear, you have no more fear of death. You welcome death each new day. Death is a passage. The Risen Christ leads us from death to life. We were baptized into His death to participate in His Resurrection. Little by little, our lives contract and our baptism and our death become one.

Life finds its fulfillment by death, through the life-giving Cross. Without death, life would not be real. It would be an illusion, a dream from which we never awoke.

I don't want to die suddenly. Perhaps to be ill for a few weeks, to get ready. But not for too long, or it would be a burden to others. And then death will come towards me. I can see death coming down the hill, climbing the stairs, walking along the corridor. Death knocks at my bedroom door. I am not afraid. I have been waiting for this moment. And I say: "Enter! But let's not leave at once. You are my guest: sit down for a moment. I am ready." And then death carries me away in God's loving kindness.

There are so, so many souls—where are they? We know something about their condition, but nothing of where they are. Are they far away? On other planets? But why would they leave this Earth that they loved, where their family and friends still live? Why leave this Earth that our Lord filled with light. They are very near to us, on the other side of the visible, in God's loving care. If we cannot see them, that is our failing. That is due to our limited and obscured spiritual awareness . . . .

Once, I was in the Church of St. Nicholas, quite close to here. I thought about all the faithful who had worshiped there since it was built, four centuries ago. There are thousands. Where are they now? Where are their souls? But suddenly I understood that they had prayed here in this church, they had venerated these icons, they had received the body of life. This is where they were, in the communion of saints and the unbounded presence of Christ. In Christ's love we are not separated. God exists. Eternity exists. Eternity is God's love in which he wants to reunite us all.

At the Resurrection, He will be all in all. Cruel time that wears away and kills, space that collides with us and separates us—these will be no more. It will be our time and our space. Because God exists. He exists. You cannot explain this. This is the mystery of faith. This is the joyful experience of faith.

ΩΩΩ

In the Orthodox tradition, as, by the way, in other religions, the personification of God is not a metaphor. Many dying people have seen the angel of death, preparing to cut the thread of life and to receive the soul into another world . . . . In our times, during his long final illness, Father Nicholas Afanasiev, one of the French theologians who renewed our understanding of the Church, repeatedly saw a 'young man' who was waiting for him.

ΩΩΩ

Professor But you cannot speak about death without speaking about hell and the biblical texts on eternal damnation.

Patriarch Eternal damnation? What is hell? Paradise and hell are within us. And far as purgatory is concerned—it has no meaning. What would purgatory be? God has prepared nothing of the kind. He receives the souls into his love, he wipes away the tears and heals the wounds. He very gently prepares the soul for the resurrection—for the moment when the soul will be plunged into the light of God.

The light of the resurrection will fill our whole being. If we accept this with humility and gratitude, we will find paradise. But if we reject it, if we are plunged into divine love while we are still separated and attached to ourselves, then we will be in hell.

Professor That is exactly what Isaac the Syrian wrote: "It is not correct to say that sinners in hell are deprived of God's love . . . . This love acts in two different ways—it is suffering for the sinners and delight for the blessed."[39]

But do we have the right to speak of hell for other people? Only God has the right to speak to me of hell. The parable of the sheep and the goats summons me directly to repentance.

I know that the Judge is also my Advocate. As St. Isaac the Syrian says, "A handful of sand in the vast ocean, that is the measure of all human sin in comparison to the loving kindness of God."[40] For St. Isaac, the only real sin is not to pay enough attention to our Lord's Resurrection, which has become ours through our baptism. What is essential, he says, is to pay attention, with our whole being, to the "joy of the love of Christ. How can Gehenna stand, when faced with the grace of his Resurrection?"[41]

Patriarch You know, of course, that Origen, one of the Church Fathers, believed that in the end, after traversing the eons and the vast emptiness, every soul turns toward God. Each soul finally understands that even the most extreme evil cannot have total hold, because God alone is infinite.

Professor It's true that in evil doing one sometimes becomes aware of a search for the infinite, as if discovering its obverse.

Patriarch The Church condemned Origen. Universal salvation cannot be automatically guaranteed. But the greatest saints have prayed that all may be saved. We cannot set any limits to the power of prayer.

Professor This is one of the most significant moments in the history of the Church. Origen's doctrine was condemned as heretical, but his spiritual heritage was retained. We could say that in the most important areas, theology finds its resolution in prayer, and not in supposedly objective speculation.

Anthony the Great wanted to know where he was on his spiritual journey. He asked Christ. Christ praised his efforts but said that there was a shoemaker in Alexandria who was more advanced. Anthony hurried to Alexandria and sought out the shoemaker. "I don't do anything special,"

---

39 Isaac the Syrian, *Ascetical Homilies*

40 Isaac the Syrian, *Ascetical Homilies*

41 Isaac the Syrian, *Ascetical Homilies*; see also Olivier Clément, *Transfiguring Time*, pt.3, ch.8, On Hell

the shoemaker said, "of everything I earn I give one third to the poor, one third to the Church, keeping one third for myself." "But I have given away everything," said Anthony, "There must be something else. Christ himself sent me to you. You must tell me everything."

"Well," said the shoemaker, "while I am working I can see the vast crowds of people coming and going. And I pray: 'That all may be saved. I and I alone am worthy of condemnation . . . .'" This prayer has been transmitted by the monks, from generation to generation right up to today. And it arises spontaneously in the heart that has been broken open by divine love. At the moment of his death, a fool-for-Christ in nineteenth century Russia refused to enter into the divine light and argued with God, "I won't enter until you promise me that all will be saved, that the whole earth will be saved."

Patriarch We see St. Paul asking to be condemned in place of his brothers and sisters. The martyrs pray for the salvation of their executioners. *What* we must announce to people is not hell, but Christ's victory over hell.

Professor Perhaps, as Urs von Balthasar said, one of the serious gaps in Western theology is that it does not sufficiently consider *what* God redeemed us from. This *what* is, quite plainly, hell. In taking on the ultimate solitude of death, in chaining himself to the experience of hell, Christ introduced light and communion into the darkness of death and isolation, at the same moment that the chains evaporated on contact with his divinity.

The Orthodox Church places this simple certainty at the center of its mystical and liturgical life. Christ, in descending to the kingdom of eternal death, has conquered death, he has destroyed death, he has replaced it with eternal life. This is why the Church celebrates Pascha with such joy. It is a definitive cry of joy because the gates of hell have been destroyed, and so they will remain, whatever the twists and turns of history, until the day the Lord returns. As the sacrament of Christ who has conquered hell, the Church is the haven in which the gates of hell will never again close on mankind.

ΩΩΩ

When you descended unto death,
O Lord who are yourself immortal Life.

Then did you You mortify Hades
by the lightning flash of Your Divinity.

How could hell endure it, when in splendor you came
and how not be swiftly shattered and plunged in dark,
blinded by the blazing glory of your light?

Like a burning lampstand, here the flesh of our God,
as beneath a bushel measure,
now lies concealed under earth
and puts the gloom of hell to flight.

Hades is wounded at its heart, by receiving Him,
whom a lance had wounded in the side.

And it groans, consumed by the fire of divinity,
for the salvation of us who sing,
"O our God and Redeemer, You are blessed."

One was the Godhead of Christ
with the Father and the Spirit,
and there was no separation in Hades,
in the tomb, and in Paradise,
for the salvation of us who sing,
"O our God and Redeemer, blessed are you, You are blessed."

ΩΩΩ

Patriarch We have quietly sketched out the first steps of the path of prayer, the path of love.

Professor And it is also the path of knowledge because prayer and love renew our minds. Tenderness (*katanyxis*)[42] and watchfulness (*nepsis*) make us aware, as one spiritual master said, "of the flame at the heart of matter and of the secrets of the heart". The path that you have traced out proceeds from tears of repentance to tears of joy; from disarming yourself to caring for others; from total trust even under the worst of circumstances to the complete peace that 'surpasses all understanding.' And so we attain joy and freedom. Freed of our own individual limitations, we find, in God, the unlimited space of our freedom. If God does not exist, we are just specks of matter, deterministically subject to the forces of nature and society. Then, what we would call our freedom is only the flight from oblivion. But if God exists, we can throw ourselves into God to become what we most deeply desire to be. We throw ourselves into God

42 [*Katanyxis* is more usually rendered as contrition or compunction, but Clément always translates this as tenderness, the tenderness of the heart that results from contrition]

like the birds soar in the sky and the fish swim in the ocean. There is no more death. There is only freedom!

Patriarch What a wonderful lightness—to be free, to be free in oneself. This requires giving up all lies, all the lies that our shameful mask of personhood stirs up and uses in self-justification—and being reborn in the Lord. We find ourselves welcomed by him, forgiven by him, and we receive an unlimited life from him, in which we are no longer separated, in which our life force reveals itself as the breath of the Holy Spirit!

Professor This is what the ascetics speak of as freedom from passion! For them, passions are the life forces that rear up in face of oblivion, seeking the absolute where it cannot be found. We hope to be saved by a woman, or by art, or by revolution. But, outside of God, the search for the absolute is a path to destruction. In fleeing from oblivion, passion opens the door to destruction. Death is secretly hiding within. And death must ultimately kill the one it encounters there, as they are not God . . . .

Patriarch The freedom that mankind celebrates is most often merely movement without content, a rejection of all restrictions that results in destruction or suicide. It is freedom *to* . . . and freedom *from* . . . . It is not freedom *for* a new life. Freedom itself can become a form of enslavement, if it does not have the light-filled center that is rooted in the infinite and in limitless love.

Professor In the liturgical texts, Christ is called the one who sets us free. By His Passion He has freed us from passion. Our misdirected energies are gathered up and transformed in the light of Pascha. They become infinitely tender and infinitely creative. The sanctified person brings light blessings to the world around her. She becomes a creator of life, justice, and beauty.

Patriarch Living water flows from her breast, according to the promise of the Gospel. This is true freedom in the Holy Spirit. But the greatest freedom is to give your life for those you love, for the one that you love. That is martyrdom. Remember what the Holy Spirit says to the Church in Smyrna, at the beginning of the Book of Revelation: "Be faithful unto death, and I will give you the crown of life." (Rev. 2:10)

Professor In the early Church, the Christians were called *aphoberos thanatou*—"those who were not afraid of death." They were supremely free, because death was not ahead of them, but behind them.

ΩΩΩ

Patriarch One of our great challenges is to renew spirituality. The popularity of yoga and psychotherapy shows that Christianity is in some way absent from the deepest questions of life. We don't have a spirituality that is both rooted in our best tradition of prayer and attuned to the person of today.

Professor Extreme asceticism, which is designed to achieve mastery over the body, no longer makes much sense for the city-dweller in our post-industrial civilization. People are worn-out and always tired, and yet they never have the experience of complete physical exhaustion. The tiredness is above all emotional. The sexualization of everything from advertising to repressed fears, that pervades our media, prevents a person from constructive self-discovery. She is bombarded by noise and images so that she lives only on the surface, as if sleepwalking. We must restore the sense of *sophrosyne*, the chaste wholeness of the spirit, and the sense of *nepsis*, watchfulness, the awareness of awareness. Because a whole civilization is becoming enslaved to the 'giants of oblivion' of which the Orthodox ascetic tradition speaks, forgetfulness, laziness, and ignorance.

Patriarch Today it is not so much a question of detaching oneself from life and fighting off passions, as of bringing peace and illumination to everyday life. Mysticism does not necessarily entail extraordinary experiences. We can live in wonder at the most elementary experiences, we can find wonder in the completely mundane. We can become aware of the face of the Risen Christ in all things and in all people. In His light, everything is passage, from death to life, from absence to presence, from time to eternity.

Professor It seems to me that we must return to the 'apophatic' approach of the Fathers, in order to bring back the sense of mystery, or if you will, the sense of the unknown, to the person of today. According to this way of thinking, God is always beyond any words, any image, any concept, beyond even the word 'God.' God is not some arbitrary being in the heavens. God is the Unknowable, the Vastness, the Luminous Darkness. And at the same time, He is our foundation, our meaning, the opening in which everything is filled with light.

We have diminished God by turning Him into a supreme being, into the keystone of all our rational explanations. We have made Him a laughingstock. And this is perhaps why so many people today are attracted by the impersonal spirituality of India, or simply seek solace in the mountains, or in the sun shining on the sea. There was a recent tragic film in which a young man desperately seeks a certain innocence, and as he dies, we hear these words from the poet, Arthur Rimbaud

> It is found again
> What? Eternity.
> It is the sea
> Joined to the sun . . . [43]

Patriarch The miracle of the Christian revelation is that the immeasurable vastness is never impersonal. It reveals love and freedom as they come toward us. They reveal themselves as countenance. Indeed, God so far surpasses the Unattainable that he gives himself to us on the Cross. He descends for us into hell. He welcomes our suicides as cries for help. A crucified God: that is the truly apophatic approach. This is much more than 'negative theology.' This is the revelation of love. Our God is the living God.

"No longer do I call you servants . . . . I call you my friends." (John 20:15) This is where a renewed spirituality should lead us. God reveals Himself in secret as the friend who accompanies us throughout our life. "Since the children share one nature of flesh and blood, He Himself likewise partook of the same nature." (Heb. 2:14) The time of servile submission is over. No more. No more the burdens that man piles onto man in fear of a vengeful God. The time has come, the time of the living and life-giving God, who lights up our lives, the God who is our friend, who, in His Son, has adopted us as sons and daughters, and who, by his Holy Spirit makes us participants in his fullness. This is the framework within which Christianity can again become a real "science of life."

ΩΩΩ

5. Politics

Talking with Lebanese friends, the Patriarch mentions his sympathy for the Arabs, and how he has been familiar with Islam since his childhood. He starts to talk about Jerusalem and then checks himself. "That is a political question and there is nothing I can say—except that I grieve and I pray." Several days later a Greek American asks him about the Vietnam War, and he refuses to take a position, other than to suffer and to pray.

---

43 Arthur Rimbaud, *Eternity*

Professor So you don't take sides politically?

Patriarch That is right. I am not a politician. Politics does not interest me. I leave it to the politicians and the diplomats—there are quite enough of them! And besides, the Orthodox live under all kinds of political systems. Some are in the West; many others are in the East. Others are in the developing world. Any political statement on my part would risk being problematic for one or another of them. And any political statement would be inconsistent with my purely spiritual role.

Professor This is a way of thinking that you hardly ever find in the West, where Christians are very involved in politics. They make a lot of noise. The Churches call for revolution. This even gets to be called a prophetic mission.

Patriarch There, as elsewhere, the Church should remember its mission. The heads of the Church must speak out in face of outrage, in prophetic language, or even act as the prophets acted, at the risk of their own lives. But I don't think they should be advocating purely political solutions. That is not their role. The Orthodox Church has never sought political power. That is one of the temptations that Christ rejected in the desert, and the Church should do likewise, because "the servant is not greater than the master." (John 13:16) This does not prevent our Church from inspiring and blessing the lives of whole cultures and whole peoples. But the Church does this through the radiance of its liturgy, through its presence, through changing the human heart. And do not forget the Church's unbroken tradition of confessors and martyrs.

Professor Martyrs, first at the hands of the pagan emperors, and then at the hands of heretical emperors. And then the new martyrs of the Muslim world, and the thousands of martyrs of twentieth century totalitarianism, in Russia, Serbia, Romania. Indeed, the servant is not greater than his master, and the true prophet pays a very high price.

Patriarch Islam was very tolerant, especially in Turkey. For five centuries we lived together with the Turks and then, thanks to Atatürk, the Greeks became full citizens in a secular state. But we have learned the cost of mixing religion and politics. The "Grand Idea," this dream of restoring the Byzantine Empire, was fatal for the Greeks of Turkey. Today (1968), we see the same confusion of religious authority and political power in Cyprus. We must state firmly: "The Byzantine Empire is dead."

For a long time already, the real Byzantium has been a spiritual Byzantium. We have suffered too much from mixing politics and religion to go down this road again.

Professor I often have the impression that young Christians are fundamentally backward-looking, with their revolutionary vocabulary and their political Christianity. They want the Church still to be an earthly power, as it was, or as it wished to be, in the time of Christendom. But the profound meaning of the biblical revelation is victory over all earthly power—in the tension between the Kingdom of God and the kingdom of Caesar. Perhaps these adolescent revolutionaries haven't seen enough suffering. They have not had the experience, so familiar to the Christians of the East, of being loyal subjects of a society in which Christians are at best tolerated—as in the Muslim world, as in the Communist world.

Patriarch That is where you learn what is important. And you thank the authorities that they have at least left you this.

Professor This is what the mindless commentators in the West call the servility of the Orthodox Church. They themselves have not suffered and they make light of the suffering of others.

Patriarch Faith is what is essential: that the Church is able to exist and to share the Eucharistic mysteries and the Gospel message. Under the Ottoman Empire, we had our own religious and civil order; our faith was respected, as were our families and our communities. And we were loyal Ottoman subjects, just as today we are loyal Turkish citizens.

Patriarch And this is the experience of Christians in Communist countries—not to take a political position, but to be a loyal citizen while remaining faithful to the Church.

Professor And when loyalty to the State and loyalty to the Church are opposed? When the State demands that the Christian rejects his faith?

Patriarch Then the answer is the confessor and the martyr. Because my Christian belief is challenged, I disobey the State, but I accept the State's punishment for disobedience.

Professor The early Christians refused to bow down before Caesar, but they still prayed for him and humbly asked him to allow their worship. This, they said, could only be for the good of the Empire and of the Emperor.

Patriarch The Church's prayer protects the world. We should be thankful for every state that allows us to pray in peace. And Christ reminds us in the Beatitudes that as Christians we have no special rights. But we should use the rights we are granted as citizens peacefully and intelligently . . . .

Professor The duality of the Kingdom of God and the kingdom of Caesar prevents history from closing in on itself. It permits the Spirit to animate history, if only with the blood of martyrs . . .

Patriarch It is only the blood of the martyrs that has made freedom and the free existence of the person possible, despite great societal forces. But if the person is greater than history, they are also responsible for history . . . . As people of the Church, as Church leaders, our job is not to offer political solutions, it is to remind people of their responsibilities. They are responsible to God for all mankind.

Prayer and Eucharist also are a form of social engagement. The man or woman who has been fed by the body and blood of Christ must be engaged in the works of society, as far as society allows.

Professor The Church works by inspiration, not by command. The Church is that added source of life, continually replenished by the celebration of the Eucharist, and by the prayers of the monks and holy fools, whom the world considers to be of no use. And yet, without them the world would disintegrate.

Patriarch But the Church cannot really penetrate this life unless it becomes one. The destiny of humanity has become an acute problem. We are threatened by the death of souls and bodies. The world no longer has time for the luxury of Christians who remain divided. The world needs an answer. And this answer can only be the revelation of Christ in his undivided Church.

Will we remain indifferent to Christ, who is suffering in the form of the millions of seemingly dead souls? Will we remain indifferent to Christ who is afflicted, in the form of those who are naked, starving, and stripped of their dignity? How can we continue with this scandalous Christian disunity, when there is no more important question than the destiny of humankind—the unification of the planet, our technical mastery of the natural world, our sciences that are uncovering the inner secrets of matter and of life?

How can we bear witness if we are divided? How dare we speak about love if we act without love? All of us leaders of the Churches should go out together into the world, as poor people among the poor. We should become pilgrims like Christ, announcing that God exists, that the Lord is risen, that love will conquer hate.

ΩΩΩ

Professor The outlines of Christian unity are already being drawn. You have done a lot of work in that direction. You have taken up the pilgrim's staff many times . . . . Today the Church is called to awaken people to their responsibilities in the new planetary city. How should the Church nurture such people?

Patriarch First of all, they can't just be full of chatter. They must be alive, living persons fed by the blood of Christ and made peaceful through silence and prayer. This will enable them to understand, prophetically, the history of which they are part. And first of all, they will understand that our epoch is that of human unity. As wars become global, they turn into planetary civil wars. The media means that we become aware of everything, simultaneously. In the past, there would be famine in India, but we did not know about it. Now, what is far away is close at hand. It must also become spiritually close to us.

Professor I see you putting this teaching about planetary unity into practice each day. You always speak the language of the unity of mankind, with all the many visitors who come each summer . . . you constantly say "all peoples are good . . . ."

Patriarch All peoples are good, all races . . . . Yes, I repeat that to them.

Professor And you tell them that you are a citizen of the world, that you belong to all people . . . .

Patriarch But I am still from the East. (He laughs). Have you noticed how I like to have this hard, white, bitter cheese with my food? I belong to the Turkish people, to the Greek people. But at the same time, I am a citizen of the world. I feel French with the French, German with the Germans, Russian with the Russians, American with the Americans . . . . I like to speak a few words to each person in their own language, even if I hardly know it. This is not about mixing everything up. It is about sharing everything. Even when the mother country makes it difficult for us, it is still our mother country. But all peoples of the world should find their place in the unity of mankind. I have believed this for a long time.

Professor You witnessed the great multinational civilizations that collapsed after the First World War—the Hapsburg Empire, the Ottoman Empire . . . .

Patriarch In my childhood in the Ottoman Empire I experienced the brotherhood of humanity. In my village, Turks, Greeks, Albanians, Christians, and Muslims, all lived harmoniously side by side. I had the same experience in Monastir, an experience that was tragically hammered home by war. I understood, definitively, that all people are good—if you only give them love and respect. Fear is what makes them cruel.

Professor The weakness of these multinational empires was that they were based on the dominant power of one race—of the Turks, of the Austrians. They never had time to become true federations. They were destroyed by the rise of nationalism.

Patriarch There are a lot of misconceptions. We need to rethink the history of these empires and rehabilitate them. In the years before the First World War, the Ottoman Empire was moving towards becoming a real federation. And as for Austria, in the Danube region, it stood for prosperity, order, freedom and high culture . . . . These empires have disappeared. But I discovered a similar experience of diversity in unity in the United States. Our Greek communities there are full of people who participate in the life of the nation without giving up their identity . . .

Professor The Americans have taken a long time to understand that they are no longer a Protestant, Anglo-Saxon nation, but a microcosm of the world . . . .

Patriarch Today, that is a *fait accompli*. The election of a Catholic, John F. Kennedy, as president made this clear. The recognition of Orthodoxy as one of the 'major' religions is another important indicator . . .

Professor The problem of Black inequality remains. This cannot be resolved simply by integration. It calls for the emergence of a new civilization, composed of many races and many cultures. If the United States achieves this . . . . But will it get there? If it can achieve this, it will become a microcosm of the universe, and at the same time it will become aware of its responsibility for the developing world.

Patriarch One can ask if such a profound transformation is possible without a powerful spiritual renewal. Technology and science aren't enough to construct a new world civilization. You cannot have a civilization without a spiritual foundation. All that results is the endless conflict between a conservatism built on fear, and a destructive search for revolution.

The undivided Church should be found at the heart of humankind, that is on the road to becoming one people. This renewed Church will make no demands. It will impose no laws. The Christian empires have disappeared, as have the theocracies. The Church will become leaven and radiance. It will radiate meaning, freedom, and love. It will nurture the brotherhood and sisterhood of mankind, in the image of the communion of the Holy Trinity. In the Resurrection, it will reveal the ultimate meaning of science and technology.

Professor That was Dostoevsky's vision at the end of his life: the brotherhood of all people in Christ . . . .

Patriarch We need to nurture this brotherhood and sisterhood, whenever we can . . . . Even here, I have done what I can so that the Christian minority can live peacefully as loyal citizens. And besides, it is impossible for any nation, anywhere, to be completely homogeneous. And this would not even be desirable. The presence of different races and religions creates an opening, the possibility of an exchange, new life.

Professor We see both movements occurring, sometimes productively, sometimes tragically. On the one hand, we see the emergence of the world citizen, as part of global development. On the other hand, every nation digs into its national and ethnic roots—perhaps as an escape from the impersonality of our technological civilization.

Patriarch As Christians, we must place ourselves at the junction of these two movements, to bring them together . . . sister Churches, brother races, this should be our message and the example we set.

Professor Perhaps this is the special vocation of the Orthodox. Orthodoxy has sanctified the widest possible range of cultures without ever asserting the dominance of any one culture. And today the Orthodox live on every continent.

Patriarch All Christians have their part to play in this. The Western Christians have a sense of their historical responsibility, that is often surprising to us. But we Orthodox have a rich spiritual life. This can offer an unexpected newness to the ethical and cultural priorities of our Catholic and Protestant brothers and sisters.

Professor You might apply the hesychast idea, the unification of the person by the 'descent' of the mind into the heart, to the whole question of the unification of mankind. Only the union of the Western 'mind' and the Eastern 'heart,' in the fire of the Holy Spirit, can reveal the true dimensions of the 'citizen of the world.'

ΩΩΩ

Patriarch To become a responsible Christian is to demand justice – not as some shibboleth but as an expression of love. "Blessed are those who hunger and thirst for righteousness sake . . . ." (Matt. 5:6)

Professor And the first principles that we should reveal are that "man shall not live by bread alone, but by every word that proceeds from the mouth of God." (Matt 4:4) It little profits a man to gain the whole world, and to lose his soul. But this soul, this captive soul seeking its freedom, more precious to us than the whole universe, has certain earthly needs for its existence. When we clothe those who are naked, when we feed the hungry, when we give shelter to the homeless, it is Christ himself whom we clothe, we feed, we shelter.

Patriarch There is a text of Victor Hugo's that has impressed me. It is in his short prologue to *Les Misérables*. It is only a few lines, but they still speak strongly to us today. Let me read it:

> "So long as there shall exist, by virtue of law and custom, decrees of damnation pronounced by society, artificially creating hells amid the civilization of the Earth, and adding the element of human fate to divine destiny, so long as the three great problems of the century—the degradation of man through poverty, the corruption of women through hunger, the crippling of children through lack of light—are unsolved; so long as social asphyxiation is possible in any part of the world; in other words, and with a still wider significance, so long as ignorance and poverty exist on earth, books of the nature of *Les Misérables* cannot fail to be of use."[44]

And consider the book itself: the abandoned child, the women driven into prostitution by dire need, the man who must steal and who is severely punished. And yet, right from the beginning, there is this bishop, this poor man in service of the poor and the promise of justice, that is inseparably linked to freedom and love, the witness to the Beatitudes. (He searches for the place and reads) "Oh You who exist! Ecclesiastes calls You the All-Powerful . . . but Solomon calls You loving-kindness, and this is the most beautiful of all your names—"

Professor Hugo expresses what is best in the French socialist and republican tradition, which is rooted in the Gospel and the evangelical poverty of the Middle Ages and the Renaissance . . . .

Patriarch Now more than ever, we need this inspiration, for the whole planet. The regions condemned to social asphyxiation—to use

44 *Les Misérables*, Prologue

Hugo's expression—cover more than half the Earth. The gap between the haves and the have-nots is getting larger and larger. It is a scandal. On the one hand, a few rich countries produce and consume more and more, without knowing why, with a fortune is spent on advertising to get people to buy things they don't need. On the other hand, millions of people degraded both physically and morally by hunger, whole regions of shantytowns, women "corrupted by hunger," children "crippled through lack of light."

Professor The revolutionary ideologies of the nineteenth century have reached a dead end. The workers of the rich countries have become the bourgeois of the developing world. Technology has made unfathomable progress, but it has no ultimate goal. This is a global problem. The spiritual underdevelopment of the rich countries leads to the material underdevelopment of the poor countries.

Patriarch This is why nurturing and forming the inner person is so important. Only through a spiritual effort can we master technology and address these two related problems: the social problem in the developing world and the problem of the meaning of life in the rich countries. The interior life and active loving engagement are not opposites. The more interior life is rooted in the beyond, the more it can nurture real service in the world in which we live.

Professor The Church should elicit this creative love in every aspect of culture. Not in expectation of a total and lasting victory in this world—that would underestimate the scope of evil—but in pursuit of the vision animated by the Holy Spirit, of humankind who need bread, but who also need friendship and beauty, who need the infinite.

Patriarch A head of the Church cannot promote or oppose revolution. His duty is to sound the alarm and to awaken the conscience when the situation becomes extreme. This is what the Pope has done in his encyclical *Populorum Progressio*. This is a prophetic reinterpretation of our world. I have publicly stated my support. I have sent him a telegram, to say that I will be with him as he leaves for South America, where there is such an urgent need for social justice. As you know, there are pockets of abysmal poverty even in the United States. I saw families of ten children huddled together in mere shacks. You find the problems of the developing world at the heart of even the richest countries. It is all linked.

Professor And what do you say about the 'theology of revolution' or the 'theology of violence' that people talk about in the West?

Patriarch The only revolution that the Church knows is *metanoia*—repentance. It is just as essential for the Church community as for the individual. As for the great upheavals of history, let everyone make their own assessment. The Church cannot take part. It is not "of this world." The Church is neither revolutionary nor counter-revolutionary. It is the Church of love. It knows that, in the end, only love can transform life. And the Church should begin with itself. Otherwise, this talk of revolution is just an excuse. The one who would be first should be last and be the servant of all. This paradoxical saying of Jesus applies to the leaders of the Churches and to civic leaders as well. But, alas, we are so often led by infantile characters, whose pride and fanaticism brings us useless violence and suffering.

Professor In France in May 1968, there was a slogan that read, "If the fathers would become real fathers, then the revolution would become an evolution." And, as I remember, a French eighteenth century philosopher said: "to avoid revolution, you must seek it out and carry it out yourself."

Patriarch We have yet to understand the revelation of the Father that Christ came to bring us. Too many Christians still act like the older son in the parable of the prodigal son.

ΩΩΩ

Professor The crisis of today is a spiritual crisis, a confrontation with the reduction of the person to a set of techniques . . . .

Patriarch The only real way out is through prayer, And prayer can also be an exorcism . . . . That is what has happened in Russia. Without anyone noticing, the Russian Christians conquered their totalitarian system. They conquered it by their faith, by their prayers, by the suffering of their confessors and martyrs, and also, as will become clear in the future, with the help of the spiritual renewal of Russian Orthodoxy in the nineteenth century and early twentieth centuries. Little by little, through prayer and service to their society, their humility, their love of their country, their presence, has triumphed over the darker, idolatrous aspects of Communism. Their victory is not yet visible. As so often the case, the obstacles remain visible in the foreground of history, when great changes have already occurred at the deepest level.

Professor Consider how great literary works have come from Russia in our time, and how many are deeply Christian in inspiration. Boris

Pasternak's *Dr. Zhivago*, the work of Andrei Sinyavsky, Solzhenitsyn's monumental body of fiction . . . . While Western literature has calmly been exploring hell, the dispossessed voices coming from Russia have announced a mysterious resurrection.

Patriarch This is the first light of dawn. What was won secretly through love will in the end emerge into the full light of history. We will understand then how the ordeal of Russian Christianity has not only protected Western Christians but has saturated history with the blood of its countless martyrs, and the patient daily suffering of its people. Purified by their patience and the blood that flowed from hatred and terror, joined by them to the freedom of the Holy Spirit, the great search for the brotherhood of mankind, that was at the root of the Russian Revolution, finds its proper place in Russia's spiritual mission, the mission of 'Holy Russia.'

ΩΩΩ

Patriarch Christianity is the religion of freedom. If Christ refused to make the stones into bread, and if Christ refused to come down from the Cross, this was in order to establish our freedom. Freedom is at the heart of the Gospel message. Faith sets us free—from fear, from death, from the powers of this world—and faith is the supreme act of freedom. I go towards Christ because I love him. Nothing compels me, except the example of his love. And love does not compel, it sets free.

This is why the life of the Church should be based on love and freedom. The Church cannot be the body that forbids or grants permission. The Church should give birth to free men and women, who are able to invent their lives in the freedom of the Holy Spirit.

And we need freedom everywhere. The loyal presence of Christians in the city, who witness, if necessary, by their blood, that the city is not God, and that the living God has a personal relationship with each human soul. This Christian presence is the foundation and the renewal of the freedom of the Spirit.

Nothing is more precious than freedom of thought and freedom of expression: but these also demand respect for our neighbor. That is to say we work to rid ourselves of our prejudices and passions.

Professor The error of the socialist or anarchist conceptions of freedom, that are so widespread among the young revolutionaries of the West, is to imagine that all evil can be defined as a social evil, and that the fundamental instincts of mankind, its vital force, are good: that it would be enough to free mankind of every social constraint and give free rein to our fundamental instincts, for the brotherhood of mankind to become reality.

But as Christians, we know, based on centuries of spiritual experience, that these fundamental instincts and this vital force have been profoundly corrupted. It requires invisible intercession and a whole ascetic practice to restore them to their true nature—which is a dynamic freedom, where the vital force, filled with light, spontaneously becomes adoration of God and love for one's neighbor.

The problem is not so much to get rid of constraints, as to replace the bonds of submission with the discipline of transfiguration. What we must bring to the world is the experience of a creative transformation of *eros*. And in this regard, we might consider monasteries to be laboratories, as necessary to the city as the scientific research lab or the artist's studio. Because our apprenticeship in the Resurrection is "the art of arts and the science of sciences."

Patriarch But it is a science that does not compel anyone to believe. It simply gives examples and offers a source of energy. As Christians, we undertake these life-giving disciplines willingly. We know that they give us profound freedom and make us more loving. But we have nothing to impose on others. And in fact, to free us of our self-sufficiency and pride, we need their criticism.

This criticism has become more and more merciless in our time. Nothing and no-one is respected anymore, not even the Pope among the Catholics. And this is good. We all need to be criticized. This is the job of the press. If the press criticizes me—that is good. It is only the lies that I reject.

ΩΩΩ

Patriarch Christianity is closely associated with the liberation of women. Jesus never spoke against women. It was a woman whose assent made possible the incarnation of God. In this same woman, the resurrection of the dead took shape. And so, for Christianity, womanhood is no longer a biological function but personal fulfillment.

We need to set women free and to ensure that they are in charge of their own lives. Every time that you witness the liberation of women, in Africa, or in Asia, in whatever political context, you can say that the leaven of the Gospel is at work.

The worst is to turn women into the object of men's pleasure. This is prostitution and is the result of extreme poverty.

Professor That is true. But doesn't a certain sort of liberation transform women into objects again? Or perhaps, transform the woman into an object for the man, and the man into an object for the woman as a result of this systematic eroticization that we see in the West?

Patriarch That may be so, but without freedom, without passing through the experience of freedom, we cannot reconstruct anything. According to the Fathers in their inspired commentary on the Gospels, the human person is defined by freedom and responsibility. What we must bring to this freedom is not external constraints but inner content, the experience of true love. All the rest will be swept away by history.

Professor The sexual orgy is denounced in the Bible, not as a matter of morality, but as a demonic caricature of worship, as the pursuit of ecstasy that devalues both the partner as a person and the personal faithfulness of the Almighty. By contrast, in the Song of Songs we find all the poetry and splendor of human love. When love is allied to the mystery of the person it becomes chaste. Vladimir Solovyov said that a person is fulfilled in showing compassion to what is inferior, in showing adoration to what is superior, and in maintaining modesty in all relationships of reciprocity. For him, modesty indicates that a man or a woman wishes, above all, to be recognized as a person, as face. Modesty veils the fascinating and impersonal mystery of sex. Modesty enables love. And in true love, as in Paradise, the soul embraces the body.

Patriarch Modesty, true and noble love, true femininity, are all born from freedom, and they all give meaning to freedom, once one understands that Christianity is not built on childlike taboos. It is built on creative love.

We have outstanding Orthodox women. Here, they are the life of our parishes. And consider the role they still play in Russia. When these women can speak, these women who serve and are faithful, they will have a lot to teach us.

ΩΩΩ

In August 1968, Istanbul became the meeting-place for a whole tribe of young people, who came from Western Europe and North America for a 'peace festival' that was banned at the last minute. The police were tolerant, the food was cheap, and therefore many of these youth stayed. In Hagia Sophia, where it was cool and spacious, they sat around or lay on the floor chatting in small groups, scarcely aware of the sacred space—a space built to express the communion of a whole people, that today seems accessible only to the solitary and silent.

Patriarch We have abandoned them! How we have abandoned them! And so they rebel against us and don't want to learn anything from us. They have rejected a past of which they no longer know anything. But we must not be afraid. Their demands are valid, even if they don't know how to express them. They challenge us to face up to our responsibilities.

Professor Their rebellion makes me think of Dostoevsky's 'Underground Man.' It is a serious search for freedom, a refusal of mandated happiness, a desperate search for the fullness of life. It is both the search for God and the rejection of God, at one and the same time.

Patriarch They reject the God of theological systems, not the God of spiritual experience. The God of the Pharisees, and not the Friend. The God of the divided Church, and not the God of Christ's Church. Let us show them the one Church as a living community. Let us become examples of life. And then, we can talk about this again.

6. Theologia

Professor People say that you are against theologians.

Patriarch What can I say? I take after my patron, Athenagoras, the apologist, not the saint. He said to the heathen, "You will find us to be mostly ignorant, small-minded people, incapable of putting the truth of our doctrines into words but trying to demonstrate this truth by the example of our lives." Perhaps he was not canonized because he said this! He also wrote that "the compassion of God's breath" is absent from no one.

Professor And what of this story about the Bosphorus?

Patriarch What story about the Bosphorus?

Professor You are supposed to have said that you would like to drown all the theologians in the Bosphorus!

Patriarch I never said that! It's a legend . . . . I simply proposed to put all the theologians on an island . . . with plenty of caviar and champagne!

Professor To get rid of them or to give them have a better place to work? They are not used to champagne. They hardly ever get drunk, more's the pity, certainly not on champagne.

Patriarch And not on the Holy Spirit! You are even worse than me! But let me answer your question. First, I wanted them to be on an island so that they could breathe a little. So that Christians from different confessions could get to know each other spontaneously and freely, without being reminded all the time, who was right and who was wrong, and without being on guard. But now I think it is time to put all the theologians on an island for deep discussions. The time has come.

Professor Now, thanks to the lengthy work of the ecumenical movement and thanks to the in depth reconciliation with the Church of Rome, which you initiated, there is a basic level of trust between Christians . . . . Fundamentally, the work of the theologians always comes second for you: it is the expression of the status quo—of confrontation in times of confrontation, of convergence in times when love has returned . . . .

Patriarch Exactly. What I hate about theology is the pride in being right. This turns dogma, and even God Himself, into a weapon to use against the others.

Professor And very soon this turns into the use of real weapons. A thousand years of religious wars are at the root of modern atheism.

Patriarch And so, theology ends up expressing the most unchristian attitudes: a refusal to disarm, a refusal to welcome. Whereas God disarmed even to the point of death on the Cross in order to welcome us. A theologian is a person on the defensive, tangled up in fear, who wants to be right, and wants the other to be wrong.

Professor I know a bishop—a man of remarkable learning. He hides behind his beard—an enormous beard, bushier than St. Gregory Palamas' beard (if you can believe the icons). And from behind his beard, he observes his Orthodox and heterodox brothers and itemizes their heresies. His world is a cacophony of heresies. He sees heresy everywhere—except, of course, in himself.

Patriarch And I don't see heresy anywhere! I only see partial truths, poorly formulated beliefs, and reductionistic statements. Or else I hear something that claims to encompass and possess an inexhaustible mystery.

Professor And what do you want from theology? Perhaps we should not speak about this anymore . . . .

Patriarch It should be alive! It should speak of the knowledge of God as the Scriptures do, as the Fathers do.

Professor And then what would theology become?

Patriarch The true theology is Christ. We discover theology in our encounter with Christ, and in contemplating the mystery. In Jesus, God tells us his name. And this name is not a philosophical concept. It is a verb and an action. Jesus means: God saves; God sets free; God gives us free rein. We can only respond to this gesture of infinite love with adoration, and by showing this same humble attitude towards our neighbor. How does God set us free? By the Cross! God himself suffered death on the Cross for us. The Infinite, the Unattainable One, experienced the ultimate loss and separation. "*Eli, Eli lama sabachthani* . . . ." So that his love would fill everything and nothing would ever separate us from his love.

Professor The Church Fathers have described, with fear and trembling, this paradox of a suffering God, of the Living God who dies in the flesh in order to conquer death by death. For Nicholas Cabasilas, God becomes incarnate in order to transcend his transcendence and convince mankind of his love—of his "crazy love"—his *manikos eros*—by suffering and dying for mankind.

Patriarch It was St. Paul who proclaimed the folly of the Cross, and exclaimed: "Where is the sage? Where is the scholar? Where is the student of this age? Did not God turn the wisdom of this world to folly?. . . . We preach Christ crucified, a stumbling block for the Jews and folly for the heathen, but for us who are chosen, he is Christ the power of God and the wisdom of God. Since the folly of God is wiser than men, and the weakness of God is stronger than men." (Cf. 1 Cor. 1:20–25)

That is true theology! The preaching of Christ crucified—and resurrected. If I call Pope Paul VI 'Paul the Second,' it's because, it seems to me, his mission is to retell Paul's message in new words. But that is our mission too—all of ours.

Professor Faced with rationalistic explanations, the Fathers of the Church, and the great Byzantine theologians, constantly cited St. Paul's words on the wisdom of this world "turned to folly . . . ." According to St. Gregory Nazianzus—the East knows him as Gregory the Theologian, true wisdom comes from the way of the apostles and from the way of Aristotle.

The Liturgy reminds us that the apostles were uneducated men, illuminated by the Holy Spirit.

> Blessed are You, Christ our God.
> You made the fishermen all-wise
> by sending down upon them the Holy Spirit
> and through them You drew the world into Your net.
> O Lover of mankind, glory to You.
> (Troparion for Pentecost)

True theology is Paschal joy. From age to age, theology is renewed by 'apostolic beings,' who live the teachings of the Church to the absolute limit, and who see the Resurrected Christ, just as St. Paul saw Him on the road to Damascus, and St. John saw Him on Patmos. And more recently there are St. Seraphim of Sarov in the nineteenth century, St. Nektarios of Aegina, and St. Silouan of Athos in the twentieth century.

The great doctors of the Church, the learned theologians, simply give structure to this experience. Behind St. Athanasius of Alexandria one can discern the desert monks. Behind the great Russian religious philosophers, one can discern the elders, the startsi, of the Optina Monastery. The greatest theologians, such as St. Symeon the New Theologian, were visionaries who expressed their visions, both intellectually and poetically.

Patriarch St. John, the beloved disciple, St. Gregory of Nazianzus and St. Symeon the New Theologian are the only saints that the Church venerates as 'theologians.' Theirs was not speculation: they lived the mystery and let their intellect sing. They were intoxicated with the Holy Spirit . . . . Consider how St. John evokes the light and life of God himself, who became our life and our light! Then consider how he portrays the humanity of Jesus, his physical gestures, his friendships—in which light and life are condensed. Once more, here is true theology: to know and to love are inseparably united. In the final analysis, to know is to contemplate in silence. To contemplate the profundity of God silently, in the Holy Spirit, through the transparent face of Christ—this is what the Fathers call true theologia.

Professor Some people have said that the trisagion hymn is a 'theology' taught to us by the angels so that we might worthily glorify the Trinity:

> Holy God, Holy Mighty, Holy Immortal,
> have mercy on us.

> Holy, Holy, Holy, Lord God of Sabaoth,
> Heaven and earth are full of your glory.

Patriarch The Word became flesh. We don't only hear His Word. We receive the Word Himself as food. Only the Eucharist allows us to fully understand divine theology and sing it out loud. The theological intellect can only be a Eucharistic intellect.

> "The mystery of the incarnation of the Word itself contains the meaning of all the symbols and all the puzzles of Scripture, as well as the hidden meaning of all creation—the tangible and the intelligible. But the person who knows the mystery of the Cross and the Tomb also understands the fundamental reasons, the logoi, of all matter and things. And finally, the one who penetrates even further and becomes initiated into the mystery of the Resurrection understands the purpose for which God created all things in the beginning."[45]

Professor For the Church Fathers, Moses is the model of the theologian. He enters into the divine darkness and, sheltering in a cleft in the rock, sees God 'from behind.' (Ex. 33:21) For the Fathers, this rock symbolizes Christ's humanity. But other great spiritual fathers and theologians, especially Gregory Palamas, use another image, that of the Mother of God. In Mary, the Old and the New Testaments are united. She reveals the Kingdom, because she is "the Mother of Life who was translated to life," as we sing in the Troparion for the Feast of the Dormition. She kept "all these things in her heart" and pondered them in silence, that is, the whole revelation of God who, in her, had become flesh and blood.

Patriarch Constantinople is the city of the Mother of God. Her icon is venerated in all the churches. You saw the Byzantine mosaic that we have at the Phanar, in the Church of St. George. At night, I often go and pray before this icon. This is not a solitary prayer—it is a conversation, a *homilia*. It would not be possible to put into words what she, the Mother of God, tells me.... We find refuge in her tenderness—that is the secret of our theology. Think how many names we have for her—hope of the hopeless, wellspring of life, joy of all creation—and how these are portrayed in the icons. Each of her names is a ray of light, illuminating an aspect of her presence.

---

45 Maximus the Confessor, *Gnostic Centuries*, 1,66

Professor God is boundless in his energies and the Mother of God, the *Panagia*, the first person to become wholly deified, is boundless in her intercession. As the *Panagia*, the All-Holy, we see her in a special relation to the Holy Spirit, the *Panagion*. She who gave her own flesh to the Word of God, now, by the grace of the Holy Spirit, seems to watch over the spiritual birth of the Word in the souls of men and women.

Patriarch You could fill many books with hymns to the Mother of God. In her, mankind welcomed the Creator. In her, the Church intercedes for all people.

Professor Vladimir Lossky, the great French theologian, said that the "let it be" of the Virgin resolved the tragedy of human freedom. Is it possible that her maternal tenderness, which she reveals to us at times of complete abandonment, is the feminine dimension of divine love? I am speaking symbolically: think how the Bible evokes God's "bowels of compassion," (Is. 63:15) almost like a womb.

ΩΩΩ

As you enter the ancient churches of Constantinople you are greeted by the icon of the Theotokos. In the narthex of Hagia Sophia, we see Constantine presenting her the city, and Justinian presenting her with the temple in offering. In the chapel at Chora, you enter under a cupola that portrays her. In this way, the Mother of God leads us to the ultimate mysteries that are portrayed in the next cupola and in the apse—the Last Judgment and Christ's descent into hell. The victorious Christ, who has conquered death, is portrayed in a translucent whiteness, whereas the cupola of the Mother of God is blue, a soft, nocturnal blue, as when the first stars are seen and the birds have gone to roost. Mary is at the center, and around her, and descending towards us as if embracing us in her tenderness, there is a garden of flowers and angels.

Patriarch The Mother of God is both beauty and wisdom. All the beauty of creation is gathered in her to become part of divine beauty. That is why the spirit of Orthodox theology is 'philokalic,' not philosophical. It is struck through with the beauty of the new heaven and the new earth that is comes to us in the Holy Spirit, in the celebration of the Divine Liturgy, and in the face of the Theotokos and of all the saints.

ΩΩΩ

Professor 'Fallen reason' divides and confuses, and it has to pass through the death of baptism, and be watered with tears, to be reborn within the loving mind of Christ. "Why," St. Ignatius of Antioch asked, "do we not all become wise? Why can we not all accept that knowledge of God which we have been given, in the person of Jesus Christ?"[46]

Patriarch Why? Let me tell you why. It is because we have wanted to make theology into a science, just as we have made the Church into a machine. But real theology requires a complete transformation of the person. It starts with repentance and it is completed in love!

Professor The Church Fathers would say "Theology without action is the theology of the devils."[47] Action, praxis, implies repentance, prayer, and active love. "It is a great thing to speak about God, but it is even better to purify yourself, for God."[48] The goal should always be 'awareness of God.' This is not speculation. It is total knowledge that unifies the whole person and resonates with the whole person.

Patriarch The Greek Fathers lived their theology. And so did the Latin Fathers, especially St. Augustine.

Professor I sometimes get the impression that St. Augustine was too passionate and too individualistic, and that his personality has overshadowed Western Christian spirituality.

Patriarch And this is precisely because, with the collapse of Western culture under the weight of the barbarian invasions, he became a massive but isolated figure. What is of lasting value is not how one or another Church Father is unique: it's the marvelous symphony of all the Fathers over time and across geography. Greek, Egyptian, Syrian, Latin—what a fantastic symphony, in which we hear the same vision, the same motifs.

Professor "God became man so that man could become God!"

Patriarch Rather than criticizing Augustine, as the Orthodox like to do, we need to make him part of this symphony. We should read him with the Greek Fathers.

Professor And we have found out that he was quite familiar with them.

---

46 Letter to the Ephesians, 17, *Early Christian Writings* (Penguin 2nd Ed.), p. 64

47 St. Macarius, *Epistle 20*, PG 34, paraphrased

48 St. Gregory Nazianzus, *Orationes*. 92.12, PG 36, 188, paraphrased

Patriarch I could continue . . . St. Thomas Aquinas did not distinguish between theology and a deeply Christian life.

Professor That is true. We tend to forget his mystical side, his taste for Dionysios the Areopagite and for *lectio divina*, that very traditional form of meditation. All the same, he was tempted to make theology a science—perhaps because the 'antidote' of Eastern thinking was no longer available. And his heirs, the Thomists, yielded to this temptation. The unity of liturgical life, mystical life, and theological thought was broken apart. Theology became a Christian way of expressing Western metaphysics, with its distinction, that goes back to Plato, between the sensory world and the world of the intellect. This led to the intellect being identified with the divine. But the true mystery is beyond intellectual and sensory apprehension, and in it, both body and soul are transfigured.

Patriarch We should leave these 'spirit-mechanisms' to the engineers! At its weakest point, Eastern Christianity also adopted this Western way of thinking, in its most impoverished form. And this resulted in a purely polemical theology which borrowed its anti-Catholic arguments from the Protestants, and its anti-Protestant arguments from the Catholics!

Professor That is what Father Georges Florovsky called Orthodox theology's 'Babylonian Captivity.' But, by the grace of God, our prayer was always nurtured by Patristic theology, whether in the Byzantine liturgy —a rich theological creation of the Patristic age—or in the 'philokalic' tradition of silent prayer, the practice of the Jesus Prayer—in which all true theology is mystical theology. And then there came the theological renaissance of the nineteenth and twentieth centuries—notably the 'neopatristic' synthesis of Florovsky and Lossky.

Patriarch We absolutely need this theological renaissance. I encourage it whenever I can. I established an Institute of Patristic Studies in Thessaloniki, several years ago. I spend a lot of time there.

ΩΩΩ

Patriarch The West and the East share the Church Fathers. They are an expression of the undivided Church. We have a lot in common with Western Christians, especially the Catholics—not only the Scriptures, but a certain way of understanding the Church, in the light of the Eucharist, a conception of holiness. We need to reach towards this continued and renewed Patristic tradition, in the East and in the West.

Patriarch In the East, St. Gregory Palamas is revered as one of the Church Fathers. The rediscovery of his thinking, in our time, is a very positive event. St. Gregory Palamas so very well expresses the reality of the Christian life, and the transformation of the whole person in the light of the Holy Spirit . . . .

Professor Yes, the transformation of the whole person, and through them, of history and the universe. The person-in-communion is not in any way separated. What is this body, if not the formation of the person from universal matter, either to become a corpse or to become Eucharist?

In Palamas, we find a wonderful balance between the sense of the person and the sense of the cosmos—through the human person, all flesh and all the earth's matter is summoned to become 'the flesh of God.' And Palamas' distinction, between God's inaccessible essence, and his energies in which we can participate, is perhaps the best understanding of the Living God and of life in God, that has ever been attained. This 'distinction' is an 'identity.' There is no boundary between the inaccessible God and the God in whom we participate. "God is wholly inaccessible," says Palamas, "and God is wholly to be participated in." God reveals himself in his unlimited self-giving, an infinite revelation of what is always unreachable. The light that shines within this personal communion is the light that transfigures the saints. The light shines from the face of the Risen Christ. This face is both completely known and completely unknowable.

Patriarch As are all faces, after the revelation of Christ . . . .

ΩΩΩ

Patriarch True theology is not opposed to love: it is an expression of love. What are dogmas if not the symbols of the experience of love? Fundamentally, there is only one Christian dogma, from which all the others are derived. That is Christ himself. God became man so that man could receive the Spirit of life, in the Church.

We cannot fight over the words any longer. We must end this war of words.

We must bathe these words in the love that they are supposed to serve, in the mystery of Christ, in the mystery of the Church.

We must encounter these words, not in their hardened husks but in their inner kernel of holiness. In the place that words collide, the saints sought understanding.

Professor The undivided Church was always reluctant to be dogmatic —and Orthodoxy has remained true to this tradition. St. Hilary of Poitiers protested that he had to put into fallible human language "mysteries that he should have enclosed within the adoration of our souls." If he put the mysteries into words, this was only to prevent the approach to them being compromised by one-sided or reductionist rational explanations.

The Church of the Seven Councils only formulated a dogma when compelled to, in order to avoid a worse outcome. And even then, the Church took care to 'crucify' human understanding through negation and antimony—the coupling of contradictory opposites. The Chalcedonian doctrine of the union of the divine and the human in Christ only states this through a series of negative adverbs, in contradictory, linked pairs.

Patriarch We receive divine love and an understanding of the infinite. Dogma protects the mystery through this 'crucifixion' of our limited understanding, but its real meaning is that of wonder in face of love. The Chalcedonian doctrine is the wonder that God so loved the world that he gave his only-begotten Son to save it . . . .

Professor And two centuries earlier, at Nicaea, the First Council introduced an apparently philosophical term into the Creed—the word *homoousios*. If you used only the language of the Bible, it was impossible to avoid a certain ambiguity that placed the divinity of Christ in question, and thus, the reality of our salvation.

To say that the Son is *homoousios* with the Father, that is to say identical in essence, without in any way being confused with the Father; then to show that this identity of essence is also that of the Holy Spirit—this is not philosophizing, this is the affirmation of the absolute unity and the absolute diversity of the Trinity as the basis of all reality and all thought.

Patriarch It means that God is love, and it reveals what that love is.

Professor Unfortunately, many Protestant theologians, and now some Catholic theologians, think the doctrines of the first Seven Councils no longer have meaning for the person of today.

Patriarch And why is that?

Professor Because they are based on an outmoded Greek philosophy and a static ontology of being.

Patriarch What Greek philosophy? Greek thought and Latin thought had no concept of the person. The Latin *persona* and the Greek *prosopon* meant not a person but a mask—at most they implied an individual. And you can set individuals side by side and never be able to conceive of true communion between them . . . .

Professor In one of his little treatises on the Trinity, St. Gregory of Nyssa demonstrates that, on the model of the Trinity, we should say that there is one Man composed of a multitude of persons. One Man-Adam that Christ has brought together in his body. St. Gregory does not mean a philosophical a = b, but a mystical identity.

Patriarch The massive accomplishment of the Fathers and the Councils was to develop a realistic theology of the person and of love. To do this, they used the philosophical vocabulary of their time, but they used it very freely—they borrowed equally from Aristotle and from Plato.

Professor And often from the Stoics . . . .

Patriarch And from the vocabulary of daily life. The word '*hypostasis*' is a building term, to which they gave a new meaning, the meaning of the unique and irreducible character of each person. They transmuted the Greek words in the crucible of Biblical revelation.

Professor And, rather than forcing God into a general science of being, they developed an ontology of the mystery.

Patriarch Love brings everything into being. But, if the dogmas of the first councils are still living and relevant to today's Church, it's not because we repeat them like fossilized formulas. We must rediscover their dynamism and their pulse of praise and wonder, so that we can express this in today's language. Otherwise, instead of awakening us to the immensity of God's love, they will cloak our minds with a false sense of security.

Professor We demarcate a geometric Trinity, parts of a distant God exiled in the heavens. But, in fact, we only truly exist within the mystery of the Trinity. All knowledge and all love is founded on the Trinity, and is fulfilled in the Trinity. If you do not have the Trinity, there is only nihilism: the nihilism of the materialistic West, in which individuals move around on the surface of non-being, or the mystical nihilism of India, in which people are swallowed up into an impersonal eternity.[49]

---

49 [See *Transfiguring Time*, pp. 32–37]

The Father is the *Arche*—the origin of all things. The Son is the Face, the Holy Spirit is Inwardness. In the Spirit, nothing and no-one is exterior to me. In the Son, the other reveals himself as face and the world reveals itself as a festival of faces. And the immense movement of life and love that brought everything into being has its beginning, its *arche*, and its end, its *telos*, in the Father.

The fact that we have being, not non-being, speaks to us of the Father. So that man, *logikos*, a word that conveys something deeper than simply 'rational,' can speak the meaning of the world, in a hymn of being that sings of the Logos which penetrates and orders all things.

The stars and the atomic particles that rotate in their orbits, the flower that becomes fruit, everything that is clothed in beauty, a man and a woman who are drawn toward each other, all things yearning for a dimly senses fulfillment and metamorphosis—all of this speaks to us of the Breath that communicates life, the Pneuma, the Holy Spirit. Father Sergei Bulgakov said that it is the Holy Spirit that makes young women beautiful. Now there is a man who tried, even if clumsily, to reinvent the message of the Fathers for the person of today.

Patriarch Yes indeed. The Russian thinkers and theologians of the nineteenth and twentieth centuries give us an example of thought freely inspired by the Fathers, both creative and faithful to Tradition. In our time, the Russians have played the same role as the Byzantine humanists of the Renaissance, who came to Western Europe after the fall of Constantinople. These Byzantine thinkers were important contributors to the Renaissance discovery of the beauty of the world and the creative power of the individuals. These had perhaps been neglected in the Middle Ages, when people were wholly in awe of God. The Russian religious thinkers, scattered around Europe after the Revolution, have fostered a great Christian rebirth, in which the human and the divine both find their fulfilment. We are not yet able to measure its full impact.

Professor The renewal of Patristic studies in the West owes a lot to the Russians. Cardinal Jean Daniélou said that he was first directed towards the Greek Fathers by Nicolai Berdyaev. The renewal of Catholic ecclesiology in the Second Vatican Council, and with it, the renewed focus on the theology of the Holy Spirit, owe a lot to the 'neo-patristic' scholarship of Georges Florovsky and Vladimir Lossky. And the new ecclesiology of communion owes much to the work of Nicolas Afanasiev.

The prophetic witness of the Russian religious philosophers continues to bear fruit. They bring a whole cosmic dimension to Christianity. They transfigure modern culture into a divino-human synthesis,

Patriarch These theologians have spread Orthodox thought to Western Europe and to America. They have renewed it through their direct encounter with the West. I have known some of them personally. I am very fond of them. I met Father Sergei Bulgakov when he was on a trip to the United States. I have read many of his books. He is a man of creative faith and a powerful vision.

Professor In his 'sophiology' he shows the world interpenetrated by divine Wisdom. He discovers the cosmic aspect of the Church—God created the world in order to become incarnate and to transform the world into the temple of his Wisdom . . . . It is very moving to be discussing Father Sergei Bulgakov in this city, whose heart is the temple of Saint Sophia, the temple of divine Wisdom. In Wisdom, Sophia, Bulgakov saw the total presence of God. Now, it is true, his thinking was not always clear . . . .

Patriarch Because he was alive and was not exploring the sterile desert. He was exploring the divine fullness, at his own peril. You cannot have productive research without overstatement and imbalance. We should not condemn mistakes: we should look for balance in a more complete understanding. We should consolidate what we have learned. That is the role of Tradition, which, for Bulgakov, was creative memory.

Professor What is Tradition, if not the Holy Spirit resting on the Body of Christ, to make real the mystery of the Resurrection?

Patriarch The Russian religious philosophers knew how to take the risks that come with renewal. They combined a sense of mystery with a sense of freedom. This is in fact the way of the future.

Professor It is however true that, in their creative exuberance, they have sometimes thrown the great Orthodox Tradition out of balance. The neo-patristic scholars had to rediscover the thread of Patristic thought. But unfortunately, if they are more rigorous, they also lack the prophetic insight of the religious philosophers they seek to correct . . . .

Patriarch You have just stated one of the great problems of our time: how do you bring prophetic insight and rigorous scholarship together? It is not easy. But there are those who are trying. For example, I can think of Paul Evdokimov. I met him in Geneva last year. He made a very strong impression on me. He has an inner light. I esteem him greatly. There is important theological work being done in Greece and Romania. And then, there is everything that is taking shape within Russia. The renewal of Russian religious thought has helped (and will keep on helping) Russian Christians to silently overcome the dark side of Communism, through prayer and through love.

Patriarch When it becomes possible to explore the specifically religious implications of this experience, it will be monumental. We are beginning to see this explored in literature, as you have pointed out.

Professor Russian religious philosophy seems to have attracted some young Russian intellectuals . . . .

Patriarch You must be patient and have confidence. I have confidence in the Russian Church. In fact, the Greeks criticize me for this and accuse me of being a 'Russophile.' But it is not about being 'Russophile.' It is about the Russian martyrs. I am overwhelmed by the blood shed by countless martyrs in twentieth century Russia. They have renewed our whole Church and the whole Christian world.

Professor These martyrs perhaps also bring us something new, that isn't specifically mentioned in the old accounts of the saints—the prayer of the martyr for the soul of the executioner. There are many accounts that witness to this.

Patriarch "Lord forgive them, for they know not what they do."

Professor For the past several years, a prayer has been circulating in Russia, a prayer "to bring comfort to the Comforter." It is a prayer of intercession for the executioners.

Patriarch And this is pure theology, when the martyr, the witness, and the one to whom they witness, become as one.

7. Leitourgia

Patriarch In Uppsala last month, we talked a lot about worship.[50] There was a working group on worship in the secular society. This is a question that I have thought about a lot. Too many Christians have become indifferent to liturgical worship, or even worse, disappointed by it. But it is in worship, and more precisely in the Eucharist, that the Church has its center. This is where the Church becomes the mystery

50 [The Fourth Assembly of the World Council of Churches took place in Uppsala, Sweden, July 1968]

of the Body of Christ and makes us all participants in the communion of the Holy Trinity.

Professor Homo sapiens is truly revealed as *homo adorans*, a liturgical being, who, through the Eucharist, becomes able to "give thanks in all things," to "eucharistify" the world, as the Apostle says.

Patriarch The first flowering tree in the gardens of the Phanar in February is filled with the glory of God. The inner ocean of a gaze is filled with the glory of God. Seized in the moment of this indescribable openness, we bring all being and all things to the Father, in Christ, in our Eucharistic offering.

Professor "Thine own of thine own, we offer to thee, on behalf of all, and for all."

Patriarch We also offer our work and our struggles, all the suffering and all the creations of humankind. We bring everything into the light of God, into the light of three suns that heals and brings peace. And the fire of the Spirit descends on the chalice, to radiate through our lives, a radiance that has no limits . . . .

Professor At the end of his *Meditations on the Divine Liturgy*, the Russian novelist Nikolai Gogol writes that, if society has not yet disintegrated completely, if mankind is not filled with hatred, one towards another, it is because of the secret power of the Eucharist.

Patriarch The Eucharist protects the world and already, secretly, illuminates it. Man-Adam rediscovers his forgotten kinship and draws life from the life of Christ, the secret friend, who shares the essential bread of life and the festive wine with him. The bread is His body, the wine is His blood, and in the unity of communion we are no longer separated.

What could be greater? This is the joy of Pascha and the transfiguration of the universe.

We receive this joy in the act of communion with all our brothers and sisters, living and dead, in the communion of the saints, tenderly watched over by the Mother of God.

And then we have no fear anymore. We have known the love that God has for us. We have become like God.

From now on, all has meaning. You, and you, and you have meaning. You will not die. Those whom you love will not die, not even those whom you believe to be dead.

Everything that is beautiful and alive will live forever, down to the last blade of grass, and the fleeting moment in which you feel yourself pulsing with the sap of life.

Even suffering and death have meaning and become pathways of life.

Everything is already alive because Christ is risen.

We have, right here, a place in which there is no separation, in which there is only love, great love and great joy. And this place is the Eucharistic cup, the Holy Grail found at the heart of the Church, and thus, in your own heart.

This is what we should be able to say. This is what worship should be.

Professor And is this not the case?

Patriarch No, it is not—or rather, it is not anymore.

Professor And yet, the other day on the Feast of the Transfiguration, I could feel the prayerfulness and joy in the church. It was a large modern church in the new part of Istanbul. Yes, the icon paintings were second-rate. But, above all, there was this joyful ease of being in the House of God. Some people were chatting while the Orthros was still being served. As the church slowly filled up, a little girl was playing, almost dancing, to the rhythm of the choir. The closer the liturgy came to its climax, the more fervent the prayer of the faithful became. People sang along with the choir, especially the *Kyrie eleison* of the litanies and the troparion of the Feast.

I was especially struck by the veneration shown to the Eucharistic gifts, at the Great Entrance, and at the moment of consecration. I witnessed archaic acts of prayer: the head bowed, the arms reaching down toward the ground, the outreached hands, palms upwards, in offering . . . .

Patriarch Yes, for the feasts, worship is particularly intense. But more often, the service is like a parade of sleepwalkers in front of a sleeping audience. We can't go on like this: these services where people are rigid and motionless, occasionally, mechanically, making the sign of the cross. No more private family baptisms, no more fashionable weddings. You mentioned the low quality of the sacred art. Just think for a moment how the liturgy at Hagia Sophia would have been, when the ambassadors of Vladimir, Prince of Kiev, said they did not know if they were in heaven or on earth. Nowhere on earth was such beauty to be found!

Patriarch Today, there is no liturgy at Hagia Sophia—and yet this silent space draws us into the divine fullness.

ΩΩΩ

Seen from the sea, Hagia Sophia is like a hidden secret. Guided by the Spirit, it is easy, in the mind's eye, to erase the minarets that insist on a remote God. And the gentle curve of the cupola suggests the presence within. From close up, this impression is confirmed. Hagia Sophia hides itself and does not reveal its extent. It is never seen as facade. Hagia Sophia is too large to be seen in a single glance—as one sees a cathedral. The curves of the arches and the cupola are out of harmony with the heavy abutting buildings, which themselves are concealed by layer upon layer of accretions. This 'outside' has no existence in itself. It does not even seek the simple balance of interior and exterior achieved by so many Byzantine or Romanesque churches. You become aware that this exterior seeks only to become, as if compelled, a 'within'—a summons to inwardness.

On the flank of this gray stone mountain there is an opening for a sort of vestibule. At its back, a mosaic emerges from the half-light, on the archway of a concealed porch: the Sun-Child contained by the nocturnal blue of his Mother's garments. This brings to mind the Christmas kontakion, by Romanos the Melodist, composed just at the time this temple was built.

> On this day the Virgin Maid goes to the grotto
> to give birth to the pre-eternal word in an ineffable manner.
> Dance for joy, all the inhabited earth, on hearing.
> Glorify along with Angels and with the shepherds
> Him who willed that He appear as a new-born Child,
> the pre-eternal God.

The Wisdom of God, to which the temple is dedicated—this is the meaning of Hagia Sophia—is this child, who seems to have summoned the light of the whole world. The Wisdom of God, the folly of the living God. While from the outside its riches seem to be veiled, you step into an interior of sudden and total immediacy. This is not a metaphysical otherworld crouching in the shadows. Here, God and man, heaven and earth, are no longer separated. The heavenly benediction of the cupola joins with the terrestrial nave, gently lighting it, the semi-cupolas and pendentives merging the two without the least discontinuity. The whole is vast and weightless, completely clear, yet tangible. The architects were masters of light. The light streams in through huge rectangular-paned transoms at the base of the cupola, and through the curved line of windows at the base of each semi-cupola, set in arches that soar in the sun.

This 'descending' movement is not all: the horizontal axis, the expression of humanity that dominates in Western European churches, is given form by the apse and the straight-walled colonnades of the nave. And yet, the cupola triumphs over all. To gaze into it is to expand and become centered, to feel the internal heavens of the heart burst into blossom. Height and depth become one.

We do not know the names of the Byzantine painters and mosaic artists. Like the Holy Spirit they remain unseen. They are hidden behind the transparency of the faces they created. The Holy Spirit is *zoopoion*: the giver of life. These artists are *zographoi*: those who by their art represent the life of the Spirit. God is Spirit and those who worship Him must worship Him in spirit and in truth. (John 4:24) But we do know the names of the architects of Hagia Sophia: Anthemios of Tralles and Isidore of Miletus. They were not so much architects as engineers and technicians. They were highly regarded for their craft, in a world that was more 'profane' than one might imagine. For example, Anthemios was renowned for his experiments with compressed steam, and Miletus continued in geometry where Euclid left off. They dedicated themselves to giving body to the *noetos*, the meaning, of numbers and shapes, in the *aesthetos* of the walls and cupolas of Hagia Sophia, so that the intelligible and the tangible, each symbolically representing the other, would together form the Temple of Wisdom. They were engineers of Wisdom, and for sixth century Byzantium, Wisdom was the Logos, the Word made flesh.

Hagia Sophia is a supreme expression of the great theological codifications of the Fifth Ecumenical Council and was built at the time of the Council. Its task was to express the modality by which the divine and the human meet in Christ. This modality is the light that deifies the flesh. It is the grace of the Holy Spirit. The Spirit abolishes the exteriority of our subjection to the fallen world. The Spirit itself is the interiority of all that exists, the Life of life. Joined without confusion or separation, to use the words of the Council of Chalcedon, the sky of the cupola and the earth of the nave are interpenetrated by light. Anthemios of Tralles and Isidore of Melitos, the craftsmen of divino-humanity, made Hagia Sophia to be a screen that captures and redirects the light, that becomes the light of Mount Tabor and is no longer exterior to us.

Earlier, I had been strolling in the Courtyard of the Janissaries, in front of the Church of Hagia Eirene, the ancient church dedicated to Divine Peace that the Turks had ringed around with bronze cannons. Once more, the smell of the wind from the sea on the old stones made me think of my childhood home in the Languedoc, in France. And once more I remembered my adolescent despair, at being bathed in the great light of the Mediterranean, but unable to reach to the core, to the heart, of my being . . . . I had to meet and welcome in this Child of silence and gold. He had taken me into the temple of his wisdom, this temple of his mad love, so that this light would no longer be that unattainable beloved. The inscription around the cupola reads: "God is the light of the heaven and the earth."

Hagia Sophia is no longer a church. After becoming a mosque, it was made a museum.[51] What a strange museum! It is so vast that it always seems almost deserted, an invitation to the solitary pilgrim. There is no longer an altar, and, from its time as a mosque, the platform of dark stone, oriented southwards towards Mecca, 'disorients' the apse. But these changes have no real importance and perhaps, even reveal new hope and new meaning. You discover that Hagia Sophia is not centered on its altar. Unlike Western Cathedrals, with their long naves that lead towards and culminate in a sanctuary in which the divine presence is concentrated, Hagia Sophia is the divine presence, in the totality of its light-saturated space. It is not so much a sacramental space like that of other churches. It is an 'apocalyptic' space, the symbol of the New Jerusalem, in which there will be no sun and no altar, because God will be all in all. Islam's harsh purification has transformed this temple of the Risen Christ into the temple of the Christ, who will come again in the glory of the Holy Spirit.

The Nativity, the first coming of Christ, only has its full meaning in the light of the second coming. And Pascha is the synthesis of both events.

No doubt, the hymn composed by Emperor Justinian, the emperor-theologian who ordered the building of the temple, was heard in Hagia Sophia for the first time, the hymn sung at the beginning of the Liturgy of the Word:

> Only-begotten Son and Logos of God,
> being immortal, you condescended for our salvation
> to take flesh from the Holy Theotokos and ever-virgin Mary
> and, without change, became man.

51 [Before being again converted to a mosque in 2020]

> Christ, our God, you were crucified and conquered death by death, save us.[52]

At every moment inside Hagia Sophia, a ray of light from one or another window brings to life a face in one of the few remaining mosaics. And so, St. John Chrysostom appeared to me above the triforium arches of a semi-cupola, his face become an immensely wise, domed forehead, his gaze one of resolute good will. This Father of the Church was a passionate defender of justice and conscience, even at the price of his own life. When the crowds rioted against the fallen favorite of the emperor, from whose tyranny he himself had suffered, and whom he had confronted; when the crowds tried to drag the dispossessed tyrant from the altar where he had sought refuge, Chrysostom calmed the emotions of the crowd by evoking the memory of the prostitute who had kissed the feet of our Lord.[53]

A man of Antioch, steeped in the Semitic sense of realism, St. John Chrysostom took Matthew 25 at its word.[54] He declared that the Eucharist had no meaning if it was not continued in the 'sacrament of the poor.' No doubt today, with the Western Church's focus on social action, he would say that the sacrament of the poor is nothing without the mystery of the incarnate, crucified, and risen God. Because if God did not become man, in human history, if Christ was not really resurrected, then our history is in vain. It is an idol that will not save us from non-being. St. John Chrysostom, the "Golden-mouth," is the one who preached about the God who could not be comprehended, in words that are even more relevant today.

The sun goes down. The molten light enters by the wide windows of the western wall to set the apse aglow at the eastern end. This light is transformed in its passage beneath the cupola, the cupola in the form of an inverted chalice. Thus the 'western' light becomes the glorious light of the Resurrection in the 'sea shell' of the eastern apse.[55] The setting sun is transformed into the dawn of the unending day of the sun of righteous-

52 The second antiphon

53 [In this striking image, the fallen tyrant kisses the feet of the altar just as the fallen woman had kissed the feet of Christ]

54 [In his writings, Olivier Clément repeatedly contrasts the 'Semitic' realism of the Antiochian Church Fathers with the allegorical tendencies of the Greek Church Fathers of Alexandria]

55 [Clément uses the architectural term 'conch' for the apse, perhaps consciously echoing the Akathist to the Mother of God: "Rejoice, O undefiled dwelling of the Word, seashell that produces the divine pearl." (Ode Five)]

ness, the Child in the arms of his Mother. (cf. Zech. 14:7, Mal. 4:2) They are also depicted in the mosaics of the apse. As we sing in the words of the ancient hymn, *Phos Hilaron*:

> "Now that we have reached the setting of the sun and behold the evening light, we sing to God: Father, Son and Holy Spirit. We sing to Christ, the joyful light of the holy glory of the immortal Father."

The earth bathed in color, the creation that secretly rediscovers paradise in this "joyful light," appear all around us in the nave, in the play of light on marble and porphyry, and in the blue fronds emerging from a ground of gold on the triforium arches.

At the time of its construction, one contemporary commentator, Paul the Silentiary, explained in his Description of Hagia Sophia, how the Byzantines saw, in this marble and porphyry, symbols of all the beauty of the earth.

> "The one who turns towards this light-green marble will think that he sees the banks of the rivers of Thessaly in flower, or a vine shooting out its young tendrils . . . . In another place, here is the deep-blue peacefulness of the sea in summer. On the capitals of the columns, foliage like curls of golden hair . . . the porphyry is like powdered stars, milk flowing over dark skin, cornflowers exploding out of drifts of snow."[56]

The embedded jewels and most of the mosaics are gone. And yet, the courses of polychromatic marble, each slab symmetrically interwoven with the next, occasionally inset with porphyry, symbolize the New Jerusalem, with its courses of precious stones. (Rev. 21:19–20) In the natural world, precious stones combine the highest density with the greatest transparency. Weight is inverted into the weightlessness of light. A precious stone is to the natural world what the eye is to the human body. And just as a person, says St. Macarius, must become wholly gaze and countenance, so in the Logos, the natural world becomes an architecture of transparency, in which light assumes the density of matter, in which matter becomes light.

Such are my meditations at Hagia Sophia, in the evening, when the light brings the marble and the porphyry to life. Then, everything is Light

56 Silentarius, Paulus, *Descriptio Sanctae Sophiae*

and everything is Life, from the motionless whirl of the cupola to the heaviness of the stone walls. For, as St. John Chrysostom tells us, Byzantium forever unites Light and Life.

Above the Phanar, past the Greek Lycée, the dense urban fabric begins to unravel. The streets become tracks, a whole hillside is taken up with vegetable gardens. And then, as you rejoin the main road that runs along the ridge, you are back in the town. I come across a church converted into a mosque—the Church of the Theotokos Pammakaristos—the All-Blessed. This is where the Patriarch had his residence for a while after the Turkish conquest of Constantinople. A side chapel has been turned into a museum of Christianity. The wall-decorations in the apse and in the cupola are still intact.

You become aware that these sanctuaries must have been completely clad in mosaics. In the very tall cupola, topped by a dome, there is the icon of the Pantokrator, of the One who holds the whole world in his hand, in an embrace that conveys life and ushers in the fullness of all things . . . .

In the fourteenth century, as the Byzantine Empire collapsed and the spirit of Byzantium turned inwards, the Pantokrator came to represent the radiance of love and sacrifice, instead of the severe God of the Old Testament. In this side chapel, His face has a soft strength and nobility. Around the Pantokrator on the supporting ribs of the cupola, the twelve prophets already announce the mystery. The Man of Sorrows and the King of Glory are one—the veiled announcement of the eternal humanity of God.

Now the meaning of the cupola becomes clear: the inverted sky is an offering of the face of the Pantokrator.

In this semi-rural suburb with its mounds of trash, vultures soar over the church, uttering their strange cries. I think of the Lord's puzzling words: "Wherever the corpse is, that is where the vultures will gather." (Matt. 24:28) There are those tourists who, consciously or not, are pilgrims. Then there are the others, who are like these vultures. They grab and plunder with their hasty glances and their captured photographic images—an expression of their inability to contemplate what they see. In this church, they don't even lift their heads to see the Christ in the cupola. It is true that this cupola, from the end of the Middle Ages, no longer makes the same overwhelming statement as that of Hagia Sophia. It hides within its own elevation. The Pantokrator no longer imposes: you have to look for Him in order to find Him.

Today, the cupola of Hagia Sophia has only Arabic inscriptions. But it is held up by four angels. You find angels throughout Byzantine art and in the Scriptures. The angelic presence makes the eternal dimension of history apparent . . . . Theirs is a spiritual, yet not immaterial, universe. Their materiality is diaphanous, yet not completely transparent. The angels' slight opacity creates an iridescence of light that becomes color and sound. In Christ, our High Priest, the earthly liturgy is joined to the liturgy of the angels, who dance around the silence. The liturgy of the angels is the only one celebrated today in Hagia Sophia. And since the cupola is without the Name and the Face, this is the liturgy of pure expectation, the liturgy of heavenly silence of which the Book of Revelation speaks.

The four giant angels of Hagia Sophia, depicted on the curved, triangular pendentives at the base of the dome, are six-winged seraphim. These, says Dionysios the Areopagite, are fire by nature, and this fire transmutes the soul into its divine form. Their wings are the symbol of the angels' wondrous flight towards "the mysteries of the divine."

At Hagia Sophia, the wings are the whole angels: the face is an abstraction, formed of an enormous golden cabochon.[57]

Golden brown wings, a dull gold from which emerges other green and blue plumage. The archeologists tell us that Hagia Sophia was mainly decorated in green and gold. Today, these colors are only to be seen in the angels' wings. The golden brown is the source of fire. The green and blue are the colors of the waters of creation. The vast wings evoke waves and clouds, the secret thunder of the great "sea of glass mingled with fire" in front of the throne of the Lamb. (Rev. 15:2)

ΩΩΩ

Patriarch The Pan-Orthodox Council should undertake a comprehensive renewal of our forms of worship, and we should be starting this work right now. The Liturgy should become an act in which everyone takes part, the drama of death and love in which everyone is transported. He smiles. Think of Wagner's *Parsifal*, think of Boris Godunov. I saw this opera performed when I was in America. What a powerful moment it was when the patriarch came out to bless Boris. It felt as though he was really a patriarch, not an actor . . . . But more seriously, you have seen the icon of

57 [Restoration work revealed the faces of the angels beneath that layer of plaster.]

the Resurrection of Christ at Chora. Imagine if all the liturgical force of this sublime and violent painting could be expressed in our worship. That is what we need.

There is a side chapel at the Church of the Holy Savior at Chora, that is now the Kariye Camii mosque. You pass under the cupola with its icon of the Theotokos and into the chapel. An angel has rolled up the sky like a tent, tearing away the fabric of time on which the twelve signs of the zodiac are inscribed. "There shall be no more time." (cf Rev. 10:6) You see the icon of the Last Judgment: Adam and Eve kneel in supplication on either side of an empty throne—the throne of implacable justice.

And then, in the apse, the secret "judgment of judgment" is revealed. Christ descends into hell like a lightning bolt; he shatters the doors of the underworld, and he seizes the lost Adam and Eve out of the tomb: he seizes all of humanity from its tomb. Christ is portrayed in a victorious leaping movement. One leg is extended to crush the *diabolos*, the one who separates, beneath the broken gates of hell with their shattered chains; with the other leg, He kicks upwards in the motion of a diver thrusting towards the air and the light. But here, He is the air and He is the light that refreshes. He grasps Adam and Eve by the wrist (not by the hand) and brings them flying from their tombs.

There is a deliberate dissymmetry in the symmetry of Byzantine art, that gives it the pulse of life, rather than a geometric immobility. In this icon, the extreme dissymmetry expresses the richness of life. At the symbolic center of the land of the dead and damned the uniting glory of God replaces the dead weight of separation. "The sky, the earth, and even hell are filled with light." The dissymmetry is resolved in the regal and gentle face, which remains supremely still amid this whirlpool of liberation.

Christ is encircled by a mandorla of three concentric circles, each progressively darker (or rather, revealing another form of light), until the darkest inner ring reveals the celestial glory of the Trinity, the star-filled divine constellation at the heart of non-being. The darkness is that of the unknowability of the Father, the source of all divinity. The brightness of the light reveals the Holy Spirit. The colors of the mandorla and the whiteness of Christ's garments point to a materiality that is not that of our world, a spiritual form of the body, of which our bodies are merely the chrysalis, another state of existence in which one is no longer imprisoned by space, in which time is filled with eternity. And here is the whole meaning of this icon: the chrysalis of this world is torn open and the cosmos emerges, in metamorphosis.

ΩΩΩ

Professor The poet Georgios Seferis wrote that all Greek philosophy can be found at Chora, in this depiction of Christ regally freeing Adam and Eve from the tomb.

Patriarch All of Christianity is there. This is the sacred drama that we should enact in worship, so that the worshipers feel that they have been freed from the tomb and thrust into the brightness of the light, into life.

Professor But this drama cannot just be a play performed before comfortably seated spectators. In studying the history of the liturgy—the leitourgia, the common work of the people of God—one often feels that, in the Constantinian era, the liturgy became a sort of spectacle, performed by the clergy in front of the laity.

Patriarch Everyone should take part, everyone should feel themselves transported. Let me go back to the example of the theater—whose origins, by the way, are liturgical. As a Greek, I love these ancient tragedies —especially Medea and the Iphigenia of Euripides. When you see them performed, you are bowled over. For a moment, you are transported. You have encountered the sacred in its raw state: that sacred astonishment, the thambos.

Believe me, most of our faithful never experience anything like this at church, not even a little bit. They do not experience this shock of astonishment at the sacred. Think for a moment about Peter's response to the transfigured Christ, on Mount Tabor: Lord, it is good for us to be here. *Kalon estin*, it is beautiful, it is marvelous for us to be here.

Alas, all too often what is found in our churches is individualistic piety, or mechanical gestures. But the only drama, the drama of which all others are mere reflections, unfolds here in the Church, when the Holy Spirit reveals Christ's death and resurrection to us. Everything is there: the drama of life, of suffering, of death, of love that is stronger than death. Everything is there in Christ, the alpha and the omega, the Crucified One and the King of All, the Pantokrator. Everything is there, from the lamb sacrificed before the foundation of the world (Rev. 13:8) to the "second and glorious coming again" that the priest recalls to our attention—because the Church, in Christ, remembers the future. Everything is there, from the birth and the preaching of Christ to the three extraordinary days in which God suffered death in the flesh, in which hell was destroyed, in which we were resurrected.

The Paschal joy is now and for always with us: this is what we drink from the chalice. You will understand that I am talking of astonishment and delight. That is why I referred to those nineteenth century operas, that sought to create a total art melding the beauty of the poetry and the beauty of the music.

Professor It is worth noting that music does not stand on its own in the Orthodox Church. The music enables the words to move our whole being, giving shape to a holistic knowledge. I found the Byzantine chant at the Church of St. George quite remarkable. It was more intense. It had more inner tension than Gregorian chant. But like Gregorian chant, it has no pathos. It lifts up the soul but breaks down any self-regarding exaltation. It is always supplication, from the heights of praise to humble beseeching, mixing the tears of penitence with the tears of joy—what the ascetics called the tears of joyful sadness.

Patriarch We have undertaken the renewal of Byzantine chant. But we need to rediscover worship as a total art, that harnesses all the creative strength of our times, that will allow everyone to take part, with all their being, in the Paschal joy that is made new every Sunday . . . .

The Pan-Orthodox Council should make this renewal a priority. We need centers for the study of liturgy, music, architecture, and the sacred arts. This should not just be about archeology and scholarly learning. We must rediscover the living Tradition with the help of artists, with the help of those in whom contemplation and creation become one, with the help of those who are so deeply rooted in faith that overflowing beauty pours out of them.

Professor And the faithful?

Patriarch They need to take part fully and to be able to fully understand. The Council should address the problem of archaic liturgical language and also clarify the role of the priest, the choir, and the people.

Professor And this will, it seems to me, allow the people to hear and to place the seal of their "amen" on the Eucharistic prayers and especially on the epiclesis.

These prayers were written to be heard, to be spoken, as a dialogue, and they only became secret in the Constantinian era, when it was feared that the crowds of barely instructed people coming into the church would betray or blaspheme the mysteries. But now that the

Church and the world are once again opposed to each other—often tragically—the faithful must regain their full dignity as co-celebrants.

Patriarch You are completely right. It should not be difficult for the Council to reestablish what is true to Tradition. Our centers for liturgical study will clarify the origin and purpose of each service. In monastic usage, the services have become over-elaborate. But we should not randomly make cuts. We need to concentrate on the essential. Our liturgical texts are infinitely rich. They combine contemplation and purity of thought with rich symbolism and biblical typology.

Let us start by making them intelligible and true to their original intention. Here I am not so much thinking of the Liturgy—this is so rich that there is very little we need to touch—but of the other services. This work should be done with care and beauty, to touch people's heart. And then, perhaps, we can create our own forms of praise, as every generation has done, in every epoch.

ΩΩΩ

Patriarch Along with the renewal of worship, we need a renewal of preaching. Enough of these pious homilies with words that no-one listens to, enough of making the Church into a synagogue, with its many rules, its lists of what is, and what is not permitted. Let us announce that God has upended all moral and pious values, that God has become our friend, so that trust can displace anxiety, so that we can become able to show a little love. Baptism should be celebrated with dignity in the midst of the assembled church. This should not be a small family ceremony. This is a person's birth into eternity.

Professor In the early Church, people were baptized on the night before Easter. Sometimes I wonder, if we want baptism to have its full significance as a death-and-resurrection in Christ, as an 'illumination' that restores us to the image of God, whether we should still baptize little children. I was thirty years old when I was baptized in the Orthodox Church. This experience still amazes me. I know how it is not to be baptized and to live in a merely three-dimensional world. And I know how it is to be baptized and to feel a new inner dimension opening up in which, finally, the soul can breathe. The crisis tearing Christian thought apart in today's world seem to me, primarily, to be a clumsy reaction to the infantilized theology in which so many of those who were baptized as infants remain trapped.

Patriarch I agree completely that those adult converts are among the most thoughtful of Christian witnesses. But those baptized as infants can, and should, become lucidly converted. The grace of baptism works in us like leaven. And, especially in the Orthodox Church, we have kept the ancient practice in which Baptism, Chrismation, and the Eucharist are not separated. So the children grow up in the presence of Christ. They are fed by love and life, and this precedes conscious awareness and religious awakening.

By contrast, for the convert, conscious awareness grows out of the absence of love, out of an asphyxiating absence of real life. We need both paths. But the baptism of the infant at once becomes communion. This requires the parents' participation in the life of the Church. The faith of the church community lends its strength to the child's relative lack of religious consciousness. Why would we not share with our children the best of what we have? They want to take part from very early on. If we refuse them, we are making their freedom an empty abstraction. By contrast, in communion they receive eternal life, which is at the heart of freedom. They receive the possibility of making a free choice, a choice that ultimately cannot be avoided, towards which we should lead them with the utmost of care and respect . . . .

And meanwhile, what a joy to have these little ones approach the Communion cup, or to have them come up in the arms of a parent. Because our Lord said: "Let the little children come to me." (Matt. 19:14)

Professor To be more precise, the issue is not so much baptism as the free and lucid decision made after the crises of adolescence. This is where we need to show that Christianity is not just a set of well-meaning moral precepts—or even a set of revolutionary social precepts! We need to reveal Christianity as a way of life, that is both open and demanding. Not as the categorical imperative, but as the revelation of what we need to 'live and have our being.' To live in fulfilment and in eternity—to live *aei en einai*—St. Maximus the Confessor expressed it so much better with his succinct Greek adverbs.

Patriarch This is why we need to emphasize the true meaning of *metanoia* and the Sacrament of Confession. *Metanoia* is the great transformation of consciousness in which everything is no longer centered on the ego but instead on God and my neighbor.

Professor In which we discover our true self, our true personhood, in communion.

Patriarch Repentance (*metanoia*) is not some sort of morbid self-abasement. It frees us, it lifts a weight from us, it recomposes us, it gives us life. *Metanoia* opens the way to our true nature, to life-without-limits in the Holy Spirit. And this is the reason that the Sacrament of Confession has such meaning. We are unhappy, but instead of proudly enclosing ourselves within our unhappiness—by denying it or by shrugging it off—instead of turning our despair into loathing of life, we offer everything to Christ, the physician of our soul and body.

The priest is there to bear witness to God's forgiveness and to hold this for us, so that the new life takes root deep in the heart, and not merely, in the form of good intentions, on the surface. Those will be quickly smothered by worldly cares and worldly riches that spring up like weeds. "So long as the unclean spirit, finding the house empty, swept and put in order, does not go and bring with him seven other spirits more evil than himself . . . " (Matt 12:44) The father confessor should know how to shine light into the very heart of a person's being. And then this light, starting from the 'pastures of the heart,' in the words of the ascetics, will, little by little, penetrate our whole existence. Little by little, the person is transformed, not by exerting her own petty strength, but by allowing the life in Christ to ripen within.

Marriage should also receive its full divine significance in the life of the Church. Each couple should understand that they are the first couple, Adam and Eve in Paradise, and united once and for all to all humanity by the new Adam. So that human love becomes, not just a poignant nostalgia for a lost Paradise, but a Paradise regained, in love that now, already, is transfiguring the world.

This is a sacrificial love: Adam's ecstatic trance enabled God to create woman from his side and from Christ's pierced side on the Cross, the new Eve, the Church, flows out together with the water and the blood. This is a victorious love, whose existence is objectively greater than the man and the woman, and whose existence is deeper than the ups and downs of their life.

Christ is its beginning, its middle and its end. This is the mystery of Christ and the Church. A man and a woman have only to draw from this well for the miracle of the Wedding at Cana to be renewed.

St. John Chrysostom sees the couple as a reflection of the unity of the Trinity, and their home as a little church of life and love. Children come as an added, overflowing joy. The Sacrament of Marriage is not only the

Miracle of Cana, the transformation of the water of daily life into the wine of joy and happiness. It is also the sacrament of human fulfillment. I tell newlyweds that they are the roots of a single tree, and this tree will yield many branches, many flowers, much fruit. The Tree of Jesse grew towards the birth of the Savior. The tree of each Christian couple grows towards the fullness of which the Fathers tell us, and when it is attained, Christ will return in glory.

ΩΩΩ

Professor Doesn't the renewal of worship also require the renewal of the icon and of icon painting, in the broadest sense?

Patriarch Absolutely! The icon is an integral part of liturgy. We cannot conceive of a church without icons. Through their prayer, these serious, light-filled faces, these images of God that have attained his likeness, guide us towards the source of their light, towards the Face of the Savior, the icon of icons. Jesus said, "He who has seen me, has seen the Father." (John 14:9) God made himself visible in the flesh. God saved me through the material world and, from that moment, the material world can represent God-made-man and man-become-as-God.

The icon contains a whole theology, because God is beauty: before anything else, He is beauty.

Professor Maximus the Confessor said that "perfect beauty receives the name of the Kingdom."

Patriarch What is a saint if not a truly beautiful person? Not the transitory and often shallow beauty of youth, but an eternal and unique beauty that arises from the heart, when the heart becomes the true reflection of the Risen Christ. The icon should resemble its prototype. In this resemblance, we recognize the presence of the sanctified person no longer separated from God. But it is not a portrait, in the flesh, of the natural person who continues in the here-and-now. Here, saintliness is always provisional. Here, our participation in the Risen Christ is also participation in the Man of Sorrows. The icon is an opening to the Kingdom of God. It represents the fully resurrected person in all the glory of their spiritual body, the communion of saints and the transfiguration of the universe. (1 Cor. 2:6–16)

Professor Yesterday, they were making a film in the nave of the church at Chora. The actors wore costumes from the Middle Ages. Between takes, they were lounging in the side-chapel, smoking, and chatting. They were attractive young men and women. But there, in front of these wall-paintings, in front of the icon of Christ blazing from the apse, their beauty seemed to be opaque and larval . . . . Their laughter and antics seemed to reveal nothing but a mediocre sketch or caricature of the person.

I suddenly understood St. Paul's distinction between the *sarx*, the flesh as existence unto death, and the *soma*, as the body promised to the life of the Spirit. (Rom. 8:5-8) Above me, in the wall-paintings, the faces gave meaning to the bodies: the bodies had become face. Around me on the floor, the opposite seemed to occur. The flesh, the impersonal dance of flesh and blood, had overwhelmed and disfigured the faces . . . .

Patriarch The iconographer always begins with the head, and the face is always centered on the gaze. But I think you are exaggerating the dualism. If you could have seen the faces of these actors in a moment of peace and trust, or simply in deep sleep, letting go of everything like a sleeping child, you would have understood that this face is also—and will never cease to be—the promise of an icon.

I often worry that today's iconographic art, which has been renewed by remarkable artists and scholars, and purged of the pietism and sentimentality of a long period of decadence, has not become, by contrast, a little too rigid, a little too hieratic, a little too modeled on the great icons of the past. The same principle applies to icons as to Patristic thought. While remaining true to Tradition and to the fundamental canons of sacred art, you must have the courage to be creative. Otherwise, we will never get beyond a form of pious archeology. The great river of life that is Tradition must take up all the discoveries of the modern world, to shed light on every aspect of life . . . . Byzantine art underwent this renewal many times, especially at the time of the Palaiologos Dynasty. You were talking about Chora. Look at the freshness, the imagination, the humanity, in the mosaics in the two narthexes!

ΩΩΩ

Kariye Camii is still inside the city walls but it is at the outer edge: the Church of our Savior of Chora, in-the-fields. But the first narthex gives the word *chora* an unexpected dimension. On the archway of the entry-door there is a mosaic of the Theotokos with the inscription *he chora ton achoritou*—the space of the one who transcends all space, the limit which encloses the unlimited. And opposite, on the archway of the entry to the second narthex, there is a mosaic of Christ with the inscription: *he chora ton zonton*, the land of the living. This Christ at first seems huge and imposing. But then you sense that the tension is peacefully resolved. The Risen Christ is young and fair-haired. The mosaics inside the two narthexes join all the aspects of life into their luminous light . . . . The games of childhood, the dance of the young women, love between a man and a woman, the love of a son for his mother, friendship, feasting, wine and flowers—everything is present in the 'land of the living.'

Nicolas Berdyaev once said that the Middle Ages tended to elevate God at the expense of the human, whereas the Renaissance and humanism elevated the human at the expense of God, to the point where the human, unrooted from the heavens, becomes disintegrated and exhausted, in contemporary art and philosophy.

But Berdyaev celebrated the ephemeral emergence, in the first Italian Renaissance, of an art that balanced the human and the divine, that bore the perfume of St. Francis of Assisi. What would he have said if he had seen Chora? The Palaiologos' renaissance is a renaissance of transfiguration, in which the divine and the human are joined "without separation or confusion."

Can the Christian renaissance of which the Patriarch dreamed make the liturgy the driving force of human culture? In which science, technology, and art, made one in paschal faith, will prepare the way for the resurrection of the dead and the transfiguration of the universe, in Christ, 'the land of the living'!

Part Three: Acts

1. Roma—Amor

At our very first meeting, the Patriarch said: "Let's not talk about me. There is no point. Let's talk about uniting the Church. That is God's will. That is the irresistible demand of all Christians. That is the only way to bear witness at a time when the world is becoming one. Today, the one Church is the *ananke*, our destiny—Pope Paul VI knows this. The Archbishop of Canterbury knows this. I know there will be problems and it will be difficult. But if we look at this in the light of unity, everything will be different."

Professor When you talk, you never separate this drive for unity from the Church's sanctification of history.

Patriarch This is the heart of Christ's high priestly prayer—the founders of the ecumenical movement have cited this so often; Pope Paul VI and I prayed this together in Jerusalem: "That they all may be one, even as Thou, Father are in me and I in Thee, that they may also be in us so that the world may believe that Thou has sent me." (John 17:22–23) We have divided Christ but kept the Communion cup. We have lost the spirit of the Gospel. And this has become the leaven of history, outside the Church, and often in opposition to the Church.

Professor This is why many of today's Christians think that ecumenism is outmoded. You should just become part of the evangelical ferment that is history: you should just become one more person in the crowd . . .

Patriarch That is one way of looking at things. But if that is all, you lose sight of the reality of Christianity: the Paschal joy and the force of the Resurrection, that we receive in communion with the mysteries of the Church . . . .

Professor Which we can sum up as what the Fathers call 'deification' or 'theosis'—terms that can be shocking to the West: "God became man so that man might become God."[58]

Patriarch There is nothing shocking in this far-reaching statement. In Christ, we receive the spirit of adoption, and this becomes our whole life. A person is never fully human except in God. (Rom. 8:14–17) So it is a mistake to think that we can find Christ only by serving people. You should at the same time receive life from the Eucharistic cup, and then share it in love for one's neighbor. This is how you reconcile the Church and Christianity!

And this reconciliation demands Christian unity. Our divisions have made our Savior unrecognizable. Remember what St. Paul said to the Corinthians: "Each one of you says, 'I belong to Paul,' or 'I belong to Apollos,' or 'I belong to Cephas,' or 'I belong to Christ.' Is Christ divided? Was Paul crucified for you? Or were you baptized in the name of Paul?" (1 Cor. 1:12–13) A Church that is fragmented into different confessions cannot reveal Christian values and give life to history. And if these Christian values are separated from the cup of life for too long, in the end they will burn out.

Professor This awareness of the tragedy and sin of our divisions, this pilgrimage towards the union of all in the one cup—perhaps these are the major events of the twentieth century. Perhaps we needed the vertiginous destruction of these mutually distrustful Christianities, in which we lived side by side, before Christians could rediscover each other as brothers and sisters, together responsible for the spiritual destiny of humanity. Christians have become a small minority in the globalizing world, in which we see the rise of mass atheism, the rise of pseudo-religious cults and the melting-pot of different peoples and races.

Patriarch In one way or another, we have all tasted the bitter fruit of our divisions. When I became a deacon, the Orthodox had, for centuries, been reduced to a minority in the Muslim Ottoman Empire. And what did the Western Christians do? They tried to take advantage of this situation by making converts, by proselytizing . . . .

---

58 [St. Athanasius the Great, *On the Incarnation*, ch. 54]

Professor The Metropolitan of Kolonia told me that when he was a young priest, if they met on the street, a Catholic priest would turn away, with obvious hostility.

Patriarch I often had the same experience during my many years in America—a country that did not have the experience of different Christianities living side by side. If I met a Catholic priest or bishop, even if we happened to be in the same railroad car, they would act as if I did not exist, they did not see me. What a big difference there is now! I used to feel this burden of distrust weighing down the Orthodox, first in the Ottoman Empire and then in America. And we hunched up in a defensive posture and became distrustful in our turn. Now, this can also be a blessing, to undergo the suffering inflicted by one's brothers and sisters. We must ensure that it is for their good. But it was more my understanding of the contemporary world that made me understand the urgency of unity, its inevitability—the *ananke*. You know, I am interested in everything, in people's delights, their discoveries, and their sorrows. I am one man among the others: I don't strive for this; it is what I am.

Professor But also a pastor, a priest, a man of prayer . . . .

Patriarch A man of prayer? Perhaps, perhaps, I don't know. In any case, you must know who you are praying for . . . . So I receive many visitors, I read the newspapers, I get a lot of letters.

Professor If I may be disrespectful . . . .

Patriarch Be disrespectful. You are here living in my monastery. You have to obey me. Be disrespectful!

Professor I would say that you are greedy for human contact. I need only have watch you opening your mail . . . or watching people strolling along the Grand Avenue of Pera in the evening . . . but then, it isn't greed anymore, it is as if you are blessing people.

Patriarch I don't know. What I do know is that I am not a churchman closed up inside the Church. I love people, I observe history. Believe me, people have never needed to understand the meaning of life as much as they do today. Everything is changing at a crazy pace. And people ask themselves: Why? The person of today is hungry. In the developing world there is famine: but everywhere there is a hunger for love and meaning. The world is in danger of destruction: not only from atomic weapons but from lack of meaning, from boredom and hopelessness. Drugs, eroticism and failed political religions—such as Communism—are not the answer. There is only one answer: the revelation of the One Christ by his One

Church! This revelation cannot be delayed. The Holy Spirit will not any longer stand for the luxury of Christianity divided, the luxury of a theological calculus based on fear and pride, the luxury of comfortable negotiations in soft armchairs. We need to respond and we have to respond as one.

Professor The signs of the times . . . the yearnings of the Holy Spirit—you cannot separate these.

Patriarch Quite simply, you must live as a Christian, and first of all you must live as a Christian, among other Christians. We are being judged. We are being judged by the spiritual suffering of our fellow humans, but also by the example of the Son of God who suffered on the Cross, for love. Are we going to disarm ourselves as He did, or are we going to rest on the laurels of our predecessors and continue with this polemical theology? For the past twenty years, the ecumenical movement, the Second Vatican Council, the Pan-Orthodox conferences and the meetings between Church leaders have all revealed the gaping wound of our divisions, for everyone to see. From this moment on, it is no longer possible to be unaware of the urgency of unity, not to be thinking and acting towards this goal, as a local Church, as a Church leader, as a Christian scholar conscious of their responsibility as a teacher.

Professor Unity is our obligation. Do you think it is now a historical possibility, or is it a miracle that will appear at the end of time?

Patriarch Unity will be a miracle, but this miracle will occur in time. And besides, we have been in the end times ever since Pentecost. As you know, every night I go down into the garden and into the narthex of the church, sometimes at midnight, sometimes at four a.m. I light two candles in front of the icon of the Theotokos and I pray for unity.[59] When will this be accomplished? When Christ is asked about the Second Coming, he says that he does not know: only the Father knows of that day and that hour. (cf. Matt. 24:36, Mark 13:32) The same applies to the unity of the Church. The future is in God's hands. God's desires are held in eternity. They enter time when the time is ripe, when time is lifted up. Our task is to make the time ripe. I have already seen so many miracles. So many things have happened that seemed impossible. My meeting with

59 ["He lights two candles in front of the icon of the Theotokos, one for Pope Paul VI and one for himself, and says out loud "the Mother wants to see her sons united." Unpublished notebooks of Chiara Liubich, quoted in *Porträt eines Propheten*, p. 20]

the Pope in Jerusalem, the Pope's visit to Constantinople, my journey to Rome. Unity will come. It will be a miracle. A new miracle that takes place in time. When? We cannot know. But we must prepare the way because a miracle is like God and is always imminent.

ΩΩΩ

Patriarch Today, transfiguring love is descending on the face of the Church. The breath of friendship is being felt, not as a distant breeze in a far-away sky, but in our hearts. Christians of every confession come to see me. They are already living the miracle of unity. Just now, there was a group of Germans, Catholics and Protestants. We all said the Lord's Prayer together.

Professor Many problems remain. The walls between Christian cultures have been broken down. The Orthodox have been scattered into the West. Slowly all the old historical cultural and psychological barriers are being taken down, by Christians living side by side in the New World. We are all being led to the "one thing necessary." But when these hard external layers are torn away, don't we have to face the real problems of the structure of the Church and the meaning of the Christian life?

Patriarch I don't deny that there are differences, but I think we must take a different approach to looking at them. How we look at these problems is first and foremost a psychological, or rather a spiritual, question. For centuries, we have had conversations between theologians and these have done nothing except to dig the opposing positions even deeper. I have a whole library of such books. And why? Because people have been talking to each other out of fear and opposition, wishing to defend or to conquer. This is not a theology of celebration of the mystery: it has become a weapon. God himself has become a weapon!

Professor It is very clear that the conversations between the East and West were never friendly or impartial—at least until the end of the nineteenth century. One has the impression that the West took advantage of Byzantium's political weakness to impose its will—at the Council of Lyon in 1274, and at the Council of Florence in 1438. Byzantium responded with guile, or, if they did make a bold and succinct statement of their traditional beliefs, as St. Mark of Ephesus did at Florence, there was no attempt to understand the other side's point of view.

Yet, until the end of the Middle Ages, both sides knew that they belonged to the same Church, and they continued to hope that this common membership would be mutually recognized—through fundamental debate in a truly ecumenical council. But, with the rise of the new cultural and political dynamics of the modern era, the Christian West went onto the offensive. The Catholic Church tried to annex fragments of the Orthodox world—this was the bitter goal of Uniatism.[60] For their part, the Protestants tried to take control of the Ecumenical Patriarchate. This led to the blind alley of the great and unfortunate Patriarch Cyril Loukaris' Calvinist catechism, which the people of the Orthodox Church rejected. And so, Orthodoxy turned in on itself in fear. If Pope Pius IX or Leo XII took an interest in the Eastern Church, it was to demand its surrender. The Orthodox Church responded in the same vein, with accusations and a catalog of heresies in 1848 and 1894. And let's not forget how much theological thought in the West was distorted by the centuries-long debates between the Reformers and the Counter-Reformation.

Patriarch That is why we must try a different approach. I repeat—I do not underestimate the difficulties. But I am trying to change the spiritual atmosphere. The restoration of love will allow us to present the problems in a wholly different light. We should express the truths that we hold dear, which guard and celebrate the wonder of our life in Christ, not by pushing others away and compelling them to admit defeat, but by sharing these truths with them. We should express this truth, in all its beauty, as a form of celebration to which we invite our brothers and sisters. At the same time, we must be ready to listen. For Christians, the truth is not opposed to life or to love—it is their fulfillment. Authentic theology is the expression of a spiritual experience. We need to set the words free—all these words used in contention. We need to set them free from all their troubled past, from all political, ethnic, and cultural hatred—from all these things that have nothing to do with Christ. Then we should plunge these words deep into the life of the Church, deep into the experience of resurrection, of which the words should be the faithful servants. We should weigh the words on the scales of life, death, and resurrection. We must confront the burden of experience that they carry.

60 ["The Russian dioceses of Poland and Lithuania—were constantly subject to pressure on the part of the Catholic kings of Poland. . . . in 1596 the Metropolitan of Kiev and the majority of the Ukrainian bishops signed an act of reunion with Rome at Brest-Litovsk. This was the origin of the "Uniate" Ukrainian Church . . ." John Meyendorff, *The Orthodox Church*, SVS Press, 1996, p.101–102]

Those who accuse me of sacrificing Orthodoxy to a blind obsession with love have a very impoverished idea of the truth. They make the truth into a self-confirming system that they own. But the truth is the living glorification of the Living God, in a life lived creatively in face of the unknown. One does not possess God—He seizes us, He fills us with his presence, according to the measure of our humility and our love.

We can only give glory to the Lord of Love with love. We can only give glory by our gifts and our sharing, and, if need be, by our sacrifice for the God who for our salvation was sacrificed, even to death on the Cross.

But let me go even further: those who accuse me of sacrificing the truth for love do not trust the truth. They lock truth up; they imprison truth like an unfaithful spouse. I say that the truth is the truth and we cannot fear for it. Let us give out the truth, share the truth, reveal its fullness. Let us welcome everything in the lives of our brothers and sisters that comes from life and love. If we persist in this, the truth will make itself known, and will overcome any shortcomings and limitations, from within, from the shared mystery of the Church.

Let us open our hearts: "Let each of you look not only to his own interests but also to the interests of others." (Phil. 2:4) We have one certain criterion: the life in Christ. Faced with a partial expression of the truth, we should ask to what extent it expresses life in Christ, but also, to what extent it jeopardizes this life . . . . So let us continue our dialogue, in love, so as always to reveal Christ's truth.

Professor In brief, unity is something that will be revealed, not something to be achieved?

Patriarch Exactly. And I use this word in its fullest sense—even though I usually prefer to speak of union rather than unity.[61] Unity is not a human reality. The essence of unity is in God—it is a divino-human reality. It is the unity of the Risen Christ, whose Body is the Church. It is the unity of the Trinity, of which the Church is the image. Christ prayed that we should all be one, in the love in which he was one with the Father. His prayer, "that they may be one, even as we are one," echoes across time and draws us in, in the love of the Trinity. (John 17:11) The unity of the

61 [The Patriarch makes a distinction between union and unity, in which union is the highest goal. We have not been able to observe this distinction as it is contrary to the usage that prevails throughout the ecumenical literature, in which unity is the highest goal.]

Church remains indissolubly present in the Body of Christ and in Christ's high priestly prayer, and we know that the gates of hell can never prevail.

Professor Fundamentally, when we talk of different Churches—I mean different confessions, not different geographic locations—this is an abuse of language. Or rather it is to note only the superficial historical manifestations. In God's love and will, in Christ's prayer and presence, there can only be one Church.

Patriarch There is only one Church. That is what the Christian people need to understand, in all their different, time-bound, confessions. And we shouldn't conjure away the differences—we should place them at the heart of the Church. After all, there were great differences, even disagreements, between the apostles, and this is still the case all these centuries later. But these different approaches to the inexhaustible truth, including these contradictory approaches—when seen from a human point of view, occurred within the one Church. All was made clear, all was reconciled, in the light of the shared Eucharistic cup. Then came the time when these differences caused (or were used to justify) the breaking up of the Church into separate confessions. We have looked for unity in uniformity, whereas, in the early Church, the differences were enormous, including the theological differences. Breaking communion made these differences insurmountable. They became systematized, and, alas, dogmatized.

Now we are entering the Church's third epoch: the epoch of love, of sharing in mutual respect, of reconciliation, until the time comes that the Lord wills us to reunite in the holy cup of his Body and his most pure Blood, until the time comes when, through great love and great effort, we will admit that our differences do not bar communion, but cry out for communion, and that they will no longer keep us apart, but will be seen as complementary approaches to the truth—as was the case in the early Church. The hour has come in which, in all our complicated inheritances, love will bury all that is dead and will set free all that is living, all that converges. And then the separation itself will be seen as providential, for all the exploration and all the creative flowering that it fostered, and thus it will be seen as fully respectful of the mystery that it has itself revealed, in a purified awareness.

Professor I am very struck by what you have just said about the diversity of opinions in the period of apostolic unity. Today, some Protestant New Testament scholars use the apparent heterogeneity of the New Testament to argue that Church unity never existed. It seems to me that you would say more or less the opposite. There was extreme diversity, but within the Church. Exegetical scholarship never relieves us of our responsibility to bring Christians back together as one. As you have shown, the mystery of the Church—of which the Eucharist is the heart—fosters the richness of diversity. And therefore, if Christians are to be united, they must take note of the thousand-year experience of the undivided Church.

We know that the Bible alone cannot be the basis of unity. The first thing we encounter are the problems of biblical interpretation. But only the Holy Spirit can give us the truly nurturing and sanctifying interpretation of Scripture, through the life, experience, and holiness of the Church. We have learned that Scripture is not only revealed truth, but it is also the history of how that truth was received within the first Christian communities, through the testimony of the Apostles, in the light of Pentecost. In the Church, the center of a never-ending Pentecost, the Jesus of history and the Jesus of faith become one. Faith is knowledge of the meaning of history, knowledge of the mystery in which Jesus joins time and eternity together, knowledge that the Church receives from the Holy Spirit. It seems to me that, as an essential part of our march towards unity, Christians should share, not only the Bible but also the understanding of how the biblical truth was received in the undivided Church.

Patriarch We find a growing nostalgia for the undivided Church in many places, especially in the Catholic Church, but also among the Anglicans and in the Reformed Churches, those that are still loyal to the original intentions of the reformers. There is a nostalgia for a return to the Church of the Apostles and martyrs, the Church of the Fathers, and the Seven Ecumenical Councils. The Pope and the Archbishop of Canterbury agree on the need to again take up the living tradition of the first millennium.

ΩΩΩ

Professor In this march towards unity, what should be the role of the Orthodox?

Patriarch If Orthodoxy draws deeply on its long tradition, it can be the humble and faithful witness to the undivided Church. When the Orthodox Churches meet in mutual respect, they give the Christian world an example of brotherhood, of the free communion of sister Churches united by the same sacraments and the same faith. As for the Orthodox faith itself, this is completely centered on liturgical worship and holiness, and it brings the touchstone of spiritual experience to the ecumenical dialogue. This should allow partial truths to be released from their limited understanding, to be reconciled into a greater understanding.

But are we Orthodox worthy of Orthodoxy? Until the work that we have undertaken these past few years, what kind of example have our Churches given—united in faith and in the communion cup, but strangers, and even rivals, to each other? And what about our noble tradition, of the Fathers, St. Gregory Palamas, the *Philokalia*—do we treat this as something living and creative? If we simply repeat formulas and use them against our Christian brothers and sisters, then our inheritance becomes a dead weight. What makes us truly Orthodox is humility, sharing, and reconciliation—not just for ourselves as just one more time-bound confession, but for the union of all, as impartial witnesses to the undivided Church.

Professor If Orthodoxy can free itself of its ethnic and jurisdictional distinctions, it can bring a depth to the ecumenical encounter that is missing at present. Orthodoxy did not experience the dissociations that have ravaged Western Christianity: splitting and opposing freedom and authority, priesthood and laity, person and communion, theology and mysticism, Scripture and Tradition, prophecy and the reality of the sacraments. In addition, Orthodoxy's 'apophatic' approach to the mystery, its sense of the oneness of humanity and the cosmos, the unlimited horizons that the path to theosis, or deification, opens up for us, these can all be valuable for today's witness to Christ. The great ruptures in Western Christianity occurred when (or perhaps because) Orthodoxy was absent.

What if these ruptures could be overcome by the emerging reconciliation of the Christian East and West? The same could apply to today's worsening split between those who reduce Christianity to its social mission, and those who emphasize the mystery and holiness, but in opposition to the world. We need all the discoveries of the East and the West if we are to show that the mystery alone can light up all of life. But if Orthodoxy can help the West to overcome its dissociations, Orthodoxy needs the West to free itself of its historic divisions, to revive its thought, and to consciously and humbly bear witness to the undivided Church. The prophetic aspect of Orthodoxy is awakened through its contact with the West.

Patriarch That is why the diaspora presents Orthodoxy with an opportunity. It can become a space in which the faith of the undivided Church emerges into awareness, in a bond of friendship with the other confessions. As members of the ancient Eastern Churches, we should open our hearts and minds to all Orthodox communities, of every race and language and nation, scattered throughout the world. May they all be advocates of the one faith, of the one thing necessary, whose renewed witness to Christ will bring about the reconciliation of all Christians.

Professor Did you not once say that the twentieth century will be the century of Orthodoxy?

Patriarch Yes, but only if Orthodoxy overcomes its historical limitations, in order to serve the cause of unity. The twentieth century will be the century of a renewed Christianity!

Professor If you look at the three historic branches of Christianity—Orthodoxy, Catholicism, and Protestantism—you find that there is a complex interrelationship in which each one, when viewed in a certain light, plays a crucial role. Based on all my spiritual experience, I believe that Orthodoxy is the spiritual axis, the axis of the ultimate integration. With Rome, Orthodoxy shares the sense of the mystery of the Church. But, like the Protestants, Orthodoxy insists on the freedom of the person in the Holy Spirit. However, Orthodoxy does not oppose prophetic witness and the sacramental institution of the Church. Orthodoxy embeds prophetic witness within the sacramental Church and looks to it for purification. Because the Holy Spirit has descended on the Body of Christ.

If we look at the Churches of the Reformation, we see that, in a certain sense, they are the prophetic axis of the Church. The Reformers did not want to break the Western Church apart. They wanted to reform it. They were rejected—in the absence of the 'Orthodox' spiritual axis how could it have been otherwise?—and this opened a long historical parenthesis. This can be closed only when Rome, rediscovering its Eastern roots, is able to acknowledge and do justice to their demands, without the mystery of the Church being threatened, or dissolved. In the meantime, the Protestant Churches are a prophetic reminder of the dangers of ritual and mental sclerosis, to Rome and to the Orthodox.

And as for Rome, Rome is the axis of the historical incarnation of the Universal Church. Only Rome can prevent Protestantism from dissolving into history, and Orthodoxy from becoming fossilized outside of history. But Rome needs the spiritual axis of Orthodoxy in order to integrate the demands of the Reformation without itself becoming protestant, in the most limited sense of the word. And Orthodoxy needs Rome in order to find its incarnational space in the world.

ΩΩΩ

Patriarch We must advance towards unity: we cannot stay with the status quo. The Christian laity all want unity. If the Church hierarchy does nothing, the laity will unite without us.

Professor But then they would risk losing the mystery itself.

Patriarch Or, at least, the mystery would be put at risk. This is why the leaders of the Church must recognize the burning urgency. The raw desire for unity is growing, in lay people and in the young. I have spent many days and many years in solitary contemplation. Now I understand that the Church leaders must get personally involved. They must step down off their thrones, to say the words that are required, and to do what is required, to break down the wall of separation, and to set the Holy Spirit free, to give the Holy Spirit a greater space . . . .

Professor And you have said those words and performed those acts . . . it seems to me that things first began to move in 1959.

Patriarch Yes. Up to that point, we had been faithful participants in the ecumenical movement, in the spirit of the Patriarchal Encyclical of 1920. In 1948, we were among the founders of the World Council of Churches. And I did everything possible to encourage the Orthodox Churches to join the World Council of Churches (WCC).

Professor But the WCC was made up only of the Protestant Churches, together with most of the Orthodox Churches. If it was easy to collaborate on moral and social questions, in-depth theological dialogue remained problematic. For one very simple reason, I think. Spiritually, the various Protestant communities have no independent existence. They only exist in relation to the Western Church that they wished to reform. Orthodoxy can only act as a mediator if it encounters the whole of Western Christianity, even if this wholeness is broken apart. An in-depth dialogue with the Churches of the Reformation requires the simultaneous, and even prerequisite, in-depth dialogue with Rome.

Patriarch That is why something new began when John XXIII became Pope in 1958. From the first time he spoke, I understood that he was suffering and that he shared the same hopes as me.

Professor John XXIII was the leader of the Catholic Church, but also a spiritual father, a sort of fool-for-Christ, and, most certainly, a prophet. You also share his suffering for the world and his prophetic hope. One of the blessings of our time is that many of our leaders are men of great spiritual and personal gifts.

Patriarch I cannot speak for myself. I don't count. But John XXIII had a great prophetic gift. And he expressed it very simply, with immense goodwill and great humor.

Professor In his Christmas message of 1958, he summoned all Christians to unity—with a humble impartiality that sounded a new note. And you took him at his word, you sent him a New Year's message that seems to foretell the future. You suggested that the heads of the two Churches meet in the East, where "God revealed himself"—a symbolic designation of the Holy Land . . . .

Patriarch And I went there on pilgrimage that same year, 1959, to visit the Orthodox patriarchs of the Middle East, and to pray for Church unity, right there, where the Church began. At the Church of the Holy Sepulcher, I could feel how the divisions between Christians have torn Christ himself apart, and this tore me apart. I could hear Christ's high priestly prayer. He asks his Father to guard, as one, not only his disciples, but all those who believe as a result of their preaching. And we owe everything to the grace of Jerusalem, where God shed his blood for us, where the Holy Spirit descended on the Church of the twelve Apostles, the mother of all the Churches. Following my pilgrimage, Patriarch Alexis of Moscow also made a pilgrimage to the Holy Land, and on his return, he stopped in Constantinople and we celebrated the Christmas Liturgy together. That same year, the Archbishop of Canterbury, Geoffrey Fischer, visited the Holy Land, and he also visited me on his return journey, before he went on to meet Pope John XXIII in Rome.

Professor And so the way was cleared for the great encounter of 1964.

Patriarch When I learned that the new Pope, Paul VI, was planning to visit the Holy Land, I was stunned. If the Church of Rome, in the person of its head, was no longer in Rome, but in Jerusalem, if the Catholic Church was going to Jerusalem in all humility and repentance, then it would be possible for all the Churches to become sister Churches.

ΩΩΩ

The message that Patriarch Athenagoras sent to Pope John XXIII for New Year, 1959, deserves recognition because its powerful impact set everything in motion—he sent a similar appeal to the leaders of the other Churches. The following Christmas, the Patriarch wrote: "Since, one year ago, the Patriarchate called for the unity of all Christians on Earth, there have been continued contacts and visits between Church leaders. These contacts, and the direct and indirect communications, demonstrate that, from now on, the Churches have begun to draw nearer, as sister Churches.

ΩΩΩ

2. Two Sisters

Professor The more we understand the split between Eastern and Western Christians, the more it seems to us to be the greatest tragedy in the history of Christianity. It decisively shaped the subsequent centuries, in which the modern world emerged. Orthodoxy and Western Christianity became two closed and mutually hostile worlds. As Western consciousness took shape, it did so in ignorance of Eastern spiritual values and the Eastern emphasis on the 'wholeness' of knowledge. If on occasion the West did launch itself towards the East, its goal was not understanding, but conquest! One could say that the Orthodox world was the first victim of colonial expansionism.

The conquest of Constantinople in the year 1204,[62] and the plundering of its wealth by Italy's merchant republics, allowed the Muslim invaders to reach Vienna. As a result of these momentous events, Orthodoxy became incomprehensible to the West. Its spiritual depths were unknown, its external symbolism was the subject of caricature and suspicion.

62 ["One of the most unfortunate occasions was the sack of Constantinople in 1204, by Western warriors during the Fourth Crusade. This act included the destruction of many Greek-Orthodox shrines and the establishment of a Latin empire in the East. 'From that day on,' writes Father Alexander Schmemann, 'the separation of the Church ceased to be a quarrel of hierarchies and a theological quarrel—it entered forever the flesh and blood of the Church's people . . . "Latinism" in the East, "the Greeks" in the West became the synonyms of evil, heresy, hostility, they became words of insult'." *The Historical Path of Orthodoxy* quoted from Helen Iswolsky, *Christ in Russia*, 1960.]

Was this ignorance fundamental to the West's great dichotomy between sacramental communion and freedom in the Holy Spirit? This is the whole drama of the Reformation and the Counter-Reformation, the split between the divine and the human. This is the driving force of modern humanism, up to and including its contemporary state of exhaustion: the dissociation of nature and grace, the desert of technological mastery, the dead world. For its part, Orthodoxy also suffered from this estrangement. It became hard for Orthodoxy to express itself, and to take its place creatively in the unfolding history of the world. We can only imagine what a complementary relationship would have been like, in which all that Orthodoxy kept sacred had been imbued with, and purified by, the Western search for knowledge—the Eucharist as the kernel of freedom; the divino-human giving life to humanism; the East illumined by the divine energies revealed through the prism of scientific research.

Patriarch These are not regrets: they are our future! The restored, undivided Church that sheds light on our planetary, scientific civilization! For years now, I have been thinking of nothing else. And, since our meeting in Jerusalem, God has performed miracles for us.

It is quite normal that the ecumenical movement began with Protestants and Orthodox drawing closer together. There are no historic disputes between us. That was not the case for the Catholic Church.

Professor There is a bitter history of ecclesiastical colonialism. And, sometimes, this has been amplified by political colonialism. Consider Italy's control of the Dodecanese, which lasted until 1945. Consider how during the Second World War, there were Croats who combined their crusading Catholicism with ethnic hatred and killed tens of thousands of Orthodox Serbs, perhaps hundreds of thousands—many priests and bishops were killed.[63] Fanatical Catholic monks would arrive in the villages and offer the Orthodox the choice of Catholic baptism or death. In either case, it was death. The Yugoslav historian who chronicled these events entitled his book 'The Great Crime.' But, in and of itself, the Uniate Movement was enough to sow fear and hatred. Catholic missionaries told the Orthodox of Greece and the Balkans that the Turkish invasion was proof, divine proof of their heresy. The relentless pressure of the rulers of Austria and Poland, the pressures of Western diplomacy and the cultural influences of the 'Great Powers' in the Middle East....

63 [An estimated 700,000 deaths, based on reasonable estimates. Author's note]

And then, after the Second World War, there was a reversal of direction. In many of the Eastern European countries—Ukraine, Czechoslovakia, Romania—the Uniate churches were forcibly dissolved and their bishops imprisoned. In part this was due to a surge of patriotism that had Orthodox overtones, but mainly it was due to official policy, with the relentless arrest and deportation of anyone who resisted the dissolution of the Uniate Church. These tragic events have all left their trace. And yet . . . .

Patriarch And yet, Rome has changed and is continuing to change. There was Pope John XXIII, there was Pope Paul VI, there was the Second Vatican Council, there was the whirlwind of change after the council. It is an extraordinary change, that carries the most extreme risks and the greatest promise. The whole Orthodox world had been afraid. The whole Orthodox world had been on guard. People said, and people still say, Rome will not change, Rome cannot change, Rome only wants to defeat the Christian East. And yet Rome has changed and is continuing to change.

The Uniates, the Byzantine Catholics in union with Rome, have also changed. In Lebanon, Patriarch Maximos IV and his theologians have made their church a model of the union of Western and Eastern Christianity. At the Vatican Council, they often defended the Orthodox viewpoint. When Patriarch Maximos IV visited the Phanar in 1964, I greeted him as 'the champion of the opening of the West to the East.'

Professor At the same time, historical upheavals and tragedies have brought millions of Orthodox to the West—the Russian Revolution, the 'exchange of populations' from Asia Minor, a massive economic migration towards the West. This Orthodox diaspora, as well as the transformation of the Byzantine Catholics, has led to a sort of intermingling of the two Churches . . . . If the great religious and secular dissociations of the West stem from the original schism between Eastern and Western Christianity, then we must heal the root problem. And this means the relationship between Catholicism and Orthodoxy. And that is what you have undertaken to do.

Patriarch It is all in God's hands. St. Paul says: "The love of Christ embraces us", and this embrace brings us together. (cf. 2 Cor. 5:14) Above all, when we live this love through the mystery of the Church, and, first of all, through the Eucharist.

Professor Despite all the divisions and all the polemics, the Orthodox and the Catholics never reached the point of denying the valid-ity of the other's Eucharist, or of the priesthood that this Eucharist presumes. We may think that some dogmatic formulations prevent us from fully sharing in the divine life given to us in the Communion cup. But these differences do not concern the deep sacramental reality of the Church.

Patriarch This deep reality is what Catholics and Orthodox must together bring back to the surface. Look at the saints of the East and of the West. They are seized by the same love of Christ. They are fed by the same divine blood. In no way do they differ.

Professor In his book, *The Spiritual Meadow*, John Moschus tells us about a monk named Stephen, who lived in his monastery to a great and saintly age.[64] One day, some young monks came to his cell to ask his advice, but he paid them no attention. They said many times: "We are here, father, please tell us something, for our salvation." Finally, he heard them, and looked at them, and said: "what can I tell you? I can tell you only one thing: all the time that you were in my cell, in my mind's eye I could only see Jesus hanging on the Cross."

We find something very similar said by St. Francis of Assisi when he was ill and dying. Because of his failing eyesight, he could no longer read. Now he loved to read the Gospel. One of the friars offered to read to him. "It is not worth your while to read to me, my son," St. Francis replied, "Now I lack nothing. I know the poor and crucified Christ."

Now it is true that the West has placed more emphasis on the Man of Sorrows, while the East has emphasized the Transfiguration. But the Cross is itself the "Cross of Light," and Christ "conquered death by death." It makes me very sad to think of those fanatical Orthodox who denounce St. Francis' stigmata as a defect of his sainthood. As though he was not transfigured in and through his stigmata! Besides, in emphasizing the illumination of the whole person by the Holy Spirit, the Eastern tradition is not unaware of stigmata. The Coptic life of Abba Macarios, *Macarios the Spirit-Bearer*, tells us that one day he was visited by a fiery seraph, just as St. Francis would be. The seraph held him on the ground in the form of a cross, telling him: "You will be crucified with Christ and you will join him on the Cross, in beauty and with the perfume of virtue." This is the same perfume as that of the blood of the great Western bearers of the stigmata, up to and including our own contemporary, Padre Pio. The Man of Sorrows and the Risen Christ are one and the same. The great-

64 *Le Pré Spirituel*, Paris, Cerf, 1946, reissued 2013

est monks know that in His image they are both "*stavrophores*"—Cross-bearers—and "*pneumatophores*"—Bearers of the Spirit!

Patriarch The saints unite us, not externally but by making real the mystery of the Church. Too often, theologians deal only with the superficial. They put into words what has crystallized on the surface of history. And so, in the end, they can only express our divisions! And there is no way of adapting to their formulations. We need to dig deep into the soil of our common heritage. To begin this great reversal, this great return, required someone at the head of the Catholic Church who would be free from all of these mental schemes and legal straitjackets. And that was John XXIII. From his very first words and acts I sensed that he would be this prophet. That is why I said of him "There was a man, sent by God, whose name was John."

Professor These words have resonated ever since. They were even used by Cardinal Suenens to begin the eulogy to John XXIII that he gave at St. Peter's Cathedral, during the Vatican Council. There was a man named John XXIII but there was also Athenagoras I.

The history of their meeting is providential. When he was still Archbishop Roncalli John XXIII was the Vatican Apostolic Legate to Turkey from 1935 to 1944. In 1939, he informed the Ecumenical Patriarch of Pius XII's election as pope, by letter. After centuries of silence, this was the first step taken towards the renewal of relations between Rome and Constantinople. During his time in Turkey, John XXIII had the opportunity to review the Patriarchal Encyclical of 1920. The Catholic press of the time had greeted it with open distrust. Its impact had also been prematurely curtailed by the military occupation of Constantinople, in 1922, by militantly nationalistic Turks who opposed any international outreach by the Patriarchate. In his Christmas message of 1958, John XXIII mentioned this encyclical: "We remember vividly how, many years ago, some leaders of the Orthodox Church were concerned for the union of all civilized nations, beginning with the search for agreement between the various Christian confessions. Unfortunately, the pressure of more urgent practical concerns and nationalistic tendencies nullified this effort, which in and of itself was good and worthy of respect. And so, the agonizing problem of the broken and divided heritage of Christ's Church continues to cause problems. Our deep sadness at this tragic state of affairs will not hinder, will not delay (for this we place our trust in God) our spiritual efforts to respond to our separated brothers' and sisters' loving invitation—"for they too bear the name of Christ on their foreheads." (Rev. 22:4)

With these words, the Church of Rome had at last responded to the Church of Constantinople's invitation, issued in 1920. And you took the Pope at his word, in your New Year appeal of 1959.

Patriarch That is not all. Because he was sympathetic to the Orthodox proposal of 1920, I had told Pope John XXIII that he should summon a truly ecumenical council, of all Christians. And I think that this was his initial intention. But the time had not yet come. He went only as far as to summon a council of the whole Roman Catholic Church, in order to set the Catholic Church on the path to unity. This Second Vatican Council started a transformation, and, as Orthodox, we are also responsible for its successful outcome. I followed the proceedings of the Council very closely. Because of the role granted to observers from other confessions, at times the Council took on the mantle of a truly pan-Christian, Ecumenical Council. What is most important is that, through the deep research they undertook as part of the Council, our Catholic brothers and sisters rediscovered the Church as Eucharistic Mystery and as the Body of Love. This is a providential convergence with Orthodox ecclesiology, and this convergence opens up a fresh approach to doctrinal problems. Love becomes the criteria for our common work.

ΩΩΩ

Patriarch Faced with a Catholicism that was rediscovering its conciliar dimension, it became important for Orthodox Churches to come together. We were united in our faith and in our communion, but in practice there was little unity to be seen. And so, after consultations with the heads of the sister Churches, and with their agreement, I summoned the first Pan-Orthodox conference, at Rhodes, in 1961. This was the beginning of a process that should lead to an Orthodox Great Council, of all the Orthodox. And this also finally enabled the autocephalous Churches to grapple with real ecumenical problems.

ΩΩΩ

The Rhodes Conference of 1961 proved to be very circumspect about relations with Rome. Those churches that lived within a Catholic world made their influence felt. The Czech and Romanian Churches feared that reconciliation with Rome would lead to a surge of 'Uniatism.' This, as we have described, had been suppressed after the Second World War. Others, such as the Serbian Church, were still traumatized by the sectarian massacres that the War had precipitated. The minutes of the conference only noted "the study of the positive and negative aspects of relations between the two Churches," in preparatory work for an eventual Great Council. The minutes noted the problems caused by "propaganda, proselytism, and Uniatism." But, on the insistence of the Ecumenical Patriarch, the minutes also called for "the development of relations between the two Churches, in the spirit of Christian Love, in line with the areas outlined in the Patriarchal Encyclical of 1920." Despite these hesitations, there were many at Rhodes who acknowledged the spiritual closeness of the two Churches. There were no official Catholic observers, even though there were observers from other confessions—a fact that speaks volumes about the long history of fear and distrust. But some Catholic theologians had been personally invited and they were always seated in the place of honor. And so, discretely, contacts were made.

ΩΩΩ

In this long, slow peace process, in this slow disarmament of the Orthodox Church that had for so long been bruised and humiliated, Patriarch Athenagoras not only encountered the deep distrust by many Orthodox of Rome and its unitary structure, that appeared to be built for conquest. He also encountered the ferocious independence of the sister Churches with regard to Constantinople, and most especially, of the most powerful among them, the Russian Orthodox Church. This would show itself in the matter of Orthodox observers to the Second Vatican Council.

The Rhodes Conference had taken a unanimous position on this question. By virtue of his position as first among equals, with the rights of presiding and acting on behalf of the Church, as confirmed by the Conference, the Patriarch considered that once the invitation was received from the Vatican, he should transmit it to the sister Churches. They should respond with their proposals and he would then negotiate a common position with them. However, the Patriarchate of Moscow took the position, expressed in long and complex negotiations with the Vatican, that the invitations to each of the sister Churches should come directly from the Vatican, given their equal autocephalous status. In the end, these doubts and hesitations, notably of those of Church of Greece, led the Patriarch to decide not to send any observers, following the principle of unanimity adopted at Rhodes. However, at almost the same time it was learned that Moscow would be sending two observers. This faux pas was blamed on delays in the exchange of telegrams between Moscow and Constantinople. The Patriarch bitterly regretted the situation but never dwelled on it. Nevertheless, for the first two sessions, of the Second Vatican Council, in 1962 and 1963, the only Orthodox observers were those from the Moscow Patriarchate.

ΩΩΩ

In 1963, as the Patriarch had wished, there was more frequent contact between the Catholics and the Orthodox, and between the Orthodox Churches themselves. In July, a Catholic delegation took part in Patriarch Alexis' jubilee celebration in Moscow. In June, the celebration of the millennium of monasticism on Mt. Athos provided the opportunity for a gathering of the Orthodox Churches on a scale unseen in modern times, with Patriarch Athenagoras presiding. The Phanar had also invited many Catholic dignitaries, and, in particular, the Western monastic orders were represented. The Benedictines were represented by their Abbot Primate. You may recall that the Benedictines of Amalfi had a monastery on Mt. Athos until the thirteenth century. Other Catholic representatives included Father Dumont of the Istina Center, in Paris, and Dom Olivier Rousseau, from the dual-rite monastery of Chevetogne, who were both important pioneers in the ecumenical movement. Speaking to the assembly, Patriarch Athenagoras pointed to the example that the spiritual courage and humility of the great monastics offered to the gathered builders of Church unity.

Patriarch I sought to explain my ecumenical outreach to the monks of Mt. Athos, who were ferocious defenders of Orthodoxy. I met alone with the assembled monks. They had been told that I was going to sell off Orthodoxy to the Catholics and the Protestants. In the Middle Ages, at the time of the Latin domination of the Holy Land, and later when the Byzantine emperors sought union with Rome in order to secure Western assistance against the Turks, the monks of Mt. Athos had borne unyielding witness to Orthodoxy, to the point of martyrdom. I wanted to explain myself to these monks, who have preserved a sacred patrimony in this sacred place, the treasure of Orthodoxy, and the whole Christian world. We talked for more than two hours. And in the end, they gave their approval. Subsequently, some fanatics in the Greek Church have stirred things up again, but at that moment of great mutual honesty, they understood me. I have the record of these discussions as lasting proof.

Professor No doubt, it is essential that we have this pillar of prayer at the center of the Church, this place where the ultimate meaning of Christianity is safeguarded—the deification of man that will hasten the coming of Christ. A place in which the demons are not 'demythologized' but are pitilessly combatted. But could it not also be a sign of decadence that the depths of fervor correspond to a narrowness of vision? Should not Orthodoxy overcome this endless oscillation between deep fervor that hints of aggression and the opening to the world that hints of humanitarian platitudes? Perhaps there are some on Athos who are beginning to understand this. They should remember that at certain critically profound spiritual moments, Mt. Athos did not hesitate to look towards Western spirituality and to adopt its creative lessons. In the fourteenth century, St. Gregory Palamas invoked the words of St. Benedict, who, "saw the whole universe like a grain of dust taken up in a ray of divine light."[65] And if someone were to reply that St. Benedict's vision belongs to the time of the undivided Church, I would point them to St. Nicodemus the Hagiorite, the compiler of the *Philokalia*, who also translated contemporary Catholic spirituality, from the *Spiritual Exercises* of St. Ignatius Loyola, to the *Spiritual Combat* of Dom Lorenzo Scupoli.

Patriarch This brings us back to the role of the monk. Theirs is not speculative theology. Their very existence is an expression of the central mystery of the Church: the experience of the Resurrection in the Risen Christ.

ΩΩΩ

In September 1963, the Christian West also wanted to pay homage to Mt. Athos. A Congress on the Millennium of Mount Athos was held in Venice under the patronage of Cardinal Urbani. Patriarch Athenagoras was represented by Father André Scrima, who brought the Patriarch's greetings and blessing to the Congress.

Father André Scrima, soon to be named Patriarch Athenagoras' personal representative to the Second Vatican Council, was one of the few people during these critical years who understood and promoted Athenagoras' vision. A young, highly educated Romanian intellectual, well-versed in science as well as philosophy, André Scrima had been part of

65 Gregory the Great, *Life of St. Benedict*, Dialogue 37

the hesychast renaissance in Romania after the Second World War—a silent deepening of faith in face of a historical disruption. As a young monk, he quite unexpectedly became the guardian of the spiritual heritage of one of the last representatives of the Optina Monastery, Father Ivan Kulighin.

He was close to the Patriarch of Romania, and at an official reception he met the Vice-President of India, who was struck by Scrima's knowledge of Hindu spirituality, and invited him to come to the University of Benares to teach for two years. On returning from India, Father André Scrima brought the hesychast heritage to a newly founded monastery in Deir-el-Harf, near Beirut, Lebanon. Soon thereafter he entered into the service of Patriarch Athenagoras. He spent many years in Paris, which gave him the opportunity to foster 'an ecumenism of contemplatives,' which silently made a powerful contribution to the reconciliation of Orthodox and Catholics—how many illustrious names were associated with this effort![66] But this forms part of an intangible history that we must leave to ripen in silence. May Father André Scrima forgive my indiscretion. In his person, the treasures of the Orthodox spiritual tradition were harnessed to support the work of the Patriarch.

ΩΩΩ

3. Jerusalem

At the second session of the Vatican Council, in Autumn 1963, there was a still tentative surge of interest in 'Eastern' theological thinking. There was an attempt to locate the legal and institutional reality of the Church within the mystery, and to define the mutually interdependent relationship of the bishops and the papacy. In his speech to the members of the Curia, Pope Paul VI announced fundamental reforms in the central administration of the Church. On December 4, there came the unexpected announcement that Paul VI would make a pilgrimage to the Holy Land.

Patriarch I was stunned by this news. The Pope of Rome would leave Rome and humbly go on pilgrimage to Jerusalem! To the land sanctified by the blood of Christ, to the place where the Spirit first descended on the Church of the Apostles. To the land where, between the empty tomb and Mount of Olives, the place of the Ascension, one can feel all the power of

66 [See *Dialogue Oecumenique*, Paris, Editions Fleurus, 1963]

the Resurrection, so that the earthly Jerusalem becomes the symbol of the New Jerusalem that we are waiting for . . . .

Professor That we are preparing, that we already experience in a moment of joy.

Patriarch Jerusalem, the mother of us all. (Gal. 4:26)

Professor The archetype of the Church is the community of the twelve apostles in Jerusalem, before they were scattered. There is Peter in the midst of the others, as the leader of this apostolic circle, this Eucharistic community, this sharing of life and, even, property. (Acts 2:12–26) It is true that Jerusalem would soon lose its unique position and its primacy. Now it is the celestial Jerusalem that descends towards us in the Eucharist, no matter where it is celebrated. When, in a gesture that fulfilled an Old Testament prophesy, Paul brought the offering of the gentiles to Jerusalem, Jerusalem was only one prestigious community among many, in the ever-increasing network of local churches. (Acts 11:27–30) When the Romans captured Jerusalem and destroyed the Temple in 70 A.D., the Christian community was scattered.

In the understanding of the early Church, the collapse of Judeo-Christianity was a sign that the presence of God had been revealed to all the earth, in the form of Christ's sacramental humanity. When the Patriarchate of Jerusalem was reestablished in the fifth century, it was a modest, local church that held the fifth rank in the 'Pentarchy', after Rome, Constantinople, Antioch, and Alexandria. And yet, there is a mystery of place, just as there is a mystery of history. In Jerusalem, the empty tomb is witness to the fact that history is no longer a closed circle, that history has been visited by eternity, lighting a fire that in the end will transfigure time. This is the fire that, they say, spontaneously lights the Patriarch's candle on the night of Pascha. What a symbol! No matter its material reality! In Jerusalem, the beginning and the end of the Church are mysteriously woven together: the *arche* and the *telos* of the Church, that is the universe on the path to transfiguration.

Patriarch This is why the pilgrimage to Jerusalem is so important for Christians. It has become a tradition for the Orthodox. It is the pilgrimage, par excellence. In the early years, pilgrims brought the festal liturgies back from Jerusalem, that had been commemorated in the exact spot where the events commemorated had taken place.

Professor How moving it is to see these Eastern pilgrims, so often simple folk from the villages, old people who have saved up all their lives for this journey. The Western pilgrims—though one should not generalize or confuse them with tourists—tend to be educated people, interested in archaeology, looking for the scientific 'proof' of the Incarnation. Those from the East don't ask questions: it is sufficient to see and touch in adoration.

Patriarch How else should it be? Adoration opens the way for the Holy Spirit to let us understand the Incarnation. Patience and adoration were what brought me to Jerusalem in 1959. Most Orthodox patriarchs will make this pilgrimage for themselves and for their people. The whole history of the Church is one long pilgrimage towards the New Jerusalem. And when the pastors of the Church bow down in worship, prostrate themselves, in Jerusalem, they bear witness to the one true Pastor who is Christ. Patriarch Alexis of Moscow has twice come to Jerusalem.

Professor I remember an extraordinary photograph that I saw in a church in Belgrade, in the early 1960s. It showed the Serbian Patriarch carrying a heavy cross, on his pilgrimage to the Holy Land.

Patriarch To walk where Jesus walked, to understand His suffering with all your being, to understand His love, to throw yourself at His feet in gratitude and repentance: that is how, believe me, Pope Paul VI made this pilgrimage. And please understand my astonishment on that day, December 4, 1963. Centered again in Jerusalem, the Catholic Church rediscovered itself in pilgrimage, plunging itself once more wholly into the mystery of Christ. With a great exhalation of freedom everything was set in motion. The Pope is no longer alone: now he has companions on the same road.

And two days later, I proposed that the leaders of all the Churches of the East and the West meet in the Holy Land, following Pope Paul's example. I was at Istanbul's Church of St. Nicholas, for the saint's feast day. I told people about the Pope's pilgrimage. I said that it was a divinely inspired decision. And I suggested that all the leaders of the Christian Churches should meet in Jerusalem—not for discussions, but to pray. "To ask, on our knees, with tears in our eyes, in the spirit of unity, on the hill of Golgotha that was watered by the blood of Christ, in front of Christ's tomb from which flow reconciliation and repentance, that the path to the complete re-establishment of Christian unity may be opened, for the glory of Christ's holy name and for the good of all humankind."

Perhaps a miracle would happen. You should always expect the miracle.

But rather quickly, after an exchange of telegrams with the Vatican, it became clear that this project could not be realized yet. People in Rome who considered themselves 'in the know' said that no meeting could occur. However, in December Cardinal Bea sent Father Duprey to let me know that the Pope had agreed to meet me in Jerusalem.

Professor Have you given up on the idea of an all-Christian congress, in the spirit of the Encyclical of 1920?

Patriarch Not at all. But first the two Churches who were closest needed to meet. Their schism led to all the other splits. Their reconciliation will be for the good of all. And besides, when the Metropolitan of Thyateira[67] went to Rome to make the final adjustments to the protocol for this meeting, I had asked him to recommend that the Pope should summon a pan-Christian conference....

"It would seem," the Metropolitan said to the Pope, using an image that Athenagoras had suggested to him,

> "it would seem that you and the Patriarch are called to climb the same mountain, the mountain of our Lord. Your Holiness will climb from one side, the Ecumenical Patriarch from the other. Those who understand the significance of this bold enterprise pray that you will both meet at the summit. That you meet on the ground sanctified by our Redeemer, close to his Cross, near his empty tomb, and, from there, you will walk together to try to rebuild the shattered bridges. Perhaps, as the first bishop of the Church, Your Holiness, with the agreement of the other Patriarchs and Church leaders from the East and the West, is destined to invite representatives of all the Christian Churches to a Pan-Christian conference."

The Patriarch was accompanied by ten metropolitans and archbishops: four metropolitans from the Ecumenical Synod, the metropolitans of Crete and Rhodes, and the three exarchs of America, Great Britain, and Australia. The Patriarch and his bishops are joined in a close interdependence.

On the evening of January 5, 1964, the Pope received the Patriarch at the apostolic delegation in Jerusalem. The two men embraced on the threshold. "We embraced once, twice, and then again, and again, like two brothers meeting again after a long separation." Then there was a brief

67 [The Greek Orthodox Exarch for the British Isles]

conversation. It was scheduled for ten minutes but lasted half-an-hour. Then the two delegations were introduced. The seventeenth chapter of St. John's Gospel was read, in Greek and in Latin. Together, everyone said the Lord's Prayer. The Pope presented the Patriarch with a chalice. The Patriarch made a short speech:

> "By the grace of God, in meeting on this holy soil, sanctified by the footsteps of our Savior, we give glory to God and the Holy Trinity for bringing us here from the East and from the West, and for calling us to meet in His Holy Name . . . . We wish with all our heart . . . that this blessed meeting in person, this tight embrace of our souls, may become the prelude to a shared communion of purpose and to a more complete submission to the Will of God, that will respond to the urgent demands of today's world."

> "For centuries, the Christian world has lived in a long night of separation. Our eyes are tired out from peering through the darkness. May this meeting be the dawn of that blessed and luminous day, in which future generations, communing from the same chalice, taste the Holy Body and precious Blood of our Savior and praise and glorify Him, the one Lord and Savior of the world, in love, peace, and unity."

> "Most holy Brother-in-Christ, look how, after seeking to find each other, we have together found our Lord. And he will come and join us on our journey, as he once joined the two disciples on their way to Emmaus. He will show us the way, directing our steps toward the goal that we both hope for."

ΩΩΩ

On Monday, January 6, the Feast of the Epiphany, [the Orthodox Feast of Theophany] on his return from Bethlehem Pope Paul VI paid a visit to Patriarch Athenagoras: a reciprocal gesture that went against traditional Roman protocol.

It was a little before 10 a.m. at the Orthodox Patriarchate of Jerusalem, on the Mount of Olives. In winter, the light in the garden of pines and palm trees is very pure. The Pope replied to the Patriarch's words of the previous day: "There is an ancient Christian tradition which locates 'the center of the world' at the place where the glorious Cross of our Savior stood, from which, 'lifted up from the earth,

He draws all mankind to Himself.' (John 12:32) It is appropriate—and Providence has granted us—that we should meet in this place, in this forever blessed and sacred center, meeting as pilgrims from Rome and Constantinople in a common prayer." Whatever difficulties lie ahead, "is it not a good omen that this meeting is taking place on this soil where Christ established and shed His blood for His Church?" The points of disagreement should be examined in good time, in a spirit of "faithfulness to the truth and loving understanding." From now on, we must proceed in love. And the Pope concluded "not with an adieu but with a till we meet again, in the hope of new and productive meetings, *in nomine Domini*."

The Patriarch presented the Pope with a bishop's *engolpion*, a pectoral medallion, that portrayed the Mother of God, the All-Holy, the *Panagia*. With the help of the Patriarch, Paul VI placed this around his neck. And then many of the Orthodox present spontaneously burst out: "*Axios, Axios, Axios!*"—"He is worthy! He is worthy!"—the traditional formula for the laity's recognition and ratification of the ordination of a bishop. This time, the Pope and the Patriarch themselves read Christ's high priestly prayer, alternating verses in Greek and in Latin:

> "I do not pray that Thou shouldst take them out of the world, but that thou shouldst keep them from the evil one . . . . Sanctify them in the truth; Thy word is truth . . . . I do not pray for these only, but also for those who believe in me through their word, that they may all be one, even as Thou, Father, are in me and I in Thee so that the world may believe that Thou hast sent me." (John 17:15–21)

At the end of the following Lord's Prayer, the Orthodox stopped before the final doxology, in the traditional Roman manner. But Pope Paul VI and the assembled Catholics continued with the final doxology in its Orthodox form: "for Thine is the Kingdom, and the power, and the glory, of the Father, and of the Son, and of the Holy Spirit, now and ever, and to the ages of ages. Amen."—the invocation of the Trinity that reigns in the outpouring of its energies. Finally, Pope Paul VI and Patriarch Athenagoras together said the final blessing and once more exchanged the kiss of peace.

That same day the two men met by chance on the streets of Jerusalem and again talked for ten or so minutes . . . .

Their joint statement gave thanks for the encounter: "The two pilgrims, their eyes fixed on Christ, who, with the Father, is the author and the example of peace and unity, and pray to God that this meeting may be the sign and the prelude of things to come, for the glory of God and for the enlightenment of His faithful people . . . ."

ΩΩΩ

The cry of "*Axios*," the assent of the people of God when the Pope put on the engolpion that the Patriarch had presented him, was like a new investiture, through the Catholic spirituality of those days in which, miraculously and for a moment, the brotherhood of the Church of the twelve Apostles was restored. And so, peace realized in love could flower, and the Pope and the Patriarch could give the blessing together, in the same gesture.

For a moment . . . but the seed was sown, to yield the fruits of patience and silence, in its own time. Trust has replaced fear and mistrust. When Father André Scrima, representing the Patriarch, came to the Congress on the Millennium of Mt. Athos, Pope Paul VI had given him a coronation medal engraved with his effigy, to give to the Patriarch. The Patriarch wore this medal in Jerusalem and showed it to the Pope, telling him, "You are always with me."

ΩΩΩ

Patriarch After so many centuries, there we were, side by side, with tears in our eyes, alone in front of the same God, the same Christ, the same Virgin Mary, the same martyrs, with a profound, inexplicable, mutual feeling of trust. Two brothers had met. The Pope is a deeply compassionate man, of intense, almost painful, goodwill. I feel deeply for him. I believe in his sincerity and in his desire for unity. I love him, I esteem him greatly, I admire him. He knows this.

There is a kind of tension in him that reveals both determination and vulnerability. Later on, when I had got to know him better, I said, "They tell me that you sleep very little, that you hardly eat, that you work endlessly, that you don't have time to walk in the Vatican gardens. I am an old man, allow me to give you some advice. Sleep a little more, eat a little more, work a little less, take walks in the gardens and occasionally, despite everything, smile."

But, above all, the Pope is so alone. And we all need brothers. That is why I wanted him to accept me as a brother, a no-good brother perhaps, the least of brothers, but a brother nonetheless.

ΩΩΩ

Professor Following this double pilgrimage to Jerusalem, you commissioned an icon to commemorate the meeting, the icon of the Apostles Peter and Andrew embracing.

Patriarch St. Andrew is the patron saint of Constantinople and, perhaps, the founder of the Church there. And, more than anything else, Peter and Andrew were brothers! Andrew was the 'first-called', and he then called his brother. St. John's Gospel tells us about this event. "One of the two who had heard John the Baptist speak, and followed Jesus was Andrew, Simon Peter's brother. He first found his brother Simon and said to him "we have found the Messiah (which means Christ). He brought him to Jesus. Jesus looked at him and said, "So you are Simon the son of John? You shall be called Cephas" (which means Peter)." (John 1:40–42)

ΩΩΩ

The pictures of Pope Paul VI's pilgrimage to the Holy Land and of his meeting with Patriarch Athenagoras I were very widely distributed in the media. And the mass-market magazines brought the Patriarch's face and tall silhouette into the humblest of homes. The emblematic embrace of the Pope and the Patriarch was spread across all the continents, in photographs that sometimes took on the resonance of an icon.

4. The Lifting of the Anathemas

Patriarch The past lives on in us. That is why we must erase this bad past, or rather, allow God to erase it—because all it does is stir up mutual hatred. In the end we came to think that we no longer belonged to the same Church, or even the same religion. In the West, people went so far as to think that the Orthodox were not Christians.

And so it was necessary to cleanse the Church of its memory of this bad past, and in this way open the future to God's intentions.

The initiative came entirely from the Patriarch. On the day of Pentecost, 1965 (June 6) the Patriarch's representative in Great Britain, Metropolitan Athenagoras of Thyateira, proposed the possibility of the reciprocal lifting of anathemas, in a speech given at Westminster Abbey: "Would it be absurd to hope that the Patriarchate of Constantinople would pronounce null and void the excommunication that was imposed on the Papal Legates by Patriarch Michael Cerularius in 1054? Is it inconceivable that the Vatican, for its part, would nullify the writ of excommunication of Patriarch Michael, placed on the altar of Hagia Sophia by Cardinal Humbert? These two excommunications mark the beginning of the schism between East and West. Historically, the facts are clear. Cardinal Humbert acted precipitously and without the agreement of the Pope, who had in fact died before Humbert reached Constantinople. This fatal ill-considered act of the Pope's representative provoked the indignation of the Patriarch and all the Eastern Church and led them to excommunicate the Papal Legates. Would it not be fitting with the spirit of charity and love to annul all such acts? Such a gesture would give a powerful boast to the reconciliation of the two Churches. It would have an extraordinary effect in healing the sixth wound to Christ's body—a wound that is still open and bleeding."

Patriarch Athenagoras made the proposal to the Pope and the Pope accepted the idea. In Rome and Constantinople, study committees worked in parallel to sort out the practical details. Constantinople had already taken the first steps by forming a so-called 'major' committee, which combined members of two permanent committees: Pan-Orthodox Affairs and Pan-Christian Affairs. The Patriarch personally participated in all the work sessions, making suggestions and reviewing the historical documentation. He was especially interested in the position taken by Patriarch Peter III of Antioch.[68]

Patriarch I especially liked Patriarch Peter's letter to Michael Cerularius. I had not been aware of it before and only discovered it in this process of research that led up to the lifting of the anathemas. Patriarch Peter explains that the Latin Church was also Orthodox (for Constantinople, Rome was always Latin, because they themselves were Rum, Romans.) All the differences in custom—the unleavened bread, fasting on Saturday, beards, etc.—were not, he said, in the least bit important.

Professor He said, "leave the beards to the barbers!"

Patriarch For him, there was only one serious problem: the question of the procession of the Holy Spirit. But even so, he thought that there should be no breach of communion with Rome. Instead, the problem should be looked at in the light of communion.

I copied many parts of Patriarch Peter's letter to Patriarch Michael for the Patriarch of Antioch—of whom I am very fond.[69] I reminded him

68 [1052–1056]

69 [Patriarch Theodosius VI 1958–70]

how precious his advice is to me, just as that of his predecessor must have been to my predecessor.

ΩΩΩ

The Joint Catholic and Orthodox Committee took a while to get organized. They drafted a common statement and then they came to Istanbul, where the Joint Committee met from November 22–24 and resolved almost all the points of difficulty. The committee needed to reconcile two very different points of view. From the Catholic viewpoint, with its concern for historical and legal precision, the act of excommunication, a healing penalty, expired with the death of the excommunicated person. And therefore, nine centuries later, there could be no 'lifting of excommunication.' By contrast, the Orthodox continued to feel the effects of a continued theological and existential sickness, that was sustained by the memory of the anathemas.

Agreement was reached to "remove these acts of excommunication from the memory and midst of the memory and midst of the Church, which memory continues to this day to be an obstacle to reconciliation in love, and to sweep them into oblivion." This was the authentic way to accomplish the shared task, carried out with real concern for each other's traditions.

But any such declaration could have no canonical significance. For this reason, the Orthodox delegation proposed the draft of a tomos to be issued by the Holy Synod of Constantinople, with the hope that a similar text would be issued by the Vatican. The Catholic delegation was not authorized to make this decision. On their return to Rome, they submitted their dossier to the Pope. Pope Paul VI approved the text of the Joint Declaration and decided to issue a papal letter. December 7, the feast day of St. Ambrose, Father of both the Latin and the Greek Church, was chosen for the solemn, public announcement of the Joint Declaration.

ΩΩΩ

On Tuesday, December 7, the Patriarchal church of St. George was filled—the crowd in the narthex overflowed out onto the steps. The Patriarch was seated on his throne, with the members of the Synod on his left. He welcomed the Catholic delegation and invited Cardinal Sheehan, the head of the Catholic delegation, to sit on his right. The deacon climbed the steps of the pulpit, in the middle of the nave, high above the assembled faithful. After reading the Gospel, he solemnly read the Joint Declaration in Greek, at the same moment that Archbishop Willebrands read it in French at St. Peter's Basilica in Rome.

At the end of the Liturgy, the Patriarch himself read the Greek text of the Synodal *Tomos* in a clear, firm voice. Its introduction, which is especially beautiful, expresses Athenagoras' bold and unwavering vision:

> "In the name of the holy, consubstantial and life-giving Trinity. 'God is love:' Love should be the God-given mark of Christ's disciples. Love is the power that draws together His Church in unity; love is the principle of peace, harmony and order in the Church; the unending and dazzling manifestation of the Holy Spirit, in the Church."

He continued with a summary of the Joint Declaration, concluding with this announcement: "We have resolved to remove said anathema executed by Patriarch Cerularius and his Synod from the memory and from the midst of the Church." As the clergy left the church, the crowd burst into applause and the Catholic bishops were greeted with the cry of "*Axios, Axios, Axios*,"—they are worthy—the same shout of popular approval that had rung out in Jerusalem to greet the Pope. The Patriarch took the Cardinal's hand and together they crossed through the courtyard and the garden to climb the steps to the patriarchal offices. At the top of the steps, they turned to the crowd and embraced many times, to renewed applause. The setting may have been less grand than in Rome, but the *ex cathedra* declaration had been sealed by the *consensus ecclesiiae*, by the fervent assent of the faithful.

ΩΩΩ

In Rome, the fourth and final session of the Second Vatican Council was coming to an end. The final texts of the Constitution on Religious Liberty and the Constitution on the Relations of the Church and the World (*Gaudium et Spes*) were especially notable for the lack of any 'Orthodox' dimension. The Byzantine Catholics and the Orthodox observers had made some important amendments, but they were not able to totally transform these texts, In the end these remained a patchwork. In his articles for *La Croix*, Andrè Scrima noted that freedom is intimately linked to truth, but the link between freedom and ecclesiology had not been made clear. Likewise, *Gaudium et Spes* left no place for the transfiguring power of mystical realism. Scrima added,

> "Humankind is expanding, perhaps it is on the verge of an infinite, cosmic expansion: but we can only overcome our essential solitude through participation in the 'infinite' of God—because we can otherwise remain completely alone, while working to conquer an 'infinite' external world."

On December 7, 1965, at the last public session of the Vatican Council, the Constantinople delegation, led by Metropolitan Meliton, took its place in the nave of St. Peter's Basilica. Before Mass, and before the Council's final texts were announced, Archbishop Willebrands read the Joint Declaration. After the final texts of the council had been promulgated, Cardinal Bea read Pope Paul VI's Papal Letter, and it too began with the invocation of love. "Walk in love, as Christ loved us," (Eph. 5:2) and concluded: "The sentences of excommunication once delivered, we wish to remove their memory from the memory and from the midst of the Church as we commit these excommunications to oblivion." Metropolitan Meliton then came forward to receive the Papal Letter from the hands of the Pope. From the altar dais, he spoke a few words that captured the significance of this event:

> "He who is and who was and who is to come," (Rev. 1:4) the Lord of History who is beyond history and has remitted history, who will come again in glory to sum up and complete all of history, has considered us worthy to take part in this sacred moment. We can inform you and the holy council called together with you, that at this very moment your brother, Patriarch Athenagoras, acting in the same spirit, has removed from the memory and the midst of the Church the sentences of excommunication uttered by Patriarch Michael Cerularius in the year 1054. In the spirit of Pan-Orthodox love and peace as expressed at the Third Pan-Orthodox Conference at Rhodes, the Patriarch has issued his declaration from the throne that was once that of St. John Chrysostom, Father of the undivided Church, at the conclusion of the Liturgy that we celebrate bearing his name, in which the gifts were lifted up to Jesus, our shared Redeemer and Lord, served in honor and memory of our Holy Father Ambrose, your predecessor as Bishop of Milan."[70]

70 [Pope Paul VI had been named Archbishop of Milan in 1954]

> "These two apostolic seats of Old and New Rome, whose judgments known to the Lord bound up the past, have unbound the present and opened a new future, voiding by their common declaration and their reciprocal act the anathemas once issued, the symbol of schism, and raising up in their place, love, the symbol of their being found."
>
> "While there remain differences in doctrine, canon law and liturgical practice, and while we have not yet attained full communion, the fundamental prerequisite for the step-by-step resolution of differences, which is brotherly love, is nonetheless officially and ecclesiastically, proclaimed between the first bishops of the East and the West . . . ."

Metropolitan Meliton then gave Pope Paul VI the kiss of peace. There was a loud applause, the loudest applause, some said, that had been heard at any time during the Second Vatican Council.

ΩΩΩ

Because of the autocephalous status of the Orthodox Churches, the lifting of the anathemas strictly concerned only the Church of Constantinople, among the Eastern Churches. But it was also the Church of Constantinople that alone had taken part in the critical event of 1054, historically circumscribed but of great symbolic import. The Patriarch had given advance notice of the Joint Declaration to the heads of the sister Churches, and they had welcomed his proposals and shared in the joyous celebration of their announcement.[71] Archbishop Nikodim, Chair of the Department of External Relations for the Moscow Patriarchate, had come to Rome for the final session of the Second Vatican Council. He had a long meeting with Metropolitan Meliton, in which he declared that the lifting of anathemas was a positive gesture that would further enhance relations between the Catholic Church and the Orthodox Church as a whole.

Besides, the Joint Declaration, the Synodal *Tomos*, and Metropolitan Meliton's address in St. Peter's all clearly demarcated the limits of this historic event. Constantinople had no intention of overstepping its historic role, which had been reaffirmed by the Pan-Orthodox Conferences in Rhodes. Both the Ecumenical Patriarch and the Pope were

71 [With the exception of the Russian Church Abroad and the monks of Mt. Athos, who expressed their disapproval by excommunicating Patriarch Athenagoras]

greatly concerned to nurture the newly established dialogue and common understanding of the sister Orthodox Churches.

ΩΩΩ

The discovery of the unity of the Orthodox Churches, based on Orthodox canonical tradition, marks one of the most important aspects of Rome's new attitude towards the East. For centuries, Rome had considered the Churches of Eastern Europe and the Middle East as no more than a cluster of weak and exotic 'Oriental Churches,' Chalcedonian or non-Chalcedonian, that one by one, fragment by fragment, should be drawn into the Catholic sphere, retaining their external rituals while 'latinizing' their soul. Henceforth, Rome would respect the otherness of the Eastern Churches, as seen in the light of their own self-definition. Despite some ambiguities in the work of the Second Vatican Council, and unresolved disagreements between the Secretariat for Christian Unity and the Congregation for Eastern Churches, the Joint Declaration definitively marked the Catholic recognition of Orthodoxy.

Professor The fifth paragraph of the Joint Declaration reads as follows: "Pope Paul VI and Patriarch Athenagoras I, together with his Synod, realize that this gesture of justice and mutual pardon is not sufficient to end the old and the more recent differences between the Roman Catholic Church and the Orthodox Church . . . ." Does that mean that the lifting of the anathemas is simply a step—a step that nevertheless is huge—in the "dialogue of love"? I have the impression that the climate has changed; that the miraculous, emblematic gesture of Jerusalem continues to yield fruit—the fruits of trust and peace. But isn't there something else, something else that the theologians and specialists in canon law fail to see because they are trapped in the conceptual framework and sociological structure of their Churches?

Patriarch Yes, there is something else. Active love, inspired by the Spirit of Christ, is always filled with a renewed theology. I only realized the full implications of the lifting of the anathemas after the fact. It seemed to me that the Holy Spirit had guided our thoughts, and our pens, far beyond the limits of our human abilities, far further than we could have hoped, beyond even the limits of love, towards a new, creative theological horizon. The lifting of the anathemas was the supreme product of a new approach to unity. First of all, it was the result of a dialogue that was consistently conducted on an equal footing, between partners. The dialogue itself was an expression of brotherhood. And then, the Joint Declaration clearly defines the profound implications of the theological research that we must jointly undertake. We have to express, or rather allow the expression of, the mystery of the undivided Church, that has continued to burn in the depths of the two sister Churches. Here, repentance and glorification will come together, step by step, to establish unity in diversity, to make the undivided Church a reality that loses none of the rich experience of the two Churches during their time of separation.

Professor You only have to pay attention to the words of the Joint Declaration:

> "Through the action of the Holy Spirit, these differences will be overcome through cleansing of hearts, through regret for historical wrongs, and through an *efficacious determination to arrive at a common understanding and expression of the faith of the Apostles and its demands*."[72]

And the Joint Declaration ends with an invitation to dialogue that will lead the two Churches to live together again

> "*in that full communion of faith, fraternal accord and sacramental life which existed among them during the first thousand years of the life of the Church.*"

Here the common criterion is made clear: the ecclesiology of the first millennium. This opens up the possibility of regaining unity not by way of sociological restructuring or conceptual readjustment—the way to which is blocked—but by first creatively rediscovering the living pulse of the undivided Church, in all the diversity of its traditions.

ΩΩΩ

5. From the New Rome to the Old Rome

After the lifting of the anathemas, the language of Athenagoras' messages became more daring, becoming an almost poetic outpouring of praise. This is how his 1965 Christmas message ended:

> "Rejoice, you prophets who have clearly heralded the Prince of Peace and Justice,

72 [Author's italics]

> Rejoice, you apostles, who have brought the world the gospel of good will,
> Rejoice, you saints, who have made Christianity the true science of life,
> Rejoice, you holy and venerable brothers and patriarchs of today, Church leaders, bishops, spiritual guides, theologians, Holy Mount Athos and all other monastic orders, writers of the living word, the fullness of the Christian world, and all you dear companions of many years, traveling on this road to reconciliation,
> Rejoice, most holy and venerable brother of Old Rome, for the treasure that we exchanged in a single moment, the treasure that had been conferred to each of us, each to the other in an exchange of pure reciprocity and love, at the cave in Bethlehem, two years ago . . . ."

His joy is the basis of a profound meditation on the meaning of the "new and constructive horizons" opened up by the lifting of the anathemas. On the anniversary of this event, the Patriarch stated:

> "From this day forward, in accordance with the Pan-Orthodox understanding of the unity of the Church, rooted in love, peace and our obedience to the will of our Savior that we all shall be one, we declare that we too, in all humility, are servants of the truth of the undivided Church, and are always ready to carry forward the work accomplished by the Joint Declaration of December 7, 1965, in new ecclesiastical acts of love, giving free rein to the power of the Holy Spirit."

This statement reveals Orthodoxy's ecumenical role with great depth and clarity. Orthodoxy is not one confession among all the others. It bears humble witness to the undivided Church, a witness that makes itself known, not by way of a return to the past, but by opening up space for the free reign of the Holy Spirit. In his Christmas messages of 1966 and 1967, the Patriarch placed a raw and prophetic emphasis on the demands of history: the poverty of the developing world, the spiritual emptiness of consumer society, the problem posed by the ultimate limits of scientific advances. He saw a world threatened by extinction, if only in the form of a prolonged spiritual extinction. And he concluded, tirelessly: "This is why our two Churches, the

Roman Catholic Church of the West and the Orthodox Church of the East bear a huge burden of responsibility and must advance courageously towards unity." [73]

ΩΩΩ

It was Pope Paul VI who took the first step. He unexpectedly announced that he would come to Istanbul in July 1967.

ΩΩΩ

Patriarch Yes, our God is the God of wonders. I would never have dared to hope for what the Pope decided to do. This was such a living, spontaneous act, of such humble and brotherly love. I had to reread the Pope's letter three times to convince myself that I was not dreaming. This act was characteristic of the Pope's spiritual grandeur. It was an unprecedented act of Christian courage. And it bore fruit in so many more ways than tomes and tomes of theological debate. The complete simplicity and good will with which our older brother, the Bishop of Rome, came to meet us was deeply moving to all of us. Ever since we have lived with the memory of the spiritual blessings that this great religious leader left in us and in these holy places. Every time I enter St. George's Church, I recall the image of our praying together in front of the altar.

ΩΩΩ

The Pope and the Patriarch's meeting in Istanbul, and the Pope's pilgrimage to the sites of the first Ecumenical Councils and the seven churches of the Book of Revelation, were full of profound symbolic meaning and a sacred momentum, that still carries us and transcends us. Such also were the meeting in Jerusalem and the Patriarch's pilgrimage to the Holy Land.

The history of the Church is recapitulated in an arc that reaches from Jerusalem to Istanbul. The Pope seemed acutely aware that it was here in Asia Minor, up and down the Bosphorus, that the mysteries of the Incarnation and the Trinity had been reverently and rigorously put into words. It was in Constantinople at the Second Ecumenical Council that "our Fathers in the faith met to confess, with one heart, the Holy Trinity, undivided and of one essence." Previously, in Nicea, the 'City of Victory,' on the eastern bank of the Bosphorus, the Church had proclaimed that

73 [Message of December 7, 1966]

the Father and the Son were of one essence, while being separate Persons, the whole paradox of the person and of love. Later, in a miraculous convergence of East and West at Chalcedon, a suburb on the Asian side of the Bosphorus, the Fourth Ecumenical Council had proclaimed the union "without confusion or separation" of God and man in the one Person of the Word.

A little further south, on the Aegean coast of modern-day Turkey, we find the ruins of Ephesus. The Pope came there on July 26, 1967. This was where the Third Ecumenical Council, reaffirming that God Himself was born in the flesh, confirmed that Mary was the Theotokos, "the Mother of God," to the loud applause of the people of the city.

In his Papal audience at Castel Gandolfo on August 2, the Pope reiterated the lessons of the first Ecumenical Councils:

> "They authoritatively laid down the fundamental dogmas of our faith, on the Holy Trinity, on the Incarnation of Jesus Christ, and on the Virgin Mary. They laid down the foundations of Christian belief. They engaged human thought in the exploration of the meaning and the theological reality of the truth revealed in the Gospels, just as the apostles had done. They gave religious language its first immutable and unequivocal expression . . . ."

In these matters, the Pope continued,

> "the East is our master, because it teaches us that the believer is called to reflect on the revealed truth . . . . By our visit to the East, we have wanted to assure people that the faith of the Ecumenical Councils in that blessed land provides a solid and broad foundation for the studies that must be undertaken to achieve perfect Christian communion between the Catholic Church and the Orthodox Church."

The places visited by the Pope summoned up the memory of the Churches founded by the apostles, where both St. Paul and St. John the Evangelist are commemorated. Before the exchange of populations in 1922, Asia Minor was the home of the seven churches of the Apocalypse—Ephesus, Smyrna, Pergamon, Thyateira, Sardes, Philadelphia, Laodicea. In Ephesus, where the Isle of Patmos can be seen on the horizon, St. John's influence remained strong. The letters to the seven churches that open the Book of Revelation convey a whole ecclesiology: an ecclesiology of diversity. Each local church constitutes the whole Church, and the communion of all the churches is given directly by the Risen Christ, who holds in his right hand the seven stars that are the angels of the seven churches. (Rev. 1:12-20) This is an ecclesiology of penitence, because unfaithfulness corrupts and the Spirit calls us to repentance: He who has an ear, let him hear what the Spirit says to the churches. (Rev. 2:29)

By his symbolic acts, Pope Paul VI completed the first steps of repentance taken by Cardinal Bea. The Pope knelt in prayer at the ancient site of the altar of Hagia Sophia, having first asked permission of the Turkish official who was escorting him. This was an act of courage, especially as the other message that he wished to send by his visit was one of friendly collaboration with the Turkish people, the majority of whom are Muslim. And, in fact, the Turkish press protested, and nationalistic students came to Hagia Sophia to kneel in prayer to Allah. But the fact remains that, at the place where the Papal legates laid down their anathemas, lies and curses, the Pope himself knelt in prayer. And, contrary to what so many of our contemporaries believe—sadly this includes so many Christians—nothing has more impact than prayer.

This personal act was completed in an act of liturgical brotherhood, initiated by the Patriarch. In St. George's Church on the morning of July 25, the Pope was named in the diptychs, the commemoration of fellow patriarchs, for the first time in nine centuries. "For His Holiness the Pope of Rome and for our Archbishop Athenagoras, that they may always follow the way of good works." This joint commemoration was repeated in Rome the following October. The Pope was again acknowledged in the Polychronion, the singing of "Many Years" at the conclusion of the Liturgy. The Patriarch presented the Pope with an omophorion embroidered with the image of the twelve apostles. And the people acclaimed "*Axios! Axios! Axios!*" In Jerusalem, in 1963, there had been only a few such voices. Here, in Istanbul, it was a unanimous outcry. One Orthodox attendee said to the Patriarch that evening: "You have given the Pope back to the Church." At the afternoon service held at the Catholic Cathedral of the Holy Spirit, the solemn exchange of words, and the Pope's presentation of the 'Charter of Unity' to the Patriarch, stating the "resolute desire" of the Catholic Church to "hasten the day when full communion will be reestablished between the Western and the Eastern Church, a first step in bringing about the unity of all Christians," marked the clear progress of the theological dialogue, the attempt to express what is at the heart of what the two Churches hold in common.

In this encounter, the most important step forward was the Pope's explicit recognition of the ecclesiology of communion. This was expressed in theological language that might well be described as 'Orthodox', because its fundamental concepts are the Eucharistic community and the sister Church. "The mystery of divine love is at work in each local Church," the Pope said. "Is this not why we have the beautiful, traditional custom by which the local Churches were called sister Churches?" And, speaking at St. George's Church on the duty of Church leaders, the Pope said: "They should grant each other mutual respect and recognition, as pastors of that part of Christ's flock with which they have been entrusted." The Pope had already used this formulation in a letter to Patriarch Alexis of Moscow which conveyed his wishes for "that part of Christ's flock that is entrusted to you." Pope John XXIII had appeared on the world stage as the Bishop of Rome. Pope Paul VI now revealed himself as the Patriarch of the West. Rather than diminishing his role of primacy, this restored his primacy to its essence, as Patriarch Athenagoras stated more explicitly: "And so, despite all human expectations, we see the Bishop of Rome in our midst, the first in honor among the bishops, the one who presides in love."[74] This was an invitation to Catholics and Orthodox to reconsider the question of papal primacy from the viewpoint of the undivided Church.

ΩΩΩ

In the course of this journey, Pope Paul sent telegrams to the heads of all the Orthodox Churches, and what he said in Ephesus was explicitly addressed to them: "This pilgrimage to the cities that were blessed by the apostles' preaching and by the labors of the Church Fathers, has allowed us, despite the real differences that have separated us, to better understand the profound unity of the faith that we hold in common, as preached by the pastors and the doctors of the Church. We exchanged the kiss of peace with His Holiness the Ecumenical Patriarch, and we would like to express our esteem and our fraternal love for you also, dear brothers in Christ. With full respect for the legitimacy of your traditions and usages, we wish to declare our desire to move forward in dialogue, in truth and in love. Through the intercessions of the Church Fathers, may

74 St. Ignatius, *Epistle to the Romans*, Prologue

the successors of the apostles bring about the coming of the longed-for day, in which we shall all be united in the celebration of the Eucharist of our Lord.

The 'Charter of Unity' that Paul VI presented to Patriarch Athenagoras stated the resolute intent of the Catholic Church to hasten this day.

[In return, the Patriarch decided to visit Rome that same year, after visiting the Orthodox Churches of Serbia and Romania. With certain reservations, the Patriarchs of Serbia and Romania approved Athenagoras' proposed meeting with the Pope in Rome. In Rome, Paul VI and Athenagoras I would achieve the impossible, in succeeding in reassuring the doubters and establishing a path to future solutions, with words and gestures that witnessed to a profound transformation in the Catholic Church. But first, homage was paid to Pope John XXIII.][75]

In March 1926, Monsignor Roncalli, who was then Apostolic Visitor to Bulgaria, visited Ecumenical Patriarch Basil III. Despite his old age, the Patriarch declared himself ready to come to Rome, to ask the Pope to convene a council to study the question of Church reunion. It took forty years, and the election of Monsignor Roncalli as Pope John XXIII, to break down the immovable walls. It took all of Athenagoras' patience and his belief in the possibility of a miracle to bring about this event, his pilgrimage to Rome. That is why, on October 27, 1967, the Patriarch prayed for a long time at the tomb of John XXIII, and then, to honor his life of service and his sacrificial death, he left three gold grains, inscribed as follows: "Unless a grain of wheat falls into the earth and dies, it remains alone; but if it dies, it bears much fruit." (John 12:24)

ΩΩΩ

Athenagoras' pilgrimage to Rome allowed the Patriarch to fully reintegrate the mystery and the glory of Rome into the undivided Church. As we have seen, the unity of the undivided Church was the vast living communion of sister Churches. But certain of these Churches had greater prestige, and their 'reception,' or conversely their refusal to 'receive' a doctrine, served as a guide to the universal Church, and made them the guardians of the faith. This was not in any way a legal authority, but rather a spiritual influence to which the councils had given canonical form, in particular, the right of appeal. After the destruction of Jerusalem, Rome rapidly became the most prestigious Church. Seated in the world's capi-

75 [This summarizes pp. 413–415 of the French text]

tal, symbol of the Church's mission carried to the heart of this world, in which Caesar commanded that he be worshiped, in which the Church's espousal of Christ was sealed with the blood of martyrs. The Church of Rome was, as St. Irenaeus wrote in the second century, "the Great Church established by the apostles Peter and Paul and sanctified by the blood of their martyrdom."

As Theodoret of Cyrus wrote to Pope Leo the Great: "In her keeping too are the tombs that give light to the souls of the faithful, those of our common fathers and teachers of the truth, Peter and Paul."[76]

Through his words and deeds, Athenagoras sought to underline the Christian grandeur of Rome. "At this holy moment, we can hear the cry of the blood of Peter and Paul and the martyrs in the Coliseum," the Patriarch declaimed at St. Peter's Basilica, recognizing the Church of Rome as the final resting place of our founding apostles Peter and Paul. On the morning of October 26, the Patriarch prayed at the tomb of St. Peter, and that same afternoon he made a pilgrimage to the Basilica of St. Paul-Outside-the-Walls, where he lit a votive candle next to the apostle's tomb. The following day he made his pilgrimage to the Papal Basilica of St. John Lateran, dedicated to St John the Evangelist and St. John the Baptist, and the Papal Basilica of Sancta Maria Maggiore, dedicated to the Virgin Mary. The Patriarch was very struck by their mosaics, the direct antecedents of those developed later in Byzantium. At the Coliseum, the Patriarch chanted the troparion for the martyrs, whose souls were "wounded with divine love." Finally, on the morning of October 28, the Patriarch visited the third century Greek Chapel at the Catacomb of St. Priscilla.

It is important that it was the Orthodox Patriarch who so solemnly recalled the equal dignity, and the inseparable roles, of the apostles Peter and Paul in early Christian Rome. Because the whole subsequent history of the Christian West is overshadowed by their separation: the Bishop of Rome claiming the heritage of St. Peter, and the Churches of the Reformation proclaiming St. Paul's radical conversion and the power of his preaching.

ΩΩΩ

Coming as it did after the Second Vatican Council and coinciding with the first meeting of the Catholic Synod of Bishops, Athenagoras' meeting

---

76 Theodoret of Cyr, Letter 113, *Nicene and Post-Nicene Fathers*, Second Series, Vol. 3, Buffalo, NY: Christian Literature Publishing Co., 1892.

in Rome gave Orthodoxy a catalytic role in the sought-for restoration of Rome to its place of primacy in the reunited Church, in the tradition of the undivided Church.

While stressing that the unity of the two Churches is already accomplished in Jesus Christ, "who is the head of the Church," (Col. 1:18) the Patriarch drew attention to the importance of the "true Bishop of Rome, bearer of apostolic grace, successor to the constellation of wise and holy men, who have distinguished this throne, that is the first in honor and rank in the body of the Christian Churches throughout the world, whose holiness, wisdom and spiritual struggles are the lasting inheritance and treasure of the whole Christian world." The Patriarch placed the Pope at the center of the Eucharistic community, not above it: "We greet Your Holiness, the Holy Synod assembled around you, the hierarchs of the Church throughout the world, the religious orders, and all the beloved people of the Holy Roman Catholic Church."

Pope Paul VI took up this Eucharistic vision, giving thanks for: "the profound joy of being here together, in the midst of our brother bishops, at the tomb of Peter, the chief of the apostles, the glory of our Church of Rome, whose people surround us in their fervor, taking part in our prayer and spiritual joy." Here the Pope evoked the presence of the apostle Peter, using the language of the early Church. The apostle's memory is sanctified and glorified by his relics, in the place of his martyrdom. And the Pope is only the "first in honor" when he is "together" with the other patriarchs, in the midst of his brother bishops, "surrounded" by his people, who "take part" in his prayer and his joy.

What is more, in defining Rome's role the Pope repeated St. Ignatius of Antioch's words that the Patriarch had used at their meeting in Istanbul. "The Synod of Bishops," the Pope said, "ensures, in a new form, the fuller cooperation of the local Churches and the Church of Rome, which presides in love." The full meaning of primacy only becomes clear with the rediscovery of brotherhood, as was also made clear by Rome's rediscovery of its patriarchal role. In the Patriarch's letter of October 6, in which he informed the Pope of his desire to come to Rome in the nearest future, he had addressed the Pope not only as 'Bishop of Rome,' but also as the 'Patriarch of the West.' At St. Peter's Basilica, the pinnacle of all churches in ceremonial honor, the two patriarchs sat enthroned on the same platform, completely equal in dignity.

Pope Paul VI honored the assembled patriarchs of the Orthodox Church by inviting them into the circle of Cardinals, the quintessential heart of the Roman Church. Meanwhile, it was the head of the College of Cardinals who was charged with opening the door of the Patriarch's car each time he arrived or left.

In their joint declaration, the Pope and the Patriarch rejoiced that "their Churches have found each other again, as sister Churches." As a model of how the Churches should relate to one another, the Pope gave the example of St. Peter's letter to the Churches of Pontus, Galatia, Cappodocia, Asia and Bithynia, which were here represented by the Ecumenical Patriarch. (cf. 1 Peter 1:1) Together with its teaching and its exhortations, St. Peter's letter brought the greetings of the Church of Rome. (1 Peter 5:13) This may be taken as the first example of a fruitful relationship that developed over the succeeding centuries – not that the relationship was without clashes and misunderstandings. In this way the early Church was guided towards a productive new way of relating—not without tensions—in which Rome, itself a local Church, does not give orders but instead is the source of teaching and exhortation. Once again, we should give the final word to the Patriarch, who, in the perspective of ultimate Church unity, spoke of the Pope as "our older brother."

ΩΩΩ

As was his custom, the Patriarch was accompanied by four members of his Synod. The Pope had specifically wanted his meeting with the Patriarch to take place in the presence of the Synod of Bishops of the Catholic Church, who were meeting for the first time. This would demonstrate to the Orthodox that the "ancient institution of the Synod," which the Orthodox hold in great honor, was being restored to the Western Church. In this way the meeting of the two Churches in Rome took on a collegial character. All the bishops of the Roman Synod took part in the Mass for Peace and Forgiveness, served at St. Peter's on October 26. That same evening the Patriarch was the official guest of the assembled Synod of Bishops, meeting in session. The Patriarch spoke of the "intense feelings of brotherhood" that he felt, "not just a passing, emotional response, but deeply, in the Holy Spirit. He praised the "pearl without price of the apostolic succession, transmitted without interruption by the laying on of hands," and he concluded with his hope for the great and holy moment in which the bishops of the East and the West will celebrate the Eucharist together, around the same altar, raising the one Eucharistic chalice.

Here the Patriarch expressed his vision of a truly ecumenical council that perhaps was the only way to remedy some of the unilaterally proclaimed dogmas that had been proclaimed since the time of separation, that acted as barriers between the two Churches.

The reaction of the people gave an added dimension to the reality of the Synod. "What impressed me most in Rome was the warm and positive reaction of the faithful. This shows how deeply the desire for reunion is rooted in the soul of the people."

At St. Peter's on October 26, the crowd acclaimed the entry of the Pope and the Patriarch, and they greeted the kiss of peace with long and loud applause. The young people of Rome gathered for the afternoon service at the Basilica of St. Paul-Outside-the-Walls. The crowd gave the Patriarch a standing ovation and the service was constantly drowned out by their cheers. The Patriarch was fond of recounting this episode.

At the Phanar, I met young Italians who had been stunned by this encounter and had made the pilgrimage to see this old Patriarch again, who had restored its pearl of great price, its East, to all of Christianity.

ΩΩΩ

If one of the profound causes of the schism between the Catholic Church and the Orthodox Church lies in a certain lack of clarity, in the West, about the Person and role of the Holy Spirit, then we should recognize that, in his response to the Patriarch on October 27, Pope Paul VI forthrightly embarked on the path of healing. He confessed that when he had visited Smyrna and Ephesus the previous year, he had been deeply moved by the words of the Book of Revelation: "He who has an ear, let him hear what the Spirit says to the Churches." (Rev. 2:17)

The Pope then declaimed a veritable hymn to the Holy Spirit, "who has made us know Christ, who has granted us to be the guardians of the truth entrusted to the Church, who has made us enter into the mystery of God and into his Truth, for the Spirit is life and internal transformation. The Spirit works marvels in many ways, the Spirit bestows grace of every kind . . . and brings unity. The Spirit dwells in every believer and governs the whole Church."

With these words, the Pope reaffirmed the reciprocity between the Son and the Holy Spirit, the reciprocity between the Church as the sacramental and hierarchical Body of Christ, and the Church as the royal priesthood of the people and as prophetic freedom in the Holy Spirit. This was a conception dear to certain contemporary Orthodox theologians. Pope Paul VI further stated, citing the Catholic theologian Father Yves Congar, one of those who have reflected most profoundly on ancient and modern Orthodox ecclesiology, that the two great motive forces of the Church are the hierarchy and the Holy Spirit—not that any attempt should be made to place them on the same level, as the sacraments, and the very institution of the Church, were the gift of the Holy Spirit. When they read these words, the Orthodox should ask themselves if the old and painful quarrel over the procession of the Holy Spirit has not already begun to be resolved.

ΩΩΩ

In this wonderful exchange of roles in Rome, we see the Pope evoking the spirit-bearing people, the *pneumatophores*, in whom the gifts of the Spirit are freely multiplied, while the Patriarch, in speaking to the Roman Synod, had evoked the Pentecostal character of the hierarchy, the bishops who carry the Spirit "as if in earthen vessels." (2 Cor. 4:7)

6. The Future

Professor Little by little, the gestures that you and Pope Paul VI have made, and the dialogue of love that you have dared to enter into, have softened the schisms in the hearts of the people. Christ's sacramental presence is already there in the kiss of peace. The chalice that the Pope gave you in Jerusalem already shows that our two Churches have the same priesthood and the same communion. You presented Paul VI with an *engolpion*, a bishop's stole, the distinctive mark of the bishop, in recognition of the full apostolicity of the Church of Rome. These symbolic gestures spoke to the reciprocal immanence of two Churches discovering, little by little, that they are two halves of the One Church. Now we are getting ready for the theological dialogue. This, it seems to me, should first take measure of what we already have in common, that is to say, the Mystery of the Church.

Patriarch The dialogue of love and the theological dialogue cannot be set in opposition to each other, not without stumbling into the most negative theology. The dialogue of love already expresses a theology because God is love. In the early Church, each Christian community was known as *agape*—love. And as far as the Schism is concerned, don't forget that it was never made official. We have removed from the memory of the Church its one strictly local manifestation, the anathemas of 1054. Now we must work to recapture the experience of the first millennium, when our differences became a productive diversity, in the unity of the one chalice. Through love, we have conquered this yesterday, that was so closed and so loaded with antagonism. We give glory to the Lord and Creator of today.

Today we are rediscovering the solid ground of our age-old brotherhood. In reclaiming love we are able to look calmly at our differences. It has happened to me, in a way as it happened to Kosmas Aitolos when he embarked on his work of preaching and gave up the contemplative life to which he had dedicated himself. My heart has been torn open by the words of the Apostle Paul to the Philippians: "Let each of you look not only to his own interests, but also to the interests of others." (Phil 2:4) From now on our theology must be distilled through love. We have been separated by pride. We will be united by love.

Professor We should not underestimate the seriousness of the issues that we still need to resolve .... The separation of East and West involves not only cultural factors—today these are outmoded and are rapidly disappearing . . . but also a spiritual choice ....

Patriarch I know this. I believe that our Orthodox Church is the faithful and holy witness of the undivided Church. But the true theological dialogue should begin inside the dialogue of love, inside the Mystery of the Church that we share in all its fundamentals. For as long as this work takes, we should let ourselves be guided by the Holy Spirit. We should pray to the martyrs of the undivided Church, to the martyrs, fathers, and saints .... And, trust me, if God, in his unfathomable wisdom, permitted this schism, it was so that good should result from it.

Professor Awareness is born from suffering[77]....

Patriarch Monks have long reflected on the deeper understanding that we gain from suffering, *ponos*, and what is true for a person's life will

77 [Clemént uses the term *souffrance*, which can be translated as suffering, tribulation, and pain, *ponos* in Greek]

be shown to be true in the life of Christianity. We will rediscover the undivided Church, but with deepened understanding. During the second millennium, the East has gained a deeper understanding of the Mystery and the West has gained a deeper understanding of history . . . . Their reunion will perhaps allow the Mystery to take on the flesh of history, leading to a great Christian rebirth.

Professor Then perhaps, the godless world that is desiccating and burning up the West, that, little by little, is contaminating all humanity . . . perhaps the godless world will turn from unknowing to knowing, to the knowledge of the Living God. And then the 'all is oblivion' of modern culture will transform into 'all is God,' as Vladimir Soloviev suggested . . . . But, for now, what needs to be done?

Patriarch We need to encourage a whole range of initiatives in which Catholics and Orthodox, especially those in the diaspora, together seek to rediscover and deepen the living tradition of the Church . . . and, as this work progresses, we should publish articles in newspapers and in popular magazines, the ones that reach the thinking public—who, however, are not familiar with the technicalities of theology. We need to get people involved. I am sure, if theology directly speaks the language of contemplation, people will become interested . . . .

Professor Catholics and Orthodox now have a common language for this dialogue—the language of the Bible as understood by the Fathers, and, if I may say, through the spiritual experiences of the ascetics. In this perspective, the truths that we are able to grasp are the least bad intellectual approximation of our experience of participation in the divine light. And our errors should be seen as clumsiness, proof of our limits, even perhaps as our refusal of a personal and ecclesial experience.

Patriarch We can distinguish between the fundamental truths that we hold in common and the other elements of the life of each Church, that are, so to speak, the local forms taken by the outcropping of our common faith. St. Paul says that the robe of wisdom is a coat of many colors.[78] In our convergence on the essentials and our respect for our diversity, we will find that the problems that divide us will no longer be the closed arenas of our theological jousts.

They will be swept up and, perhaps, resolved in the rising tide of unity. When the sap rises, you see which branch bursts into flower and which branch remains bare. So, let the sap rise. And then we shall indeed

78 [The reference is unclear]

see. The two problems of the *filioque* and papal infallibility, these are the only important ones.

We will talk to serious theologians. They will not erase two millennia of the experience of the Church with one stroke of the pen. We will speak to them in the same spirit in which Patriarch Peter of Antioch wrote to Michael Cerularius after the dispute of 1054. He explained to the Patriarch that the Roman Church was Orthodox, that we were one Church, that these difficulties were of no importance, except for the addition to the Creed, that is to say, the question of the procession of the Holy Spirit.

Professor Peter of Antioch also seems to have sensed the emerging conception of the Church in Rome. He wrote to the Patriarch of Grado, near Venice, "the head of a single Church, the blessed Pope of Rome, does not agree to be bound by the agreement of his fellow patriarchs with regard to the Mysteries . . . he wants to impose his own will."

ΩΩΩ

Patriarch And infallibility! . . . but, after all, in a way, why not? He smiles. After all, we are all, each one of us, infallible in what we do best. Don't tell the chef who is counting out peppercorns that she is not infallible. And what about you when you teach theology . . . .

Professor Well, you know, since the recent upheavals in France, people don't want to hear infallible, *ex cathedra* teaching.

Patriarch But it's not about appearing infallible! When you teach a theology class and try to express the living tradition of the Church in your own particular way, I know you are not trying to appear infallible, but in fact, you are infallible. In the union of all, in love, the person is infallible—each person is infallible in their unique vocation, in their personal awareness, as a member of the Body of Christ on whom the Spirit has descended.

Professor All the same, papal infallibility is something else for our Catholic brothers and sisters. As the successor of Peter and the Vicar of Christ, when the Pope speaks *ex cathedra*, he is expressing the infallible truth that is the foundation of the Church, with the grace of the Holy Spirit.

Patriarch Well, we'll have to consider the infallibility of the Pope to be part of the infallibility of the Church, and the infallibility of the Church to be part of the infallibility of the truth. It is true that the nineteenth century formulations are very onerous, and unacceptable to us, but the

Second Vatican Council re-emphasized the meaning of the Church as the gathering of the Christian people, under the care of the bishops. Episcopal conferences and the meetings of the Synod lead to the real interdependence of the Pope and the bishops, and this begins to renew the relationship between the priest and his people.

Professor One could say that, following *Humanae Vitae*, the Catholic Church is experimenting with 'reception,' in the Orthodox sense of the word. It is an uncomfortable experience because it is all new . . . .

Patriarch Each side takes up fixed positions: the West likes the clash of 'opposites.'

Professor Only the Anglo-Saxons know how to take part in a tension-free drama. Even where there are tensions they tend to systematize them, to avoid the tyranny of one voice or of a majority. Sadly, they are mostly Protestant . . . .

Nevertheless, the Catholic Church is changing. With the rediscovery of the communion of local Churches and the rights of the individual conscience, perhaps Rome will again in the end, become, in the words of St. Ignatius, "the Church that presides in love." Here too we must stress the importance of gestures. Pope Paul VI's pilgrimage to Jerusalem, as he himself said many times, was an act of repentance of the whole Church, of its head and of its members. And the Pope's visit to Istanbul demonstrated that the Rome has rediscovered the concept of sister Churches . . . .

Professor As Orthodox thought meets this evolving Catholic thought, it will be important for the Orthodox to clarify their conception of the throne of Peter and of universal primacy. Not to score polemical points, but to fully understand and take on board all the experience of the first millennium. I say all the experience, in the same sense that the Fathers of the Seventh Council, measured the impact of a Council by "the pope's confirmation" (they used the word *kanonisein*) by the "agreement of the patriarchs," and by the "general interest of the Church," by which we can understand the support of the people of God.

The Eastern Church's first concern has always been to avoid having the legal power of the institution take priority over the sacramental mission of the bishops, because both carry equal full weight. In addition, the legal power of the institution does not overrule the prophetic vision of those apostolic witnesses, who speak with strange authority, and who like St. Paul, speak of things that cannot be told, which men may not utter. (2 Cor. 12) The apostolic glory of the Church resides not only in the apostolic succession, but also in the guarding of this apostolic message by the whole people of Christ, and in the experience of the Resurrection that is, so to speak, distilled in those ascetics and spiritual masters whom the Orthodox tradition calls apostolic.[79] Thus, next to the apostolicity of St. Peter, we see these other dimensions, the apostolicity of St. John and of St. Paul. And Paul debated with Peter as his equal . . . .

Patriarch If we arrive at the reunited Church, the Bishop of Rome will, incontestably, be the first in honor and the first in rank in all the Churches spread throughout the world. But he will not be above all the Churches. Rather, he will be at their center, at the center of their fraternal communion, guarding the integrity of that communion, defending the Universal Church against any 'parochial' threats. Presiding effectively in love . . . .

*Professo*r Byzantine theologians accept that the Bishop of Rome has the same role among the other bishops as Peter had among the other apostles. But they also stress that, according to the Fathers, every bishop, and all the bishops together, sits on the throne of Peter. The *forma Petri*, the rank of Peter, is not absent from any bishop's province, as Pope Leo the Great tells us.[80] What is more, each baptized Christian who confesses the faith of Peter is Peter, in their witness. In this context, we perhaps need to reconsider the formulations of the First Vatican Council on the infallibility of the Pope's *ex cathedra* pronouncements, *ex sese non ex consensu ecclesiae*, of themselves and not through consensus.

Patriarch One might say that when the Pope speaks *ex cathedra* he claims to express the mind of the Church, which is wholly guided by the Holy Spirit. And therefore what he promulgates is not subject to any democratic consultation, precisely because it distills the 'sense of the Church,' as lived by the whole people of God, of whom the Pope is summoned to be the voice, to the extent that he is in full communion, a complete co-worker with the episcopal college and all the Christian people . . . .

Now, we need to carefully look at Peter's trajectory in the Gospels. St. Gregory Palamas tells us that Peter typifies the 'new man,' the pardoned sinner. Christ gave him assurances and promises about the Mystery of the Church, against which the gates of hell would not prevail. But Peter

79 For the 'apostolic' monks, see *On Human Being*, pp.74–75

80 Leo Epistle 14:11, PL 54: 676

refused to accept that the Messiah he had just confessed could be a crucified Messiah. (Matt. 16:16) And the Lord censored him harshly: "Get behind me, Satan! You are a stumbling block to me, because you do not think the thoughts of God but the thoughts of men." (cf. Matt. 16:23) Whereas the Lord had promised Peter to come to his aid, so that he, Peter could strengthen the faith of his brothers, Peter denied him. And the cock crowed. And Peter repented and wept bitterly. (Luke 22:31–34) The Risen Christ forgave him: "Do you love Me?" "Feed my lambs," and he re-established Peter in the first place among the apostles. (John 21:15–16) We see Peter in the first place in the Book of Acts. But Christ gives Peter another warning: "Another will gird you and carry you where you do not wish to go." (John 21:18) And John, the beloved disciple, who knew the secrets of the Master's heart, to whom the Lord entrusted his Mother, is the one who will remain until the Lord comes. (John 21:23)

If the bishop in the Church is the model of Peter, he is far from the power and the glory. He is only there to remind the Church that it only lives through God's forgiveness and has no power other than the Cross. And if Peter's successor should forget that his fundamental act of witness is that of the pardoned sinner, then, as in the West in the sixteenth century, other prophets will arise, to "oppose him to his face," "because he was plainly at fault," as Paul did in Antioch. (cf. Gal. 2:11) And John is him who will remain.

"Peter turned and saw following them the disciple that Jesus loved, who had lain close to his breast at the Supper and had said, "Lord who is it who will betray you?" When Peter saw him, he said to Jesus, "And him, Lord? Jesus said to him, "If it is my will that he remain until I come, what is that to you? Follow me." (cf. John 21:20–22)

ΩΩΩ

Professor Despite so much painful tension, our Church has managed to maintain the balance between the prophets and the apostles, between the apostolic succession and the 'apostolic' spiritual masters, between the sacraments and freedom. I find myself asking if we don't owe this balance strictly to our theology of the Trinity. Because the Church is participation in Trinitarian communion. I mean the original balance that our theology reveals and adores, between the Son and the Holy Spirit, that St. Irenaeus compared to 'the two hands of God' . . . . Because the Father is the sole source and origin of divinity.

In the Latin theology of the Middle Ages, the Person of the Holy Spirit seems to issue from the Person of the Son. Isn't this the fundamental reason why all the various forms in which the Spirit is manifested in the Church—personal freedom, prophesy, the royal priesthood—were subordinated to Christ's sacramental presence and its guarantors—that is to say, the hierarchy? In the medieval Latin way of thinking, in the same way that the Spirit proceeds from the Son (this is the famous *filioque*), so prophesy proceeds from the guardians of the sacrament. It becomes controlled by the hierarchy. One might even say, it became the monopoly of the hierarchy. At the limit, in the extreme formulation of 1870, there is only one prophet left, the Pope, the Vicar of Christ.

Patriarch We need to be careful about drawing brilliant, hasty, and systematically unsound conclusions. First of all, don't forget that the filioque formula and its theology were already rigorously set forth by St. Augustine. We can find similar arguments in the works of the Cappadocian and Alexandrian Church Fathers. Despite this Augustinian theology, the Church remained united for six or seven centuries after Augustine, even while this theology slowly gained ground in the West.

Professor Maybe so. But how regrettable that the Western theology did not have the same sense of balance that the East displayed, from Theodoret of Cyrus to St. Gregory Palamas. These Fathers told us that the working of the divine, the diffusion of the divine essence through the divine energies, is holiness and is Spirit. All the rest, including the created spirit of man, is part of the material world. The Fathers told us that holiness and the divine energies come to us from the Father, by the Son, through the Holy Spirit, or, if you will, from the Father and the Son. But the Holy Spirit, whose workings are always anonymous and concealed in the life the Spirit communicates to us, is not unilaterally dependent on the Son. The Son and the Spirit are interdependent. The Son came so that we could receive the Spirit, in his Nature, in his Body. And the Spirit descended on the Son from all eternity.

The Spirit "hovers over" the waters in order to make them receptive to the creative Word. The Spirit descends on Mary to make possible the Incarnation of the Word. The Spirit is Jesus' messianic anointing and the power of his Resurrection. The Spirit descends on the Church, at Pentecost, as on a new Creation, so that henceforth the Word has its spiritual birth in the human heart, and the God-man becomes God-humanity and

God-universe. For the Christian, what is the world and history, if not a great symbiotic Incarnation and Pentecost, before the victorious sign of the Cross . . . .

Patriarch You may be right. But in that case, this is a terrible condemnation of us Orthodox! While everything in our Church is made for welcoming the Spirit—the sacraments, doctrine, spirituality, the Church structure—we have made it a weapon of polemic debate, a weapon with which to humiliate our brothers. We can't just talk about the Spirit. The waters of life are renewed in the cupped hand offered to the lips of your sister. The waters of life are squeezed out of the hand that closes around them.

Listen. Can we not say that the Spirit, given to us by Christ, proceeds from the Father by the Son, *dia Uiou, per Filium*? Because, in the end, the Spirit is love and cannot remain outside, or other than, the Son.

Professor Yes, we can say this, but on condition that we don't give a causal sense to *per Filium* . . . yes, we can say with Dionysios the Areopagite that the Spirit proceeds from the Son and ascends with Him to the Father. At Great Vespers of Pentecost, we sing that the Spirit proceeds from the Father and abides in the Son.

I am not so much bothered by the *filioque* as by the one-sided relationship that it seems to establish between the Spirit and the Son. We should make clear their mutual dependence, their reciprocal relations.

Patriarch I like this idea of reciprocity. It answers love with love. We don't tell our Catholic brothers that they are wrong, but that there is an even greater love. You know that the Son is there when the Spirit proceeds from the Father. Then consider that the Spirit is there when the Father begets the Son. The Three Persons are always there, as Trinity in unity. That is the marvel.

> "Come, all peoples, let us worship the Godhead in three Persons, the Son in the Father, with the Holy Spirit. For the Father begat the Son before all ages, co-eternal and equal in Majesty, and the Holy Spirit was in the Father, glorified with the Son: a single power, a single essence, one Godhead, which we all worship saying, "Holy is God, who created all things with His Son, with the cooperation of the Holy Spirit. Holy and Mighty, through Whom we have known the Father and through Whom the Holy Spirit came into the world. Holy Immortal, the Paraclete Spirit, which proceeds from the Father and abides in the Son: Holy Trinity, glory to You." (Great Vespers of Pentecost)

ΩΩΩ

Professor In Paris, on Pentecost in 1968, in the midst of a major crisis of civilization, some sixty Catholics and Protestants, priests, pastors and laity, celebrated an ecumenical intercommunion. They wanted to reply to the spiritual turmoil with an exceptional, prophetic gesture. They also wanted to demonstrate that their revolutionary brotherhood, their fight for a more just society, was rooted in the newness of the Holy Spirit. In fact, this gesture is no longer an exceptional one. In Western Europe and in North America, little groups are taking shape outside the Churches, in the underground as they say, practicing intercommunion and declaring that there is no longer any problem.[81]

But the Orthodox seem to be among the most reticent. For us, the Eucharist, together with the Confession of Faith, is what fully constitutes the Church. The Church is not, first and foremost an institution or a book. It is unity in faith and love founded on the Eucharist. That is why, for the Orthodox, any attempt to 'relativize' or 'spiritualize' the Eucharist is seen as an attack on the Church itself, an attack on the Church that in its most vital essence is the Body of Christ, in which the sanctification of humankind is accomplished by the Holy Spirit.

If the problem of intercommunion rarely arises in predominantly Orthodox countries, this question causes a lot of confusion in the Middle East, where Orthodox and Byzantine Catholics live side by side, and in the diaspora, where our small Orthodox parishes risk being obliterated, swept away in the mass of Catholic and Protestant Churches. This, I think, is why you published an encyclical in 1967, to reaffirm that, even if the Orthodox in the diaspora must sometimes use Catholic or Protestant Churches to celebrate the Liturgy, this does not mean that they can receive Communion or the sacraments from a non-Orthodox priest. The Orthodox Church has not taken any decision in this direction, and there is not yet full communion between the Orthodox Church and the other Churches.

But our position on this question cannot be one of self-satisfied immobility. Our theologians refuse intercommunion with a serenity that seems to me to be a little pharisaical. Our position is so static that its full meaning is not properly understood. In the West it tends to be

81 [See *The Underground Church*, edited by Malcolm Boyd, New York, Sheed and Ward, 1968]

seen as a retreat into exoticism. One day a young Catholic woman came up to the Communion cup in the small French-language Orthodox parish that I attend. Before Communion, the priest asked her if she was Orthodox, and then turned her away. I was asked to go and explain the situation to her. She was in tears. She said: "I completely believe what you believe, I accept everything that was said in today's Liturgy. So you do not consider Communion to be the sharing of a fraternal meal?" I had no explanation for her, at least, not then and there. To her burning pain of being rejected there was no response. I felt bad and I was ashamed, that is all.

Patriarch The theologians have had their say on this question. But the people also have something to say. There is something profoundly right about their instinct. I am not a theologian and I listen to the voice of the people. Thousands of people, men and women, come to see me from all across the world. Let me tell you: aside from some groups who are stuck in the past, people want intercommunion, especially the young people. The movement is irresistible. This is true even in those Orthodox countries that appear to be on the sidelines. You find it in in the countries that suffered most under the state atheism of their Communist regimes. People there don't first say, "I am Orthodox," they say, "I am a Christian." We must listen to the wordless groans of the Spirit. (Rom. 8:26–27) Only Communion in the one cup will make us capable of bearing witness to the Risen Christ.

"That they all may be one, as we are one." How can this high priestly prayer set humankind on fire, if we first do not set the Church on fire and burn up all the barriers? The Catholics and the Orthodox have argued for centuries whether the Eucharistic bread should be leavened or unleavened. Now we are facing vast upheavals in the world and yet we continue to argue over fermented bread. That is why youth reject us. Youth may be simplistic. They may see us from the outside, in a harsh light. But their judgment can shed light on us.

We talk of love but we do not live love. We claim to have the greatest love, but as for ourselves, it is absent. I would like to see the impatience of youth reach the theologians, so that they examine themselves in youth's unyielding gaze. So they see themselves as they stand on the sidelines of history discussing the fermentation of bread. So that they see that they have become so unfeeling as to allow millions of souls to die of hunger, without their showing the least concern.

I'm not saying this to get the theologians and the Church leaders to gloss over the problems, or to frame the Mystery as one possible point of view among many others. But I am not sure that the demand for intercommunion necessarily implies forgetting the true meaning of the Eucharist. The thousands of men and women who came to see me are not looking for the lowest common denominator. They are seeking Christ. They want to plunge their lives into the life of Christ, to become those who love their neighbor, those who serve mankind.[82] They are no longer interested in disputes. They know nothing of modern biblical interpretations and they are not concerned with Papal infallibility.

They believe in the Risen Christ. They are hoping for the living waters of life, and they know that they can only receive them if they receive them together in Communion, for the salvation of the world.

The theologians and the Church leaders must hear these voices. The tears of the young woman turned away from the Communion cup must burn their hearts. And then, with hearts on fire, the theologians and the Church leaders will begin to look at these problems differently, and they will find the path.

Woe to the theologians, woe to the Church leaders, if Christians unite despite them, if the most ardent youth share the bread and the wine underground, away from the Church! Then, life will be torn from its source, love will no longer be an opening to eternity, and brotherly love, and fatherly love, will turn into fratricidal war. In the place where the successors to the apostles bear witness to God's gifts, there will be no-one to receive them! In the place where brothers celebrate the Feast of the Meeting of the Lord, they will no longer taste the Fountain of Immortality.[83] What an unimaginable disruption of the Church this would be! And how much more serious than the barriers that separate the different confessions today.

ΩΩΩ

Patriarch What can we as Orthodox do, right now? The proposed intercommunion between Catholics and Protestants seems to us to be a

82 [The image is of the bucket descending into the well and being drawn up full of water]

83 [In the Russian Orthodox tradition, as the faithful take Communion, we sing "Receive the Body of Christ, taste the Fountain of Immortality." In Greek Orthodox practice, this hymn is sung during the Paschal period.]

mixed blessing. We can recognize the prophetic urgency. But we fear that this will not bring the Catholics the very best of the Reform tradition: its biblical heritage and its sense of freedom. Instead, it risks bringing the worst aspects: a conception of the Church and the Eucharist that does not take full account of our Eucharistic union with the Risen Christ.

That is why I think that only intercommunion between Catholics and Orthodox can bring these developments back in balance, by strengthening Catholicism's living tradition, so that it takes on only the best of the Reform tradition.

Professor But wouldn't it be better to speak of full communion between Catholics and Orthodox only once we have reached agreement on the fundamental issues? Rather than this new concept of intercommunion, which seems to be more a form of diplomacy than of ecclesiology. We could attain this full agreement if we can recognize the changes that are occurring in the Catholic Church, and if we know how to respond to them.

Patriarch I think that we must retain the term intercommunion. Catholics and Orthodox believe in the same Eucharistic and ecclesial Mystery. Now they must begin the in-depth theological dialogue. This is not the consequence of the dialogue of love but its embodiment, the dialogue conducted from within the body of love. You can imagine that, at a certain moment, the convergence of understanding on what is fundamental will make it possible, or rather compel us, to establish intercommunion de facto. This would be like love breaking through, so that everything else is resolved into abundance in its brilliant light.

My most burning desire, my prayer, is one day to share the consecrated Chalice with the Pope.

Today, our unity has become a historical possibility. I can't say when. I hope for it. I fight for it. Unity may occur unexpectedly, like every great event, like the return of Christ who said He will come like a thief in the night. The Catholic Church is swept up in a whirlwind. Anything is possible.

Professor One could say that in this moment the Catholic Church is reliving the whole spiritual history of the West since the schism. You could say that, in the whirlwind, it has swept up the Reformation, the French Revolution, and Socialism, by way of wrenching juxtapositions and polarization. It is as though the Catholic Church has a presentiment of integration and transfiguration, and yet is not able to bring this about by itself.

Patriarch This is why John's boat must draw close to Peter's boat, so that the net of the Church does not tear. (John 21:11) Today, Rome needs Orthodoxy in order to open itself up to liberty and life, without losing the sense of mystery. If we do not accept the role to which God has summoned us, we will become a sect of Old Believers, on the margins of history, and Western Christianity will shatter once more, perhaps beyond repair. If we know how to answer God's call, a Catholicism united to Orthodoxy will be able to re-assimilate the best of the Reform tradition, and the best of the revolutionary movements for freedom and justice, and human history will rediscover its meaning and direction around this great, central axis of divino-humanity.

Professor How, in reality, can we achieve Catholic-Orthodox unity? We both share the faith of the Ecumenical Councils. We share the hard-won definitions of the Trinity and of Christ's humanity and divinity, that were worked out with such care in the debates of the Ecumenical Councils and in their decrees. These are our common heritage. The *filioque* emerged well before the schism. It seems to me that, above all, we need to share our theology and experience of the Holy Spirit, in order to find the right formulas for moving forward. The teachings, the doctrines, on the sacraments will not cause any great difficulty, if we place them in the framework of the Mystery, the Mystery of the Church as the Body of Christ. We are left with the dogmatic pronouncements of the nineteenth century, especially the teachings of the First Vatican Council on papal infallibility and the Pope's "immediate" and "truly episcopal" jurisdiction over the entire Church.[84] Here, in the eyes of the merely human, the obstacles seem insurmountable.

Patriarch But why should this be? These definitions were the unilateral pronouncements of the Western Church. They should be studied by a joint commission as part of a truly ecumenical council that reunites Catholic and Orthodox bishops, the authentic image of the divine and apostolic foundation of our two Churches. And, what is more, as the apostolic truth of the Church resides not only in the apostolic succession but also in the fullness of prophetic witness, the other confessions will send their representatives, and it will be a pan-Christian Council. All will repent. All will pray for the coming of the Holy Spirit, and the Holy Spirit will visit our minds and inspire our hearts.

---

84 See *You Are Peter*, pp. 63–64

How and in what circumstances can this all happen? We cannot know. Unity is in God's hands. Right now, everything is changing very quickly. Eastern Christianity is under great stress. Many Orthodox are suffering through grave ordeals. New and more subtle temptations may arise, as well as new possibilities. Unity will be forged in the heat of the moment. The Holy Spirit is not only light; it is celestial fire.

ΩΩΩ

7. *Audiatur et Tertia Pars*[85]

Professor Your ecumenical outreach is most commonly understood to have reached its peak in reconciliation with Rome. But it seems to me that you never lost track of the pan-Christian concerns expressed by your predecessors and in the Encyclical of 1920. In your great pilgrimage for unity in 1967, you went not only to Rome, but also to Geneva and London.

Patriarch When I had the idea of meeting the Pope in Jerusalem, I also proposed that the leaders of all the Churches should meet on Golgotha, to pray that the Church be reunited. The Constantinople Patriarchate was one of the initiators of the ecumenical movement, in the first decades of the twentieth century. For my part, I have done that I can to bring the other Orthodox Churches into the ecumenical movement. Now I am hoping that the Catholic Church will, more and more collaborate, with the World Council of Churches. If the Catholic Church joins the World Council of Churches, then what I call the 'union' of Churches will have been achieved.

Professor 'Union'—that is to say unity in action, in the common service of mankind . . .

Patriarch Let us go out into the world together to serve humankind . . . . We have much to learn from the Protestants in this regard. But this evangelical *diakonia* of Christ in the temporal world will not bear fruit unless it is sustained by Christ's total presence in the Eucharist. With the Eucharist we are no longer talking about 'union' but what I call 'unity' in the sacramental sense—full communion in the same faith, in the same chalice. If the World Council of Churches is, providentially, the vehicle for 'union,' I see the dynamic of "unity" in our reconciliation with Rome. If the Catholic Church joins the World

85 [Let the other side also be heard]

Council of Churches, this will give momentum to the movement for 'unity' which, up to now, has been very difficult to set in motion.

Professor And why is that?

Patriarch Because, as Orthodox, we can hardly begin a dialogue with the Protestants in the absence of the Catholics. The Reformation is a drama played out within Western Christianity. In reconciling with Rome, the Orthodox have cauterized its roots, aiding in the transformation of Rome.

Professor Without Rome, there are no psychological barriers to the encounter between Orthodox and Protestants. But this encounter is lacking full spiritual depth. The Orthodox and Protestants do not share the burden of the historical disagreements that tragically weighs down our relations with Rome. For example, in France the Protestants have welcomed the Orthodox with enormous generosity and open-mindedness—for which we cannot thank them enough. And yet, the spiritual encounter is more difficult and not without its disagreements. The words we use do not always have the same exact meaning. Both sides emphasize freedom in the Holy Spirit, and many of our Protestant brothers and sisters are in agreement with us when we explain to them that, for us, freedom is not the self-expression of the isolated individual but the creative expression of persons in communion . . . .

Patriarch Real freedom is love, the love that we receive in the Eucharist . . . .

Professor This is exactly the point at which the words we use no longer have the same meaning. Protestant theological 'existentialism' is close to our way of thinking. We find parallels in the Church Fathers and in the Russian religious philosophers. But we rapidly discover that, in Orthodoxy, this 'existentialism' has a realistic sacramental and mystical dimension. When we say that the divine light penetrates a person's entire being and the entire cosmos, when we speak of our oneness in the Body of Christ, these are not images that we are describing, but the reality. And we discover that there is a piece missing between the Protestants and us ...

Patriarch And this missing piece is Rome.

Professor Rome is where the Reformed Churches need to rediscover their mission and their ecclesial roots. Without Rome, our dialogue with the Protestants is either superficial, and risks turning into a sort of anti-Catholic rhetoric, or it leads to misunderstanding. When Lutheran theologians in the sixteenth century, tried to establish contact with the

Patriarch of Constantinople, they were not able to find the Greek terms in which express their explanations of Luther's theology of justification.

They began by speaking about resurrection and new life, returning to the mystical origins of the young Luther's thinking. Unfortunately, Constantinople had never received the translation of the *Augsburg Confession* that Melanchthon had sent in 1555. It was only twenty years later that the Lutherans began their discussions with the Greek Orthodox. In the meantime, Lutheran communities had begun to take shape apart from Rome. These communities were battling the Anabaptist sects that placed their emphasis on the inner light, and the living Christ in each person, and rejected all and any external Church organization. And so, the Lutherans began to define the theology of justification by means of legalistic language. Now, for the Orthodox, the Church is a mystery. For the Lutherans, mystery and mysticism came to be synonymous with either monastic pride or a false and destructive claim to inspired individualism. They could only form a solid organization, it seemed to them, by expressing their raw faith—*sola fides*—in legal language. And for this reason, the negotiations between the learned doctors of Tübingen and Patriarch Jeremias II in 1574 rapidly reached an impasse.

Patriarch They would have had to return to St. Augustine and show how his doctrine of justification—which no doubt was heavy handed—is wholly part of the mystery of the Church.

Professor Shaped by his opposition to Rome, Melanchthon went in the opposite direction. He emphasized Augustine's conception of Christ's *justitia aliena*—an externally imputed justice received by an arbitrary-seeming grace. And for this reason, he struggled to translate the *Augsburg Confession* into Greek.[86]

Professor It has often been said that the Christian West, and in particular the Protestant West, conceives of the relationship between God and man in legalistic terms that derive from the Epistle to the Romans. On the other hand, the Christian East prefers to speak in terms of new birth and deification. While there is some truth to this distinction, one should not forget that these conceptions coexist and complement each other, in St. Paul's writings and in the Church Fathers. Many of the Fathers wrote commentaries on the Epistle to the Romans. You could begin with St. John Chrysostom, who often speaks of justification. And St. Augustine himself is a witness to the undi-

86 [Also known as the *Confessio Augustana*]

vided Church. What is important is that all these symbolic approaches hint at the mystery without ever claiming to master it. The mystery is greater than any conceptual approach.

ΩΩΩ

Professor I value the balance between mystical realism and internal freedom in our Orthodox tradition. The Church is founded on the rock of the Risen Christ, who is revealed to us in the sacraments, by the Holy Spirit. There is something objectively real about the fullness that we are offered—this expression of the holiness of the Church. Not that we receive an object. We commune with Someone. In the Holy Spirit this life becomes our own. And here, all is inner freedom. The fullness of the Church becomes the most personal of experiences.

It sometimes seems to me that the great sixteenth century reformers, and their disciples above all, rejected by Rome and unable to remain fully rooted in the Church, tended to give a subjective coloring to the fullness of grace, while they objectified what should have remained inner freedom. In the face of challenges from the Anabaptists and the 'enthusiasm' of direct inspiration, they chose a subjective confession of faith in place of eucharistic realism. They systematized the mystery of God's freely-given love into the doctrine of double predestination.

Now, Calvin was a great theologian, steeped in the thought of St. John Chrysostom. He never ventured to preach the doctrine of double predestination to the people of Geneva. But, as he pushed back with all his force against Rome, he failed to see that the whole Church is predestined, that is to say, all of humanity, in Christ. Our personal response to this predestination is a secret love that can only be expressed in adoration and prayer.

Patriarch The prayer that all may be saved!

Professor On the other hand, when Gottfried Arnold translated the Macarian Homilies in the eighteenth century, and German Lutheranism encountered Orthodox spirituality in one of the key mystical texts of the Eastern Church, what resulted was a form of pietism, in the absence of the objective experience of the mystery. There was a real spiritual awakening, but its subjectivity could not find its expression in a real Eucharistic community.

We have to wait until the era of German Romanticism and philosophical idealism, before we can begin to see the outlines of an ecumenical opening, thanks to the Holy Alliance. The Holy Alliance[87] has a bad name, because it is readily confused with Prince Metternich's counter-revolutionary Concert of Europe, the quadruple alliance of Austria, Prussia, Russia, and the United Kingdom, together with France. But, in the Holy Alliance, Tsar Alexander I had sought to bring together the best elements of revolution and tradition.

In Spring of 1814, when the Russian troops occupied Paris after a fierce battle, the people of Paris feared that the Russians would take revenge for the burning of Moscow, in 1812. But Tsar Alexander asked only that the Orthodox Easter liturgy be celebrated at the place where Louis XVI was guillotined, now the Place de la Concorde. With the Tsar's support, contact between the Orthodox and the Lutherans became more frequent. And so it was that Franz von Baader discovered the Orthodox Church in his travels in Russia.[88] For him, the Orthodox Church had remained true to the original spirit of Christianity and was the foundation of the undivided Church, on which Catholics and Protestants could meet and reunite. From this point on he devoted himself to revealing the fundamental internal relationship between 'Eastern Catholicism' and 'Western Catholicism.' For him, Protestantism was an essential dimension of Western Catholicism. He wanted to promote 'coordination' between the East and the West—not the subordination of one to the other but coordination, a reciprocal integration that would allow the rupture of the sixteenth century Reformation to be healed, on both sides.

Baader was an unusual man. He also believed that Orthodoxy could help the Christian world overcome the mindless clash between science and religion. Rather than subjecting reason to a philosophical system, Orthodoxy imbues reason with the mystery. If only Orthodoxy could awaken to the awareness of its own intellectual riches, it would open reason up to infinite possibilities in the light of the Logos. To this end, Baader wanted to set up an institute in Moscow. By a strange coincidence, it was in reading Baader that Vladimir Soloviev and Nicolai Berdyaev discovered

---

87 [The alliance of Austria, Prussia and Russia, formed after the defeat of Napoleon, signed in Paris in 1815]

88 [von Baader was a Bavarian Catholic who was strongly opposed to conservative Catholicism. In 1840 he wrote a famous article in which he stated *audiatur et tertia pars*, the third witness, that is to say Orthodoxy, must also be heard.]

Jacob Böhme, the great Lutheran mystic, with his experience of the inner light and his perception of a dynamic and feeling God.[89]

Patriarch These links between the Orthodox and the Lutherans are so important! In the twentieth century, much of the impetus that gave birth to the ecumenical movement came from the Lutheran Church. In the ecumenical movement, the Stockholm Conference of 1925, summoned by the great Archbishop Söderblom, and the Orthodox Encyclical of 1920 came together. Nathan Söderblom called for a renewed understanding of Orthodoxy and his call was heard by the leading German theologians.[90]

ΩΩΩ

Patriarch Along with the Lutherans, it is important to note the important role of the Anglicans in the early years of the ecumenical movement. Even though the Anglican Church was deeply influenced by the Protestant theologians of the Reformation, it has retained its fundamental continuity with the undivided Church. There are of course many points for theologians to argue over, and we will hear from them in the systematic dialogue that we propose to have with the Anglicans. But what most interests me is the life of the Church. I went to England for the first time in 1930, as part of the Orthodox delegation to the Lambeth Conference.[91] What struck me was the liturgical piety of the Anglican High Church—the aroma of the undivided Church arising like incense that one feels in their worship and spirituality. There is a constant thread that runs through the history of the Anglican Church, at times more or less apparent, nurtured by the Scriptures as elucidated by Church Fathers. This thread is, one could say, an intimate knowledge of the Church Fathers, and especially the Greek Fathers, in which erudition is intermixed with a quiet love of Tradition. And there is also the spiritual experience, which, as in Orthodoxy, is closely tied to the liturgical participation in the mysteries of Christ. The vital reality of this worship must be the starting point of our dialogue with the Anglicans. Archbishop Ramsey is in agreement

---

89 [For Böhme, God is "the movement of the strings and the wind in the organ, (to which) ideally all creation responds in harmony." *Mysterium Magnum* or the Great Mystery, being an exposition of Genesis]

90 [Archbishop of Uppsala, Sweden, from 1914–31 and recipient of the 1930 Nobel Peace Prize]

91 [The meeting of the worldwide Anglican communion at Lambeth Palace in London]

with the Pope and me on the need to reestablish Church unity on the basis of the undivided Church of the first millennium.

Professor In the Anglican Church, you find movements coexisting, that elsewhere are fiercely opposed. There is a Catholic dimension and a Protestant dimension. But it seems to me that these are juxtaposed, rather than integrated, and this juxtaposition comes at the price of doctrinal compromise. No doubt, the Anglican Church needs to explore the limits of Western thought for the tradition of the undivided Church to re-emerge, in this spiritual soil, not as nostalgia for the past but as a creative future. Here, perhaps, Orthodoxy can play a catalytic role, in the context of a global rapprochement of the Christian East and West.

ΩΩΩ

Professor In the tradition of the undivided Church, we find both the sacramental aspect of the Church and the aspect of personal freedom in the Holy Spirit—both apostolic succession and apostolic witness. Apostolic truth permeates the whole life of the Church and gives birth to spiritual witnesses. I wonder if in this we cannot find a way to overcome the opposed viewpoints of the 'horizontal' so-called Catholic conception of the apostolic succession and the 'vertical' so-called Protestant conception of the descent of the Holy Spirit.

Patriarch For that to happen, we would need theologians who are a little more mystical, and mystics who are a little more open to ecumenism! In the consecration of a priest or bishop, the laying on of hands demonstrates the 'horizontal' continuity, but those laying on their hands humbly implore the 'vertical' descent of the Holy Spirit, and the Holy Spirit 'rises' from the assembled laity, in their enthusiastic acclamation of the consecration—"*Axios! Axios! Axios!* He is worthy!" For us Orthodox, this opposition between the vertical and the horizontal has little meaning. All the more, because our mystics, our holy men, explode all systematic thinking to find themselves in direct contact with the hidden God. The God who eludes all theological formulations, just as His Church eludes all ecclesial formulations. I myself have encountered such holy men . . . .

Professor And you, yourself have the sensibility, simplicity, and freedom of a holy man . . .

Patriarch Enough of that! I am just an old bureaucrat . . . . But make no mistake—our holy men speak of the need for the baptism of the Holy Spirit . . . .

Professor Like the Pentecostals!

Patriarch And the Pentecostals certainly have something to say to our desiccated Christian world . . . . Our holy men do not overthrow the order of the Church. They ratify it and they purify it. But they know by experience that this Church order is not a mechanism. It is the living transmission of the life that flows from the Communion cup . . . .[92]

Professor For some Protestant interpreters of Scripture, such as Bultmann, the Church is reborn, at every moment, in the personal choice that binds each believer, in this moment, to the paradoxical Cross of Christ. Here we see the apogee of Protestant existentialist thought, that excludes any historical and collective continuity. But we believe that the Holy Spirit's invitation to faith has descended on the Body of Christ, and has impregnated the sacramental Body of Christ, and has forever impregnated and sanctified each person who is a member of the Body of Christ. I like this almost crude image of impregnation! It makes me think of the oil that plays such an important role in our worship and in our liturgical practice. The cruder the image, the richer it is, the more wisdom it contains.

Patriarch What loneliness, what emptiness without this communion! Sometimes it scares me the extent to which the reformers, who were completely right in their initial demands, ended up by rejecting all these concrete manifestations that unite us to the Living God—the icons, the veneration of the saints and the Virgin Mary, the whole sacramental aspect of the Church . . . . They have retained a heroic, naked faith, an extraordinary knowledge of the Bible, and a personal and social ethic that, perhaps, alone has made the modern world livable . . . .

Professor The first Calvinists had an almost iconic reverence for the Bible! We give an icon to the newlywed couple. They give a Bible. They used to give an enormous, heavy Bible, that imparted liturgical gravity to the act of reading. A solitary old man reading his Bible. This is as beautiful as Rembrandt's final portraits. If *Roma* would only transpose itself into *Amor*, and if at the same time, the people of the Bible would only encounter the people of the icon!

Alas, in some intellectual circles little remains of this old Calvinism. Instead, you find feverish thinking and a fear of the material world. I remember one person saying to me, with veiled disgust: "and so, after you

92 [In this dialogue, the holy men are called *pneumatikoi*, a single, compact term for the spirit-filled *geronta*]

have taken Communion, do you drag something along after you?" I learnedly explained to him that it was not something, but the life of Someone . . . I was wrong! More and more I love the material world, the world of things impregnated by God.

Patriarch This person needed to find tenderness, joy, and beauty in the House of the Lord, and many brothers and many friends. And the Mother of God. Father Sergei Bulgakov once said about the first ecumenical encounters that, perhaps, his mission was to reveal the face of the Mother of God to the Protestants. "Christianity without the Mother of God," he said, "is not the same Christianity." He was right. The Theotokos and the saints do not stand between the believer and their Lord. They carry us toward Him, they carry us along in their prayer and in their love. They witness to the illumination of all of life in the Incarnation, right to the very roots of life, the love of a mother for her child.

Professor Certainly, one can understand the reaction of the Reformation to the way that the veneration of the Saints and the Virgin Mary had degenerated in the late Middle Ages. In fear of God, in fear of Christ, people sought a more immediate, more accessible means of mediation. The doctrine of storing up good works, it's an image from the banking world! The legalistic definition of merit gave a certain concrete reality to the intercession of the Saints, as something separate from the one Mediator, who sits at the right hand of the Father.

More generally, absent the influence of the East, the emphasis had been placed on works, on a rather mechanical approach to the sacraments, on hierarchy, on the authority of Peter's keys, on the two swords. And hence the Protestant reaction.

Patriarch Paul speaks out against Peter . . . .

Professor Apostolic witness speaks against the apostolic succession.

Patriarch But in the first Christian centuries, both Peter and Paul were venerated in Rome, as the two heads of the Church. This is what we will be able to rediscover through the rapprochement of the Catholic and the Orthodox Church.

Professor And for this reason the Orthodox Churches should take stock, globally and dynamically, of the Churches of the Reformation. We recognize them as Churches. But it would be wrong to claim to be able to measure their ecclesiality. Even more so since, if I can be so bold, the ecclesiality of the Reformation is the work of the Holy Spirit and the work of the Holy Spirit cannot be transcribed. Rather than confining these Churches inside the limits within which they have been historically bound, we should invoke a renewed vision of the history of Christianity. In this vision, the Reformation would not be an unfortunate accident caused by a transitory decadence, as the Catholics have so often thought. Nor would it be a new Pentecost descending after a 'lapse of memory' lasting more than a thousand years, as some have written.[93] Instead, it would be the result of, or the victim of, the great schism between the Christian West and the Christian East. The reformers sought the fullness of the Holy Spirit. But they sought it within the mental structures of their adversaries. Two systems were placed in opposition, but the unthinkable, the 'archaeology' of theological thought, was not placed in question.

This did not prevent the Reformers from bringing fresh life to many aspects of Christian tradition. Reform theology compels us to rediscover the biblical and existential aspects of patristic thought, to re-emphasize the importance of the invocation of the Holy Spirit in our sacramental approach, to re-establish full community participation in the Eucharist. In brief, it compels us to re-activate the 'spiritual' dimension of the Church, that is to say, our opening and obedience to the Holy Spirit. I am certain that the Protestant Church will take hold in those Orthodox countries where the Church will not, or cannot, give the Holy Spirit its full arena. Consider the implications of the current surge of baptisms in Russia . . . .

But Orthodoxy, in its turn, can ask the Protestants to take those two complementary dimensions of the Church—mystery and mysticism—more seriously. They are mystery in the sense that, in the Holy Spirit, the Church is the Mystery of the Risen Christ. They are mysticism, not in the sense of extraordinary individual experiences, but in the sense of the transformational awareness of living, not just in face of Christ, but in Christ.

Patriarch Orthodoxy's witness to the undivided Church and the sacramental convergence of Catholicism and Orthodoxy should, little by little, lead the Protestants to discover their own ecclesial roots. The Protestant communities will come to recognize themselves as mysteriously part of the Universal Church, manifested historically as a sacramental institution that is not a human invention, whose existence was prepared and willed by Christ, and then filled with the grace of Pentecost.

Professor And so we will begin to resolve the old conflicts . . . .

---

93 [Clément cites the Swiss theologian J.J. von Allmen]

Patriarch Of faith and works, for example . . . .

Professor Of Scripture and the Church, of Tradition and the Word of God. Beyond all scientific research, or rather, by means of it, the goal of Christian exegesis is to reveal the spiritual intelligence of the Scriptures "in harmony with the Eucharist," as St. Irenaeus of Lyons said. Tradition is to the Scriptures what the epiclesis is to the Eucharist: the illumination of the Holy Spirit, without which history would remain incomprehensible and the Scriptures a dead document from the past. Tradition is the living apostolic message speaking across generations to announce and prepare Christ's return. The Bible is the voice of Tradition speaking across human cultures: and this makes its interpretation absolutely necessary. Without this living Tradition, the Bible would not have been written. The book would have remained sealed. Without the Bible, the endless stream of life would fall silent or turn mad. Tradition finds its ratification in the Bible —as the Creed says, "according to the Scriptures," and the Bible reveals its meaning in Tradition!

Professor The saints are the ones who understand the spiritual meaning of the Scriptures. Should this be demythologized? Yes, indeed, and the Church Fathers have taught us how to discern both the letter and the spirit of Scriptures. But this must be according to the criteria of those who see, not those who are blind, according to the criteria of saintliness.

ΩΩΩ

8. The Misunderstandings of Chalcedon

Orthodoxy has an East and a West. If you ignore its Western dimension, that of research, humanism, and personal awareness, you will be unable to grasp the elevated thought of the Byzantines, starting from Alexandria and Antioch, or the icon of Christ of Sopotchani, the platonic fluidity of Rublev, or, more recently, the testimony of the Orthodox diaspora and Albert Camus' suggestion that the twentieth century was more that of Dostoevsky than that of Marx.

Orthodoxy is only the 'East' for the Latin or Lutheran world. By contrast, Orthodoxy is the 'West' for the ancient Christians of Africa and Asia who separated from the undivided Church in the fifth century. At the heart of this rupture there stands the Council of Chalcedon in the year 451, one of the most inspired councils.

To understand Chalcedon, you must put it in the context of the huge debates of the first councils, in which the mystery of Christ was defined, little by little, antinomic opposition by antinomic opposition. If God had really become man, and had descended onto earth, Christ must be *homoousios*, of one essence, of one substance, consubstantial, with the unoriginate Father, the source and the *principia* of divinity. This the Council of Nicaea proclaimed in the year 325, in opposition to the Arians.

But the Lord had to take on all of humanity, because "whatever is not taken on, is not saved." In opposition to Apollinarius, who argued that, in Christ, the human intellect was replaced by the Logos, the Council of Constantinople had reaffirmed the full humanity of the Lord, in the year 381. God and man are not simply juxtaposed in Christ but form a new unity, by which all of humanity is illuminated with the light of the divine. In opposition to Nestorius, for whom there was only a moral likeness, a linkage, between the man Jesus and the man of God, the Logos, the Council of Ephesus had reaffirmed, in the year 431, the divino-human unity of Christ, and had proclaimed Mary to be, not only the mother of Jesus, but, thereby, the Theotokos, the mother of God. Having overcome the 'Judaizing' tendency that focused exclusively on Christ's humanity, another danger arose, that of the ancient Eastern spirituality that was so much a part of this Middle Eastern world, in which spiritual gnoses flowed into one another. Here there arose the risk of dissolving Christ's humanity (and thereby our humanity) into the divine, "like a drop of perfume in the ocean." The Council of Chalcedon was summoned to combat this notion, propagated by Eutychius. This was the council of divino-humanity.

Applying the dogmatic understanding of the Persons of the Trinity, the hypostases, to the Incarnation (the hard won understanding of the earlier councils that guarded the paradoxical mystery of the Trinity), the Council of Chalcedon declared that in the person of Christ, the human and the divine were united without confusion or separation, in the "hypostatic union;" and that the fullness of human being was contained in this deifying union. This was not the separation of God and man of the Semitic religions, where the transcendent God was beyond reach, nor was it the fusion of man with the divine, of Indian spirituality. This was the living exchange of communion, in which the more a person is united to God, the more they are filled with God, the more they realize their own true nature.

Here was the crux of the drama. In the tradition of Alexandrian Christian thought, the word 'nature,' *physis*, did not mean so much the actual reality of the divine, or the human, as the material existence of the Incarnate Word. In the antinomy of the Incarnation, in which these two natures or signs, the human and the divine, are united without confusion or separation in a third term or sign, those in the Alexandrian tradition understood the word *physis*, nature, to designate the unity of Christ. The Chalcedonians emphasized the duality of two natures. Those in the Alexandrian tradition, in Egypt and elsewhere, could not understand this new language. They remained loyal to the formulation of their great patriarch, Cyril of Alexandria, on the "single nature" of the incarnate Word. They felt that the sacramental encounter with the divine, this overwhelming moment of contact with the flesh of God in the Eucharist, was itself put at risk by the Chalcedonian formulation.

The misunderstandings were amplified by politics. The emergence of strong ethnic tendencies in Egypt, Syria, and Armenia drove these local Churches to separate from the Church of the Byzantine Empire. The Chalcedonians came to be seen as Melkites, that is to say, Imperials. This separation found its expression in Severus of Antioch's systematization of Cyril's thought. This rigorously upheld the divino-human character of the *mono-physis* of the Incarnate Word, in opposition to Eutychius. But the result was two opposing conceptual systems. The one, Chalcedonian, insisted on the two natures united in the one person of Christ. The other, non-Chalcedonian, placed the emphasis on the divino-human unity of Christ, in one nature. Passions ran so high in the following century that the non-Chalcedonians were unable to grasp the import of the Fifth Council, which reinterpreted the Chalcedonian definitions in the light of Cyril of Alexandria's thought, and definitively clarified the terminology.

In the seventh century, the emperors' efforts to re-engage the 'dissident' Egyptians and Syrians by offering a dogmatic compromise—with the goal of securing the frontiers of the Byzantine world against the invading Persians and Arabs—only resulted in further misunderstandings. Maximus the Confessor's magnificent synthesis, as ratified by the Sixth Ecumenical Council, should have brought down the wall of division. Maximus revealed the divine energies transfiguring the humanity of Christ, opening the paths of eternity to mankind through

Christ's deified and deifying Body. Maximus emphasized that the Lord's human freedom, or will, found its fullness of expression in love. It freely and spontaneously joined itself to the will of God. But these words had for a long time already ceased to have a common meaning. The Middle East fell under the sway of Islam, and the Christians of Syria and Egypt used up all their strength simply in enduring and transmitting the essentials of their faith to the next generation.

ΩΩΩ

Let us recall one small event in 1923 that was a sign. After the massacre of the inhabitants of 'Little Armenia' in Cilicia, Armenian refugees arrived in Corfu. These refugees had no priest. The Orthodox Metropolitan of Corfu gave them Communion. This was the future patriarch, Athenagoras.

ΩΩΩ

Patriarch There is nothing that would prevent re-union with the non-Chalcedonian churches in a very short time. These Churches have preserved the structures, the spirituality, and the fundamental doctrines of the great Patristic period. Their liturgical practices and traditions are in many cases closer to apostolic practice than our Byzantine rites of today. The fact of their survival in a harsh environment for more than fifteen centuries, cut off from the mainstream of Christianity, is the best proof of the authenticity of their faith.

Professor Since we began the theological dialogue with these Churches, we have confirmed what some suspected. They are in no way monophysites. When, with Cyril of Alexandria, they speak of a single nature in Christ, they mean a simple existential and personal reality. But what is contained in this reality is the divino-human—although with a heavy emphasis on the deified flesh of the Lord. In this archaic form of expression, which is very close to that of the Bible, the flesh stands for all of humanity and all of the cosmos. The tragedy of these Churches is their cultural estrangement after Chalcedon. Cyril's powerful intuitions found their place in the dogmatic definitions of the succeeding councils. Today, the non-Chalcedonian Churches are in the process of discovering the whole thought-edifice of the seven councils and its Byzantine elaboration, especially in the Palamite synthesis.

They can now assess to what extent this 'Chalcedonian' theology is also 'Cyrillian,' with its focus on the real acquisition of the Holy Spirit through participation in the "spiritual body" of Christ. Palamas even uses the terms "the flesh of God," "the flame of glass," from which the uncreated light radiates, expressions that were dear to the thinking of Alexandria.

When all is said and done, what we express, more rigorously, in the concepts of Person (hypostasis) and Nature, they point to in the real existence of the Incarnate Word. Where we speak of the "hypostatic union" of the divine and the human, they speak of a simple divino-human reality. Where we evoke the union, in the one Person of the Word, of the divine will and the human will, of divine energy and human energy, they speak of one divino-human volition and one divino-human action. And every time they make clear that this reality, this action, this volition is the expression of a composite "union."

Patriarch Agreement is not difficult. There is no problem of ecclesiastical structure. We have the same apostolic succession, the same sense of the Church as the Mystery of the Risen Christ, the same communion of sister Churches in the bosom of the universal Church. There has been huge progress in the dialogue with these noble and ancient Churches in the past few years. Discretely, in almost complete silence . . . . Now it is time to shake off the historical inertia and reach the goal.

"Look at this island," the Patriarch said to me on Halki: "It is *Proti*, the 'first' of the Princes' Islands that one reaches when coming from Constantinople. We have a summer camp there for our young people. But now there are also many Armenians on *Proti*—they are the largest ethnic group there. Recently, the Armenian patriarch came to Halki for the Feast of the Dormition. He was welcomed as Patriarch to the main Orthodox Church. And young Armenians took part in the summer camp. That is how the union is prepared—*de facto*!

ΩΩΩ

9. New Rome, New Jerusalem

Patriarch When I was elected to the patriarchal throne at the beginning of 1949, I found the Orthodox Churches completely isolated from each other. They all shared the same doctrines and the same Eucharist, but there was no unity. It was as if the patriarchs had only to exchange three letters a year: once at Christmas, once at Pascha, and once on the feast day of each patriarch. As I had no feast day, they only wrote to me twice a year. In the absence of any sustained relationships, there was a tragic history of accumulated misunderstandings.

I set out to change this situation. I began to write to each patriarch regularly. I sent delegations. And then I visited them. In 1959, I visited the Holy Land for the first time and I met the patriarchs of Alexandria, Antioch, and Jerusalem. In 1960, Patriarch Alexis stopped in Istanbul on his way back from the Holy Land, and we celebrated the Christmas Liturgy together. He had anticipated very bitter and hard discussions, but we settled everything, quickly and amicably, in a half-hour meeting. I remember his astonishment. But the time for arguments was past. The only thing that counted was the unity of Orthodoxy. Then we held the three Pan-Orthodox Conferences on Rhodes, as well as the great gathering of Churches for the millennium of Mount Athos. I was not so much trying to accomplish some specific result as to plant the seeds of brotherhood. Finally, I visited Yugoslavia, Romania and Bulgaria in 1967. In 1968, at the fourth Orthodox Conference in Chambésy, Switzerland, we agreed to plan for a Pan-Orthodox Council.[94]

When I started there was union but no unity. Now we have both union and unity, and little by little we are beginning to speak with one voice. In the beginning the patriarchs wrote to me twice a year and I wrote to them three times a year. Now we exchange letters on a regular basis. I hold them all in equal esteem, whether I am writing to the youngest, Germanos of Serbia or Justinian of Romania, or to the oldest, Alexis of Moscow. Of course, I am the oldest of them all. I listen to them. I am interested in what they have to say. I try to console them and comfort them. In the beginning, everyone was distrustful, just as with our conversations with Rome. Everyone was afraid. They did not dare. They told me: "If you convene a Pan-Orthodox Conference, the Russians and the other Churches of the Soviet Bloc will dominate it. But we have held four Pan-Orthodox conferences and a theological conference, and the Russians did not attempt to dominate—and besides, how could they! It is a mistake to reduce the state of Orthodoxy to a dual between Constantinople and Moscow. The Romanian Church, the Serbian Church, the Bulgarian Church, the patriarchates of the Middle

94 [The Holy and Great Council of the Orthodox Church finally took place in 2016, without the participation of Antioch, Russia, Georgia, and Bulgaria]

East all have their positions. The Romanians, Serbians and Bulgarians are more and more attentive to that inner voice that comes from Byzantium, from the spiritual Byzantium that has sown its seeds of light in each people.

And besides, the charge of dualism is spiritually unfounded! I try to act as one who serves, as one who serves with only the power of love. There is no dualism in love, there is no spirit of opposition. Remember what St. Paul said: "Love is patient and kind; love is not jealous and boastful . . . love does not insist on its own way; it is not irritable or resentful; it does not rejoice at wrong . . . love bears all things, believes all things, hopes all things, endures all things." (1 Cor. 13:4–7)

Professor Since the beginning, the Church has always recognized one local Church that "presided in love," as the universal center of agreement and concord. In the Acts of the Apostles, Jerusalem plays this role. We see the Apostle James preside over the council that resolved the dispute between Peter and Paul. This role was then given to Rome, while Constantinople took the second place in the rank of the patriarchates.[95] The communion of all the Churches was summed up in the 'Pentarchy'—the five patriarchates under the leadership of Rome. After the Schism, the Ecumenical Patriarch, recognized by the councils as Patriarch of the New Rome, assumed the primacy, the 'presidency of love,' of the Orthodox Church, and the Pentarchy continued, restored to its full number in the sixteenth century by the elevation of the head of the Russian Church to the rank of patriarch.

The problem is that the structure of our Church has changed significantly, *de facto*, in modern times. In the early Church, the communion of all local eucharistic communities was ratified through a hierarchy of 'centers of concord.' Each civil province of the Roman Empire corresponded to a metropolitan province, presided over by its bishop. Each church province had to convene all its bishops twice a year, in the Spring and in the Fall, and nothing could be done without their agreement.[96] Later, the provinces were grouped together into patriarchates, based on areas of cultural unity. These often, but not always, corresponded to the administrative sub-divisions of the Roman Empire. Thus, Rome assumed the leading role in the Latin-speaking world; Constantinople in the Greek-speaking world; Alexandria in the Coptic world and Antioch

95 [According to Canon 3 of the Council of Constantinople, 381]

96 [Citing the Canon 5 of the Council of Nicea]

in the Syriac world. To this list one must add Jerusalem, which came only in fifth place, despite being the mother Church of all. One might suggest that this was to remind us that the New Jerusalem is to be found everywhere, in every Eucharist.

These patriarchates constitute the "pillars" of the episcopacy, in the same sense that St. Paul spoke of St. James, St. Peter, and St. John as the "pillars" of the apostolic community. (Gal. 2:9) Finally, Rome was the center of universal concord, not above the Pentarchy but at its center, and at the center of the college of bishops. The intent of this living hierarchy of centers of concord, or centers of dialogue, is expressed in Apostolic Canon 34:

> "That the bishops of every nation must acknowledge him who is first among them and account him as their head, and do nothing of consequence without his consent . . . . But neither let him (who is the first) do anything without the consent of all; for there will be unanimity, and God will be glorified through the Lord in the Holy Spirit."

Notice how this text concludes with a doxology to the Trinity, which is the basis of all communion.

Patriarch Synodality has been, and still, is the basis of our Church. As you are aware, I can do nothing without the agreement of my synod, and the same applies to each Orthodox patriarch. When I was Archbishop in America, I organized the diocese in the spirit of Nicea, with regular meetings of the synod, and with conventions in which bishops, priests, and laity took part.

Professor Today, the Orthodox Church needs to resolve a situation that is the reverse of the burning concern in Catholicism. The Catholics want to re-introduce synodality. For the Orthodox, the question is how the unity and the universality of the Church should be expressed. The Orthodox Churches are fiercely independent, in reaction to anything that might resemble an 'Eastern Papacy,' but also out of national pride. In particular, some Russians think their Church should assume a de facto leadership role, on account of its size, while the primacy of the Ecumenical Patriarch should become a purely honorary role, of no practical importance.

Patriarch The Russian Church has never claimed to deny the 'rights of seniority' to the patriarchates of Antioch, Alexandria, or Constantinople.

And Constantinople is their mother church, that brought them the light of Christ.

Professor Not that they did not want to! In 1652, Patriarch Nikon set up five altars in his monastery in 'New Jerusalem.'[97] The five altars represented the five patriarchates, but under the primacy of Moscow! For Nikon, the rights of seniority had been superseded by the divine election of Moscow. Now it is true that for many Russians in the sixteenth century, the proof of Russia's divine election was the fact that the Byzantine Empire had fallen and Russia was now the Orthodox Empire. The doctrine of the Third Rome identified Moscow with the third empire, the sacred, messianic kingdom. These dreams were soon revealed to be deceptions. Things fell apart a few years after Patriarch Nikon's claim to primacy. He condemned the Old Believers and excluded them from the Church, in part because they upheld a theocratic view of the state, only himself to fall victim to his own theocratic ambitions, with his dream of uniting the temporal and the spiritual powers, the "two swords," in his hands, as patriarch and monarch.

All of this is very significant. The tension between God and Caesar is an immovable bedrock. Rome had its primacy confirmed by the First Ecumenical Council at the same time that Rome lost its Western Empire. When Byzantium inherited this primacy, the Eastern Empire was becoming weaker, to disappear completely in 1453. The mark of divine election is not revealed in strength but in a certain historical weakness.

Patriarch That may all be true. Nevertheless, our spiritual kinship is deeply inscribed in the memory of the Church. The Ecumenical Patriarch's primacy of honor translates into service of two kinds of presiding on the one hand, and of initiating on the other. This double service always requires the agreement of the sister Churches. The Patriarch seeks and safeguards their consent. Respect for the primacy is constantly earned though creative self-denial. Nevertheless, the primacy is an essential element of the structure of the Church. The primate belongs to no one national Church and is freed from ethnic constraints and national pride. However legitimate these may be, they narrow our horizons. The primate's mission is to safeguard the universality of Orthodoxy. This is what is implied by the term 'ecumenical.' His role is to foster relations between the sister Churches, to make sure that they do not become iso-

97 [The Patriarchal monastery on the Western outskirts of Moscow, Novoierusalemskii Monastir]

lated, to encourage them to work together and to bear witness together. They have recourse to him in exceptional situations. He doesn't challenge the initiatives taken by sister Churches. He supports them through his coordination.

And, ever since the fall of the Byzantine Empire, he is the one who, after consulting with the sister Churches, summons conferences and Pan-Orthodox councils, and he guides their work. The primacy is a service of love. It draws from our constant care for the other pastors and for the whole Church. It is essential for the first-in-honor to be able to speak to the heads of each local Church in the name of the Universal Church. Not to give orders: to act in service of the fullness of each local Church, reminding them of their responsibilities towards Orthodoxy as a whole.

ΩΩΩ

Professor There is a mystery to Constantinople. The Emperor Constantine wanted to establish the *Altera Roma*, the Other Rome, here. The Roman aristocracy was very attached to the old pagan traditions and had been sulking ever since Constantine's conversion. Constantine wanted his New Rome to be the receptacle of Christianity, and he placed the whole of the Greek and Latin humanist tradition at its service. He wanted to transplant the sacred roots of the Old Rome into Christian soil, not to tear them up, to re-orient them in all their mystery towards Christ. So he placed Constantinople under the guardianship of Flora, the personification of the Roman Empire (in Greek, *Anthousa*) and he brought the old Trojan talisman, the wooden statue of Pallas-Athena known as the Palladium, that was said to have fallen from the skies. Like Rome, the new city had seven hills, and one of them was named the Capitol. The old senatorial families were enticed to come to Constantinople to form the nucleus of a new *Populus Romanus*. The most famous statues from all the cities of Greece were placed in the public squares, to make the New Rome closer to its Greek roots than the Old Rome, a synthesis of the Western tradition.

This was the home that Constantine prepared for Christianity because, as we read in the Book of Revelation, the honor and glory of all nations will enter the New Jerusalem.

I have walked and climbed along the old city wall many times. It was immense, running from hilltop to hilltop and receding into the horizon. I was reminded of the Great Wall of China. I suddenly understood the similarities. This was not just a wall. This was the outer limit of civilization, or, one might say, the protection of the heart of civilization. This heart, when seen in the light of the ancient universal city that Rome had embodied, is the city of cities, the city par excellence, the *Urbs* and the *Polis*. Here the Roman ideal meets the New Testament vision of the ultimate city that descends from heaven to transfigure the earth. Akin to the Great Wall of China, perhaps, stretching from sea to sea, demarcating the boundaries of the vast space enclosed by the definitive and total city. Byzantine historians compared the very existence of the city, holding back the forces of historical and spiritual chaos, to 'Alexander's Wall,' the Great Wall of Gorgan of Northern Persia, which had held back the pagan forces of Gog and Magog.

One can never overstate the extent to which the wall of Constantinople protected the cultural flowering of Western Europe. But it was breached twice. Once, from the West, in 1204, and once from the East, in 1453. We see here, in opposition to Byzantium's divino-human synthesis, the accidental alliance of the increasingly humanist and rationalist West, and the Islamic East, which proclaimed the ultimate transcendence of the one God.

Today, this wall looks more like a geological curiosity, a fault-line, an outcropping. Its watchtowers are cracked by earthquakes and slowly crumbling. Children have worn paths in the dust. The Byzantine Empire is dead.

Patriarch And no doubt it had to die, if the seat of the Ecumenical Patriarch was to become purified and spiritualized, to remain at the center of Orthodoxy, not out of power but out of service. Constantinople has kept the faith of the Seven Councils intact, and three of those councils were held here. It has transmitted this sacred inheritance to Central and Eastern Europe, to the Slavic peoples of the Balkans, to the Romanians, and to the great Russian people. And so Constantinople became the Mother Church. Constantinople guarded this inheritance throughout the Ottoman era. The Church was the ark that protected the Christian peoples' language and culture. The councils summoned by Constantinople on a regular basis kept Orthodoxy intact, in face of challenges from Rome and from the Reformation.

Professor During the Ottoman era, the Ecumenical Patriarch was the spiritual guide and the secular protector of the Christian people, in face of the ruling powers. This tended to favor the interests of the Greek Orthodox, often at the expense of the Orthodox Slavs. This led to a certain confusion between religion and politics: when the Turks executed Patriarch Gregory V in 1821, it was because he was the 'ethnarch,' the designated political leader of the Christian community that was in revolt throughout the Empire. But God set the patriarchate free from these ambiguous privileges. Today, the patriarch is no longer the second-in-command that he was in the Byzantine Empire. He is no longer the 'ethnarch,' the political and religious leader of millions of Orthodox people. He is the Ecumenical Patriarch, impartially serving all the Orthodox, and the unity of all Christians.

Patriarch The Byzantine Empire and the Ottoman Empire are dead. Now, thanks to Atatürk's revolution, we live in a secular state. How I wish that the gates of the Phanar could be opened, to show that we have turned over the pages of history. They have been closed since Patriarch Gregory V was hanged from them in 1821. In the Byzantine period, the Church of Constantinople formulated the canons and deepened our faith. In the Ottoman era Constantinople faithfully guarded the inheritance of the Church, adding precision where needed to the understanding of the mystery of the Church. Now Constantinople's role is to share and to bring new life: to help Orthodoxy the world over bear witness to the undivided Church. For the union of all, let us pray to the Lord.

ΩΩΩ

Professor It seems to me that the only significant deepening of our understanding of the Christian faith since the Patristic era, is that brought about by St. Gregory Palamas in the fourteenth century, the new understanding of the essence and energies of God, the Palamite synthesis ratified in Constantinople by the Councils of 1341 and 1351. This exploration of how immanence and transcendence interrelate, this thinking that traces deep and hidden movements like a seismograph, this encounter of the person and the cosmos in the divine energies—these speak to our contemporary theological concerns. These discoveries were communicated from generation to generation like a hidden fire. Perhaps today in the sought-for reunion of East and West this flame, this fire, will burn in history and in the cosmos.

Patriarch Empires pass away but the saints endure. They are the heavenly roots of this Church, the roots of the humble community founded by the Apostle Andrew in the original Byzantium, which, thanks to the workings of providence, suddenly became the seat of the Ecumenical Patriarch. This Church is built upon the blood of martyrs and is sanctified by them, the martyrs of the East and of the West. It is built upon the inspired preaching of the Church Fathers, St. Gregory the Theologian, St. John Chrysostom, St. Gregory Palamas, and upon the spiritual ascesis of the great monks, such as Symeon the New Theologian. It is built upon the service rendered by those patriarchs of blessed memory, who have such an important place among the defenders of the faith. Even though they are little known in the West, we must recognize the great patriarchs who served here, in every age, from Patriarch Jeremias II in the sixteenth century, to Patriarchs Callinicus VI and Joachim III in the nineteenth and twentieth centuries.

Professor You mentioned Byzantium's apostolic foundation. While the importance of Rome and Antioch is closely linked both to their role in history and to their apostolic foundation, it is Constantinople's historical and spiritual importance that led to the recovery of the story of its possible apostolic foundation . . . . Not that this in any way prevents St. Andrew from being the patron saint of Constantinople!

Patriarch St. Andrew the First-Called, the brother of Peter . . . the brotherhood of Peter and Andrew, of Rome and Constantinople, enabled the Church to define the faith of the first seven councils, and tomorrow, it will enable the Church to rediscover its diversity in unity.

Professor Today while gathering the scattered and isolated Orthodox Churches, St. Andrew the First-Called summons Peter to enter once more into this vast, symphonic communion of sister Churches, and to assume the first place, or more correctly, to reassume it. Everything that Orthodoxy has done to define the true meaning of primacy has prepared the place for Rome, in the rediscovered unity of East and West. In this regard as well, New Rome has played a sacrificial role.

ΩΩΩ

Patriarch Above all, Constantinople is the city of the Mother of God. There are countless sanctuaries, icons and hymns dedicated to her. From the time of Constantine to the sack of Constantinople by the Western crusaders in 1204, Constantinople was one vast shrine. The most precious relic, the symbolic meaning of the first Palladium having long been forgotten, was the protective veil of the Theotokos at Blachernae. The Mother of God saved the city many times. For example, in the wars between the

Empire and the combined forces of the Persians and the Avars, their assault on Constantinople was repelled by the intercession of the Theotokos. That night, at Blachernae, Patriarch Sergius, surrounded by the people of the city, sang an unending hymn of gratitude, the Akathist to the Mother of God:

> O Champion General, we your faithful
> inscribe to you the prize of victory,
> as gratitude for being rescued from calamity,
> O Theotokos.
> But since you have invincible powers,
> free us from all manner of peril,
> so that we may cry out to you,
> Rejoice, O Bride Unwedded.[98]

ΩΩΩ

Patriarch It was at Blachernae, on Christmas Eve, that St. Andrew the Fool for Christ saw the Theotokos spread her robe to protect the city and all her people. Now the Church of St. Mary of Blachernae has been destroyed and her robe has been stolen.[99] But we still have the holy spring, the *hagiasma*, that we venerate. And the Mother of God still spreads her veil over the spiritual Byzantium, the Byzantium of many springs.

Professor Here the most profound mystery of Constantinople is unveiled, the mystery of the New Jerusalem symbolized by Hagia Sophia. Proceeding from the Temple of Wisdom, the mystery came to embrace the whole city, the city that had gathered up all the splendors of the earth, with which to weave the wedding garment for the Bride, the Bride who cries out with the Spirit, "Come, Lord Jesus, Come." (Rev. 22:20) And He is coming, and the city is already the reflection of the "Holy City Jerusalem coming down out of heaven from God, having the glory of God, its radiance like a most rare jewel, like a jasper, clear as crystal." (Rev. 21:10–11)

That is why the Mother of God is the city's sovereign. St. Gregory Palamas says that she sums up all the beauties of the earth and, even now, imbues them with eternity. That is why Constantinople became one great shrine, assembling those material fragments that already radiated the coming of the kingdom, interpenetrated as they were by the presence of sanctity. That is why Constantinople sheltered so many monasteries

98 *Kontakion* for the Akathist to the Theotokos
99 [In the assault on Constantinople in 1453]

in the heart of the city, where monks wearing the angelic robes, resolute citizens of the New Jerusalem, sent up their unceasing prayers.

Made in the image of the original community of the apostles in Jerusalem, which is also the ultimate community, these communities bore witness to active love, which does not seek to possess for one's own good but, instead, serves the poor. These monasteries played an important social role. But they also gave birth to pure contemplatives, who appeared, here and now, as bathed in the light of the final transfiguration. Such, at Stoudios, were St. Symeon the Studite and his disciple, Symeon the New Theologian.

The witness of the monks was an opening of the New Rome to the New Jerusalem. Their living prayer still rises. I visited the ruins of the Stoudios Monastery, where nothing remains but the walls of the Church of St. John the Baptist, the man of the desert, the ascetic, the friend of the Bridegroom. The roof has fallen in. The long nave of the basilica ends in an apse. Or to be more precise, the form of the apse is sketched by the two curved wings whose center, like the roof, is missing: it is now an opening into the vastness in which the sky becomes the apse.

Never have I felt as strongly, as in front of this transfigured wound through which the celestial light flows, that a church is built not just of stones, but of prayer. The stone church has fallen, but the church of prayer is still standing.[100] A church built by the *Akoimitoi*—those who never slept—who took each other's place in an unending chain of psalmody. A church built by confessors of the faith at the time of the iconoclastic controversy. A church built by the two Symeons, witnesses to the divine light.

A small but faithful flame still burns next to the ruins of the monastery, in the form of the Church of St. Constantine and St. Helen, where we had gone to serve the Paraklesis before the Feast of the Dormition. It is a modern church, but all along its walls are inset carved stones from Stoudios. At this church, the liturgy evoked the mystical self-baring of the monks in whom the liturgy had its origins, rather than imperial pomp and grandeur. The Palestinian liturgy of the Saint Sabbas Monastery, near Jerusalem, was brought to Byzantium by the monks of Stoudios.

---

100 [There is an untranslatable play on words between *pierre* (stone) and *prière* (prayer). The seventeenth century mystical poet, George Herbert gives us a possible solution: "And truly brass and stones are heavy things . . . but groans are quick and full of wings." Sion, *The Temple*, 1633]

For me, what is greater than the mystery of the New Rome, is the mystery of Constantinople as the New Jerusalem. This is a symbol that is even more meaningful now that its physical manifestations have been destroyed. Islam placed a veil over Byzantium. Islam veiled Byzantium with the veil of the Unattainable, as if veiling a beautiful woman who had been untrue to her highest calling. Stripped of their altars, in the omnipresent light that fills their interiors, Hagia Sophia and Hagia Eirene have become even more powerful symbols of the New Jerusalem, the New Jerusalem in which there are no more altars, because God is all in all. And yet, close to the holy springs, in humble churches in which a few Byzantine icons of the All-holy Theotokos have been preserved, there still rises, chanted by a faithful people, the prayer composed by the monks, the prophets of the New Jerusalem.

To become the center of prayer and service that it is today, Byzantium had to undergo a divine pedagogy, like that of the chosen people of the Old Covenant, in which earthly disappointment leads to spiritual enrichment.[101]

Patriarch That is why we must remain in Byzantium. The Patriarchate is in very cramped quarters in the Phanar. We could establish ourselves in the New Town. The Church of the Holy Trinity has ample land and buildings there. Or we could move to the banks of the Bosphorus, to Arvanut-Koÿ. But we must remain in Byzantium. If necessary, we will give up the gardens of the Phanar. Our place is here, where the mystical voices still sound, where, through glory and through tribulation, the New Rome has become a humble symbol of the New Jerusalem.

ΩΩΩ

10. In Conclusion

First Edition, 1969

A book that describes the destiny of a living and creative man has no end. Everything continues to flow: the gathering of Orthodoxy and its awakening to new, ecumenical frontiers, the rapprochement with Rome, the synthesis of history and mystery.

101 [For the divine pedagogy of the Old Testament, see *Transfiguring Time*, Part II, God and Time]

Will Athenagoras' wishes be realized? Will he live to see the ecumenical Orthodox Council that he has worked so hard to prepare for? Will he share the single cup of blessing with the Pope? Or will he learn once again, to use an expression of Nicolas Berdyaev's, "that the only high place in the hierarchy, in this world, is to be crucified for the truth."

The most important step, however, has been taken: henceforth nothing can prevent the discrete and sure-footed encounter of the Christian East and West, in which Christianity again becomes "a science of life."

"The Kingdom of Heaven is taken by force and the violent seize it" (cf. Matt. 11:12)

Afterword

Second Edition, 1976

You head west towards Europe, through the old city walls of Byzantium, across the brutal slash of the multi-lane highway, and you arrive in the gardens of silence. Cemeteries without walls, monuments placed among the pines and cypress, narrow dusty stone paths .... Most of the cemeteries are Muslim, a few are Christian. And then, low, discrete, and bathed in silence, you come upon the Monastery of the Virgin, the *Zoodohos Peghe*, the Life-giving Fountain. You enter the courtyard. It is completely paved with gravestones, the memorials of working people and craftsmen. At the far right-hand corner there is a crypt dug into the ground. You take a few steps down to discover the clear spring, infinitely transparent, both virginal and material, under a large vault. You have the same impression as at Lourdes, of the earth made transparent by the Virgin Mary, the "life-giving" fountain.

In Istanbul, which is both secular and Muslim, the Orthodox Church has become marginal and hidden away, the guardian of hidden springs, dispersed at its very center, and therefore, more than ever, it has become the sign of the final Transfiguration.

In front of the holy spring, the *hagiasma*, you find the small cemetery of the patriarchs. Here is the white tomb in which Athenagoras rests. Here, once and for ever "close to the Theotokos," lies the one who, having lost his earthly mother at age thirteen, loved to pray before the icon of the Theotokos. They tell me that the Patriarch's tomb is covered in flowers. In wintertime, when I visited, whole truckloads of daffodils are brought to Istanbul. Their white, pure, and musky perfume rises over the city squares, just as it rises from this tomb. The tomb of one who lives.

ΩΩΩ

Metropolitan Meliton, who, at the last, was Athenagoras' closest friend, recounted Athenagoras' final hours. He died in the night of July 6,1972, in the Greek Orthodox Hospital of Baloukli, in room number 12, where I went to pray in his memory. It is a room like all the others, with the vernacular simplicity of the Orthodox buildings here. He knew he was going to die. The Metropolitan had talked to him about going on a trip to Vienna where he could be treated by the best doctors. "No," he said, "I know I won't be going to Vienna. I need to prepare for a different journey." On the last evening, his shrunken body had already yielded to death, but his mind was still sharp and clear. The Patriarch asked to make his confession. He slowly spoke the prayers of repentance, the prayers of faith and love, and then, filled with peace and joy, he received Communion from the hands of Metropolitan Meliton. After this, he declined to eat and asked to be left alone. But not until he had asked for the Metropolitan to come back, so he could thank him. Then he was alone, to die. Alone with the One God—he was a monk, a *monachos*.

ΩΩΩ

In 1969 this book ended on an almost anxious note. Would the Patriarch live to see his work completed in the world, or would he again suffer the trials of Job, the seeming defeat of the cross? Now we know that he would undergo an ordeal. The Patriarch's final years were difficult and painful, whether in regard to reconciliation with Rome or the gathering of the Great and Holy Orthodox Council. With regard to Rome, the Patriarch did not succeed in defining, and above all in getting the whole Orthodox world to assent to, the ways and means of the "dialogue on fundamentals"—even though the "dialogue of love" should have shown the way and had in fact already shown the way.

Athenagoras' impassioned language, the necessary and reckless language of love, a prophetic language that ignored the weight and slow march of history, hit up against and unsettled the many Orthodox who had jealously guarded the integrity of their faith, and who were reluctant to relinquish their great distrust of Rome. Discontent and tension grew at the heart of the Orthodox Church. Many of the monasteries of Mount Athos no longer mentioned the Patriarch in their diptychs. The Russian Church, which could have provided support to Athenagoras, also distanced itself from Constantinople and pursued the path of a direct, even privileged, relationship with Rome. At the end of 1968, Moscow admitted to Communion all Catholics living within the vast Soviet Union, without consulting Constantinople or any of the sister Churches. As the target of all conservatives, Athenagoras had to limit himself to formal acts of Eucharistic concelebration with the sister Churches, without being able to get agreement on forming a mixed commission for theological dialogue with Rome. Meanwhile, most other Christian confessions had already created such mixed commissions.

In Rome, despite the intense exchange of letters between the Pope and the Patriarch, interest in rapprochement with the Orthodox was drowned out as the Catholic world embarked on its tumultuous initiation into the freedoms of the Second Vatican Council, in which faith itself was thrown into question, against which some organs of the Vatican hardened in opposition.

And so Athenagoras lived his final years torn between conflicting realities. On the one hand, he could feel the growing demand for 'spontaneous intercommunion' among the young, and in his heart he shared this imperative, and wanted to bring it into being at the highest level, between the Pope and the Patriarch. This would be a hammer blow of love, in which, he believed, the great Sun of the Eucharist would burn away the last remaining clouds of the schism. But Pope Paul VI responded only with a friendly reticence.

And on the other hand, the Patriarch encountered the adamantine cohesion of Orthodoxy, in which dogma cannot be compromised, because the dogmas of the Church are not a constraint but life-giving light. Communion, therefore, is not a means to an end: it is the seal and the demonstration of complete unity of faith. This unity must be fought for. The hidden sicknesses in the body of the Christian must be relentlessly revealed, and cauterized, rather than acting as though they do not exist. The Orthodox Church, still distrustful, did not permit Athenagoras to undertake the necessary theological dialogue with Rome. Athenagoras died without being able to reach at the top of his symbolic mountain, the Holy Grail, the one Chalice of the finally accomplished union.

It was only with the very clear ecclesiological definitions formulated by the new patriarch Demetrios I, in November 1973, on the question of primacy in the Church, that the Orthodox world was finally reassured and misunderstandings were banished. In 1975, the new Patriarch was able to obtain agreement from all the sister Churches on the formation of a Pan-Orthodox body and a mixed commission to engage in fundamental dialogue with Rome—the goal that had eluded Athenagoras to the end.

Fellow hierarch and friend of the late Patriarch, his successor's right-hand man, Metropolitan Meliton came to Rome in December 1975 bringing this important news. And then Pope Paul VI, prostrating himself and kissing the feet of the Metropolitan, in a stunning and meaningful gesture, once more embraced Athenagoras'—and St. John's—'theology of symbolic acts.'

What a profound definition of primacy and what a recompense for the death of the great prophet, in part rejected by his own, whose prayer and whose spirit most certainly inspired this event.

ΩΩΩ

Should we then say that Athenagoras succeeded only in transforming distrust into friendship, leaving the tasks of building the lasting theological foundations to his successor? This would be to ignore the already notable ecclesial benefits that resulted from the "dialogue of love." One has only to refer to the *Tomos Agapes* (the *Book of Love*), simultaneously published by the Phanar and the Vatican in 1971, which records all the exchanges and meetings between Athenagoras and Pope Paul VI.[102]

The *Tomos Agapes* constructs a veritable 'theological space' to which we should freely refer ourselves as we take up the challenge. The Pope and the Patriarch were able to rediscover a common language, in the space between their two Churches—the language of the Scriptures as illuminated by the Fathers, faithful as they were to the breath of the Holy Spirit, that has never abandoned the Church. The dialogue should take place "with faithfulness to the traditions of the Fathers and to the inspiration of the Holy Spirit," a formula that suggests the creative and eschatological continuity of the true Tradition. And in the documents of the *Tomos*

---

102 [The Introduction to the German translation of the *Dialogues with Patriarch Athenagoras, Portrait of a Prophet*, cites the *Tomos Agapes* extensively]

Agapes, we can already see Pope Paul VI insisting on the reality of the local Church as a full eucharistic community, in an exchange of opinions in which oppositions are revealed as complementarities.

And we see Athenagoras emphasizing that the primacy of Rome is not placed in question by the Orthodox, only the dogmatic form that it was given by the declaration of papal infallibility of 1870. The Patriarch is supported by the Pope in reaffirming St. Ignatius of Antioch's expression of the primacy of Rome as "presiding in love"—a formulation dating back to the foundation of episcopacy—a service, a *diakonia*, aimed to guarantee the free flow of communion between all the local Churches.

While it was necessary to clarify Athenagoras' language on certain points, as his successor has already done; and to make clear to the West that Orthodoxy is Athos and Athenagoras (as he himself, so profoundly a monk of Athos, knew and said); the theological dialogue, born of the encounter in love, is, and can only be, faithful to the great Patriarch's inspiring vision. And in particular to his demand, so many times reiterated in his correspondence with Paul VI, that the Church should confront, not concepts and systems, but what he called the "lived" ecclesial experience, as expressed at the limits of sainthood.

Patriarch Athenagoras has joined the communion of saints, that draws together the Churches of the East and the West. How similar, how convergent on all points, are the "lived" saintliness of a St. Thérèse of Lisieux and a Saint Silouan of Athos, even to their most simple statements on humility and love.

In the area of inter-Orthodox relations, the final years of the Patriarch were likewise heavily clouded. For reasons that are hard to define, the Moscow Patriarchate blocked the progress of the pre-conciliar realignment of the Orthodox Church around the patriarchal throne of Constantinople—whether these reasons were more properly political, or more properly ecclesiological. Moscow emphasized the autocephalous Churches' independence and freedom of initiative. In the summer of 1968, following the success of the Pan-Orthodox conference at Chambésy, the Russian Church refused Athenagoras' visit, which would have capped his tour of all of the sister Churches of Eastern Europe. At the end of that same year, as we have discussed earlier, Moscow, for reasons of 'economy,' opened its Communion to the un-pastored Catholics of the Soviet Union, without consulting the other Orthodox Churches. This was despite the common commitment, at Chambésy, to act together in matters of ecumenical relations. However, the clash between the 'Second' and 'Third' Rome was most evident in regard to the Orthodox diaspora. This clash was one of opposing ecclesiologies. For Constantinople, the Orthodox Church is an organic whole, in which the patriarchate, as a guiding and coordinating center, is charged with a specific *diakonia* of unity and universality. Therefore, Constantinople should take under its protection the communities of the diaspora, those Orthodox who are far away from the canonical territories of their Mother Churches. For Moscow, the Orthodox Church is a confederation of independent Churches, in which each Church has the same right of independent action, and each Church should care for its distant scattered flock.

At the first Rhodes conference, the question of the diaspora was referred to the future Great and Holy Council. But in 1970, Moscow proclaimed the autocephaly of the Russian Metropolia in America, after hasty negotiations, and without consulting Constantinople or the sister Churches.[103] This act was all the more contentious because there were Orthodox of other origins and other patriarchates in the New World. They could only become joined in a local Church with the agreement of all the Mother Churches. Alerted to the negotiations at a late point in the process, Athenagoras proposed this solution to Moscow. But Moscow chose to ignore the pre-conciliar path on which Orthodoxy was embarked. Neither the Constantinople Patriarchate nor the majority of the other Orthodox Churches recognized this new Orthodox Church in America, and the jurisdictional situation in the New World was further complicated rather than improved.

ΩΩΩ

Here we have encountered a significant problem. Despite the success of the Pan-Orthodox conferences that Athenagoras had convened, despite the initiation of a pre-conciliar process in 1968, when it comes to serious decisions, some of the Orthodox Churches continue to act as if the renewal of conciliarity was only a matter of words, a pleasing utterance that calls for no commitment. This mismatch between language and life, between principles and practices, is one of the most serious problems for Orthodoxy today. The most fundamental formulations, such as participation in Trinitarian love in the Church, come to be mere stereotypes

103 [This led to the formation of the autocephalous Orthodox Church in America in 1970]

that puff up collective pride, and that are in no way consistent with the very cold relationships between sister Churches.

In the diaspora many of the sister Churches pursue short-term policies with no other goal than their immediate interests. Hence the tortuously difficult position of the Patriarchate of Constantinople, the guardian of the unity of the Church, which can only suggest, point the way, and implore, in its total respect for the freedom of the sister Churches. As Metropolitan Maximos of Sardis has written, in the tradition of the Christian East, primacy is a primacy of diakonia, of service that scrupulously safeguards "the principle of conciliarity and collegiality in the actions of the Universal Church, and the principle of non-intervention into the internal affairs of the sister Churches."[104]

If the Western Church is tempted by an ethics without mystery, the Eastern Church is tempted by a mystery without ethics. For this reason, for Athenagoras, the re-gathering of Orthodoxy had to be accompanied by a prophetic renewal, that would give birth to an ethics of love: not an ethics of legality contrary to the spiritual sensibility of the East, but an ethics of love and creation. The renewal of the impulse of unification and innovation in the Holy Spirit, that we find in Hagia Sophia, in Rublev's icon of the Holy Trinity, in the icon of the Descent into Hell at Chora, in the heroic boldness of the great Russian religious philosophers of the twentieth Century—the impulse that, from time to time emerges to bridge the 'Eastern' distance between language and praxis, between mystery and history . . . . But this can only be the work of several lifetimes and probably requires a full rapprochement with the West.

Athenagoras gave the essential kickstart to the dialogue between Orthodoxy and the Western confessions, while Patriarch Dimitrios and Metropolitan Meliton have captured this momentum and harnessed it into a necessary and deep process of reflection. Similarly, with regard to the gathering of Orthodoxy and the quest for a renewed creative spirituality, and a creative and ethical ecclesiology, Metropolitan Meliton sought to replace the crowded agenda of the Rhodes Conference by the single, dynamic theme of divino-humanity. This is of central importance not only for Orthodoxy, but for all of Christianity, for the encounter of the religions of the world, for moving beyond ideologies, for the emergence of a planetary civilization.

---

104 [Metropolitan Maximos of Sardis, *The Ecumenical Patriarchate in the Orthodox Church*. Thessaloniki: Patriarchal Institute for Patristic Studies, 1976]

ΩΩΩ

These difficult years laid the Patriarch bare and drew him, through the trials and unyielding faith of Job, to the "one thing necessary," to becoming a person of dispassion and light. More than ever, his spiritual life focused on the secret friendship of God, on the mystical revealed in the things of everyday life, on transparency revealed in the density of matter (for this reason, the Book of Revelation tells us, the celestial Jerusalem will be built of precious stones, of matter both adamantine and transparent.)

In face of extreme adversity all became calm for Athenagoras, all was illuminated in the presence of the Friend, the Unattainable become Countenance, the Abyss of the Godhead revealed as love. After the Patriarch's death, they found a small leather prayer bracelet with wooden beads, that the Patriarch used in reciting the Jesus Prayer: "Lord Jesus Christ, Son of God, have mercy on me." This bracelet now belongs to Metropolitan Meletios, the Patriarchate's representative in France. I have held this small object in my hands. It is steeped in memories and prayer, in the prayer life that Athenagoras, with the modesty of those who truly pray, never revealed.

At the end of his long life, the Patriarch had found "the place of the heart," the prayer that is one with breath. Everything revealed the presence of the Friend, even the mouse nest that appeared in his cell in the last months of his life. He shocked his attendants by refusing to drive the mice away. He tamed them, he fed them—the one who did not like mice became like St. Francis!

At Pascha, three months before his death, Athenagoras was already ill and confined to his cell. But, without anyone knowing, he got up and silently came into the packed church. He took part in the service as a simple monk. And when, on leaving the Church, he passed through the familiar and deeply respectful crowd, a very tall, very thin figure wearing, not the purple robes of the Patriarch, but the simple black *exorason* of an Eastern monk, then, said Metropolitan Meliton who witnessed the scene, "he was no longer the Ecumenical Patriarch, he was the grand old man, the *starets*, the *geronta*, of Orthodoxy."

A *geronta*. A prophet. One of those who have known how to touch the heart of the people of today, far from the intellectual circles, of those unbelievers, of those half-believers who are nevertheless strangely susceptible to the words and hammer blows of the Gospel. The Patriarch did not fear these countless neighbors, these others, who are so often unknown to the Church. He did not get tangled up in their ideologies. He welcomed them. He respected them for their freedom. He showed how this freedom was completed in creative love. He spoke not the *law*, but the *intent* of the law. Like John XXIII, he overthrew the wall of division. And he overthrew that other thousand-year-old wall, built on ignorance, incomprehension and distrust, that separated the Christians of the East and the West.

ΩΩΩ

We must conclude with the encounter that will never end. The Patriarch had a vivid sense that we are living through a sort of historical apocalypse in which the words East and West will take on a new meaning. Far from the geography books, they rediscover their whole symbolism of beginning and ending. The sun rises and sets at all points of the globe. The West can no longer be solely defined by the high culture of Latin or Germanic Europe, which was imprinted with the spirit of Rome or the Reformation. It has become a planetary non-culture that, through its technologies and ideologies, challenges humanity to confront the ultimate questions: through the spiritual imperatives that its technologies and ideologies conceal; through the spiritual deserts that its technologies and ideologies engender.

Let us recall these words of the Patriarch, chosen from many others: "Today history can no longer avoid the ultimate questions. Science, technology, the emergence of a planetary humanity, all call for meaning. Humanity ponders the secrets of the universe and stumbles up against the door of the mystery—to discover God, or desolation." Since Athenagoras' death, the Patriarchate of Constantinople has repeatedly returned to this theme as, for example, in the encyclical issued by Patriarch Dimitrios I on the twenty-fifth anniversary of the World Council of Churches: "In our desire to respond to the problems of humanity, we must not forget this fundamental truth: the men and women of today are intently seeking an answer to the unavoidable, overarching question that transcends all socio-political problems. What is the meaning of human existence, of the living human being, of this spiritual person straining towards an ultimate reality?"

For Athenagoras and for his successors, only a reunited Christianity that has rediscovered the full spiritual power and the creative spirituality of the undivided Church, can respond to this quest for meaning. The Christian East, itself also invaded by this planetary nonculture, has no other purpose than to bear witness in the whirlwind of time, to bear faithful and unyielding witness to the *I am*, who was in the beginning. And thus to become the deepest memory for a West that is hurtling the whole earth into a history-without-remembrance. To bear humble and unyielding witness to the Christ, who triumphed over this death and this hell that we desperately try to escape, the Risen Christ who offers humankind the lifegiving Spirit, and, yes, life and liberty.

This witness, Athenagoras said once more at the end of his long life, concerns not just to the Orthodox or Christians, but all mankind, because all are resurrected in Christ. Our task is to bring them to this knowledge, to set free in them the inseparable power of their humanity and their deification. These last times, said St. Francis de Sales, are those of the unchaining of the saints!

For this encounter, for this sharing, for this *martyria* to occur, it was necessary for the Christian East, the Patriarch thought, to overcome its historical limitations, its fears, its mistrust, its thousand-year-old inferiority-superiority complex towards the *rotten* but fascinating West. Then could begin, passing beyond the opposing temptations of relativism and retreat, the apprenticeship in dialogue in which one no longer constructs thought *against* the other but *with* the other, in which one is only fully oneself in the act of welcome and the act of giving. "Our most holy Orthodox Church cannot and must not conceal the treasures of her faith and the riches of her tradition: she should offer herself to the world, in the spirit of humble service, with the goal of the transfiguration of the world in Christ.

For Athenagoras the time had come—the *kairos* that is always here, that always invites us—in which this encounter should be enacted in the Christian world, the encounter between the searching West and the immutable depths of the East, that themselves open a path towards other spiritual depths, those of the spiritual worlds of Africa and Asia. One of the Patriarch's consolations in the last years of his life was to have seen a truly spiritual rapprochement emerge between Christianity and Islam.

The Christian West finds its full resonance in taking charge of history and in the almost tragic but very pure and acute experience of its saints. The Christian East finds its full resonance in its saints, where there is a living and cosmic dimension that comes as a shock to the Western mind, but historically the Christian East is cramped and sometimes semi-petrified. Together, guided by the communion of the saints, the Christian East and West can elucidate a divino-humanism, in which God and man are no longer opposed, but united in freedom and the Holy Spirit.

ΩΩΩ

Patriarch Athenagoras I, 1886–1972. It is deeply moving to place historical markers on a human existence, a human destiny that we encounter like a great ship sailing in uncharted territory, far from the ports, forging its path towards the unknown that is Love. It is our task to decipher this existence by means of our too-human understanding. The prayers of the Church commit him to God's *Eternal Memory*, and now our awareness of him should also pass through the presence of eternity. In striving so to do, I have been granted to be so bold as to write:

Athenagoras I of blessed memory

Olivier Clément
29 March, 1975
Synaxis of the Archangel Gabriel

Appendix

JOINT CATHOLIC-ORTHODOX DECLARATION OF HIS HOLINESS POPE PAUL VI AND THE ECUMENICAL PATRIARCH ATHENAGORAS I

Following is the text of the joint Catholic-Orthodox declaration, approved by Pope Paul VI and Ecumenical Patriarch Athenagoras I of Constantinople, read simultaneously (Dec. 7) at a public meeting of the ecumenical council in Rome and at a special ceremony in Istanbul. The declaration concerns the Catholic-Orthodox exchange of excommunications in 1054.

1. Grateful to God, who mercifully favored them with a fraternal meeting at those holy places where the mystery of salvation was accomplished through the death and resurrection of the Lord Jesus, and where the Church was born through the outpouring of the Holy Spirit, Pope Paul VI and Patriarch Athenagoras I have not lost sight of the determination each then felt to omit nothing thereafter which charity might inspire and which could facilitate the development of the fraternal relations thus taken up between the Roman Catholic Church and the Orthodox Church of Constantinople. They are persuaded that in acting this way, they are responding to the call of that divine grace which today is leading the Roman Catholic Church and the Orthodox Church, as well as all Christians, to overcome their differences in order to be again "one" as the Lord Jesus asked of His Father for them.

2. Among the obstacles along the road of the development of these fraternal relations of confidence and esteem, there is the memory of the decisions, actions and painful incidents which in 1054 resulted in the sentence of excommunication leveled against the Patriarch Michael Cerularius and two other persons by the legate of the Roman See under the leadership of Cardinal Humbertus, legates who then became the object of a similar sentence pronounced by the patriarch and the Synod of Constantinople.

3. One cannot pretend that these events were not what they were during this very troubled period of history. Today, however, they have been judged more fairly and serenely. Thus it is important to recognize the excesses which accompanied them and later led to consequences which, insofar as we can judge, went much further than their authors had intended and foreseen. They had directed their censures against the persons concerned and not the Churches. These censures were not intended to break ecclesiastical communion between the Sees of Rome and Constantinople.

4. Since they are certain that they express the common desire for justice and the unanimous sentiment of charity which moves the faithful, and since they recall the command of the Lord: "If you are offering your gift at the altar, and there remember that your brethren has something against you, leave your gift before the altar and go first be reconciled to your brother" (Matt. 5:23–24), Pope Paul VI and Patriarch Athenagoras I with his synod, in common agreement, declare that:

a. They regret the offensive words, the reproaches without foundation, and the reprehensible gestures which, on both sides, have marked or accompanied the sad events of this period.
b. They likewise regret and remove both from memory and from the midst of the Church the sentences of excommunication which followed these events, the memory of which has influenced actions up to our day and has hindered closer relations in charity; and they commit these excommunications to oblivion.
c. Finally, they deplore the preceding and later vexing events which, under the influence of various factors—among which, lack of understanding and mutual trust—eventually led to the effective rupture of ecclesiastical communion.

5. Pope Paul VI and Patriarch Athenagoras I with his synod realize that this gesture of justice and mutual pardon is not sufficient to end both old and more recent differences between the Roman Catholic Church and the Orthodox Church.

Through the action of the Holy Spirit those differences will be overcome through cleansing of hearts, through regret for historical wrongs, and through an efficacious determination to arrive at a common understanding and expression of the faith of the Apostles and its demands.

They hope, nevertheless, that this act will be pleasing to God, who is prompt to pardon us when we pardon each other. They hope that the whole Christian world, especially the entire Roman Catholic Church and the Orthodox Church will appreciate this gesture as an expression of a sincere desire shared in common for reconciliation, and as an invitation to follow out in a spirit of trust, esteem and mutual charity the dialogue which, with Gods help, will lead to living together again, for the greater good of souls and the coming of the kingdom of God, in that full communion of faith, fraternal accord and sacramental life which existed among them during the first thousand years of the life of the Church.

BIOGRAPHIES

About the Author

Olivier Clément

Olivier Clément (1921–2009) was born in the Cévennes region of southwestern France. Growing up in an atheist family, he was influenced by the philosophical streams of the day. In 1952, at the age of thirty, he was baptized into the Orthodox Church at the Russian Orthodox parish of Saint-Denys in Paris. An educator by profession, he was professor of History at the Louis-le-Grand *lycée* in Paris and Professor at the Institute of St. Sergius in Paris. He was an Observer at the Second Vatican Council. Through his writings, he became known for pioneering a renewal of Orthodox theology and spirituality, while spearheading a renaissance of religious intellectualism and mysticism. He was a faithful supporter of Christian unity, a fervent advocate for interfaith dialogue, and a firm apologist for the engagement of church and society. He became personal friends with Pope John Paul II, Brother Roger of Taizé, Vladimir Lossky, Paul Evdokimov, and Fr. Sophrony of Essex. He also became personal friends with Ecumenical Patriarchs Athenagoras and Bartholomew, producing book-length interviews with both. He was the author of more than thirty books, among which *The Roots of Christian Mysticism* and *On Human Being* have become standard texts in Orthodox theology and spirituality. Olivier Clément died at the age of eighty-seven on January 15, 2009. (Adapted from the Introduction by John Chryssavgis)

About Rev. Dr. Chryssavgis

Rev. Dr. John Chryssavgis

Rev. Dr. John Chryssavgis, Archdeacon of the Ecumenical Throne, was born in Sydney (Australia) and lives in Harpswell (Maine, USA). Following studies at the Universities of Athens (Greece) and Oxford (UK), he cofounded St. Andrew's Theological College in Sydney, where he also taught at the University of Sydney. In 1995, he was invited to teach at Holy Cross School of Theology in Boston (Massachusetts, USA). Currently, he serves as theological advisor to the Ecumenical Patriarch on environmental issues and as senior theological advisor to the Department of Ecumenical Affairs in the Greek Orthodox Archdiocese of America. His numerous publications focus on the early church and the desert tradition, as well as on the theology of the environment and the role of the church in the world. His latest books include *Creation as Sacrament: Reflections on Ecology and Spirituality* (Bloomsbury, 2019) and *The Letters of Barsanuphius and John: Desert Wisdom for Everyday Life* (Bloomsbury, 2022).

About the Translator

Jeremy N. Ingpen
After a career in management consulting and affordable housing, Jeremy N. Ingpen started translating the work Olivier Clément in 2013. His published translations include Clément's *Transfiguring Time* and Michel Evdokimov's *Two Martyrs in a Godless World*. He has also published translations of the poems of Rilke, Anna Akhmatova and Paul Eluard. He is a doctoral researcher at the Institute for Orthodox Christan Studies, Cambridge, UK.